READINGS

This series from Three Essays Collective focuses on works of scholarship which touch upon issues of contemporary concern. They address a wide range of themes in history, society, politics, culture, education and the media. South Asian themes predominate in, but do not exhaust, the scope of these publications. They are intended to familiarise readers with current debates in their respective fields, even as they enlarge areas of enquiry.

OTHER TITLES

Aijaz Ahmad, On Communalism and Globalization: Offensives of the Far Right (New Edn.)

Amar Farooqi, Opium City: The Making of Early Victorian Bombay

Archana Prasad, Against Ecological Romanticism: Verrier Elwin and the Making of an Anti-Modern Tribal Identity

Ashraf Aziz, Light of the Universe: Essays on Hindustani Film Music

Barbara Harriss-White, India's Market Society: Three Essays in Political Economy

Biswamoy Pati, Identity, Hegemony, Resistance: Towards a Social History of Conversions in Orissa, 1800-2000

Brinda Karat, Survival and Emancipation: Notes from Indian Women's Struggles

Jackie Assayag and Véronique Bénéï (eds.), Re-mapping Knowledge: The Making of South Asian Studies in India, Europe and America, 19th-20th centuries

John Saul, Development After Globalization: Theory and Practice for the Embattled South in a New Imperial Age

KN Panikkar, An Agenda for Cultural Action and Other Essays (Second Edition)

Kristoffel Lieten, Views on Development: The Local and the Global in India and Pakistan

Meera Nanda, Breaking the Spell of Dharma and Other Essays

Meera Nanda, The Wrongs of the Religious Right: Reflections on Science, Secularism and Hindutva

Mukul Dube, The Path of the Parivar: Articles on Gujarat and Hindutva

Omar Khalidi, Khaki and Ethnic Violence in India: Army, Police and Paramilitary Forces during Communal Riots

Patricia Jeffery and Roger Jeffery, Confronting Saffron Demography: Religion, Fertility, and Women's Status in India

Paul R. Brass, Forms of Collective Violence: Riots, Pogroms, and Genocide in Modern India

Radhika Desai, Slouching Towards Ayodhya: From Congress to Hindutva in Indian Politics (New Revised Edn.)

Shereen Ratnagar, The Other Indians: Essays on Pastoralists and Pre-Historic Tribal People

Sunil Kumar, The Present in Delhi's Pasts

Utsa Patnaik, Republic of Hunger and Other Essays

Vasudha Dalmia, Orienting India: European Knowledge Formation in the Eighteenth and Nineteenth Centuries

Vijay Prashad, The American Scheme: Three Essays

Zaheer Baber, Secularism, Communalism and the Intellectuals

FORTHCOMING

Angana Chatterji, Violent Gods: Hindu Nationalism in India's Present—Narratives from Orissa

Michael Witzel, The Aryan Question, Pro and Contra

Shubh Mathur, The Everyday Life of Hindu Nationalism: An Ethnographic Account, 1990-94

Sunil Kumar (ed.), Demolishing Myths or Mosques and Temples?: Readings on History and Temple Desecration in Medieval India

Vidya Bhushan Rawat, Popular Culture and DailyLife in Ayodhya

Muslims in Indian Economy

Muslims in Indian Economy

Omar Khalidi

Three Essays
COLLECTIVE

First Edition September 2006

ISBN 81-88789-50-X

Three Essays
COLLECTIVE

B-957 Palam Vihar, GURGAON (Haryana) 122 017 India
Phone: 0 98681 26587, 0 98683 44843
info@threeessays.com Website: www.threeessays.com
Printed at Glorious Printers, New Delhi

To My Sisters

Hamida
Habiba
Humaira
Hafsa

CONTENTS

PREFACE AND ACKNOWLEDGEMENT

There is no dearth of books on Muslims in India. Since the 1870s to the early 21st century, literature on Indian Muslims can easily fill many library shelves. However, only a few works deal with the economic condition of the community. Within this small body of literature, most are confined chronologically and spatially. This work hopes to fill in the lacunae by treating the question of Indian Muslims in Indian economy in a systematic way to the extent that data is available. It uses a variety of sources such as government reports, academic studies, socio-economic surveys, and the like. Wherever needed, the author interviewed a variety of administrators, politicians, community activists, and journalists to produce a picture that approximates reality. The study is conceived as more than a mere academic exercise. The audiences I have in mind are India's movers and shakers: legislators, administrators, politicians, leaders in business and industry, and the like.

I am greatly indebted to the Indian Muslim Council-USA for funding the research for this book. To my wife Nigar, I remain ever grateful for her numerous sacrifices allowing me to complete yet another book. The Three Essays Collective's Asad Zaidi and Nalini Taneja deserve my sincere gratitude for bringing out the book expeditiously.

INTRODUCTION

What is the economic condition of the Indian Muslims at the dawn of the twenty first century? What is the demographic profile of the community? Which are the areas of considerable Muslim population? What is the percentage of its population in agriculture, industry, service and the tertiary sector? How do Muslims fare at the national level? Does the Muslim economic condition differ from state to state, given the regional imbalances in the country resulting from unequal development? How does Muslim economic condition in the early twenty first century compare with the recent and distant past? To what extent can the political changes account for these variations? How does the economic profile of the Muslims compare with the majority Hindus, Dalits, and minorities like Christians, Sikhs and Parsis? Historians, politicians, journalists and others agree that Muslims in general lag behind other communities. Does Islam, or Islam as interpreted and lived, have anything to do with it? If so, to what degree? What is the role of the State in this matter? Did public policy as formulated and implemented by the colonial state favor or disfavor Muslims as a group? What is the record of the post-independence central and state governments? Have they been favorable to Muslims? Is there a consistent pattern of discrimination?

Or is the state simply neutral, if not indifferent? Answers to these questions require a dispassionate reading of contemporary history to locate causes leading to the present state of the Muslims. Understanding these causes is not only a matter of academic enquiry; it is also necessary for the appropriate corrective measures that need to be taken, both by the community leadership and by the State.

The present study is conceived as a systematic narrative, although not entirely in chronological sequence. The study will inter-weave description with interpretation and analysis. It uses a variety of sources ranging from government documents, legislative debates, and memoirs, correspondence and speeches of the main actors who shaped policies in the last several centuries. Avoiding cumbersome academic jargon, it uses common terms and phrases to draw a picture of Muslims in the Indian economy that is comprehensible to audiences beyond the academia. The first chapter gives a brief overview of the pattern of Muslim livelihood in the medieval and early modern era, and then moves to an analysis of Muslims' employment in the colonial government of India. The following chapters are in depth surveys of the Muslims' economic conditions in the states of Uttar Pradesh, Delhi and Bihar in northern India, and Andhra Pradesh, Karnataka and Maharashtra in the Deccan. The states selected are on account of the following reasons: these are areas where the various Muslim dynasties ruled the longest—the Delhi Sultanate, the Mughals and their off shoots in the north, and the Bahmanis and their off shoots like the Adil Shahis, the Qutb Shahis, the Nizams and the Mysore sultans in the south. Unlike Assam, Bengal, and Kerala, for instance, the overwhelming majority of Muslims in these areas have Urdu as their mother tongue. Even though divided by normal divisions of class, sect, and gender, Muslims of these areas represent the most homogenous of all Muslim communities in India, thus justifying the study of a group united by common historical and cultural experience. It is therefore that much easier to work out the commonalities, and also underline regional variations to arrive at a more complex picture of Muslims in Indian economy.

Problems of Data

Just about anyone who speaks or writes about Indian Muslims complains about the paucity of reliable data or empirical studies on the economic condition of Muslims. What percentages of Muslims are engaged in agriculture, industry, and professions? No one really knows. It is partly because all three spheres of economic activity are largely in private hands. Then there is a large segment of the population engaged in the unorganized, informal sector that does not pay income tax, thus escaping even the most rudimentary documentation. During the colonial period, the government published data on the educational condition and economic levels of many population groups in general and shares in state employment in particular from the 1870s to the 1940s. Evidently, the Nehru administration decided in 1949, shortly after independence, not to cross-tabulate economic and religious/ethnic group data because it felt that such statistics heightened communal and caste sensitivities during the colonial era.[1] However, it is clear that exclusion of caste, community data in the national economic life did not decrease casteism or communalism, nor did it promote a caste-free society.[2]

But, it is evident that this policy was never fully put into practice in so far as data on employees directly on government pay-roll were concerned. *First,* Nehru himself informed the chief ministers about the declining number of Muslims in the central services in the 1950s.[3] Following his example, Minister of State for Defense, Mahavir Tyagi, made a similar remark with respect to the Muslims' falling percentage in the armed forces roughly about the same time.[4] Since the 1950s, on several occasions, government ministers have either given statistics in the legislatures or made them otherwise available as will be seen in the book. *Second,* the application forms for government employment at both central and state levels almost always ask for religious affiliation from candidates. Since religion is a category of information sought in the employment forms, presumably the information thus collected is tabulated and documented. *Third,* the state-sponsored Gopal Singh Panel was able to collect data about the share of the minorities in various sectors of economic activity, made available to it by government agencies in the early 1980s. *Fourth*, the National Sample Survey Organization, under the Ministry of Statistics and Program Implementation conducted surveys regarding the differential development rates of various groups in India, twice, in 1987-88[5] and in 1999-2000,[6] obviously at the behest of the Central government. *Fifth*, emulating the example set by the central government, the governments of Karnataka, Andhra Pradesh, and Bihar sponsored detailed surveys of minorities in their states in 1984, 1994 and 1999, 2004 respectively. *Sixth*, in addition to the state-sponsored surveys already completed, three chairmen of the Minorities Commission told the present writer that they are persuading the government of Delhi, Maharashtra, and Uttar Pradesh to go along with the examples set by other states in conducting similar surveys. *Seventh*, in June 2005, Prime Minister Manmohan Singh constituted a High Level Committee for Preparation of Report on Social, Economic and Educational Status of the Muslim Community of India chaired by Justice Rajindar Sacchar. The Committee's Member Secretary, Abu Saleh Shariff, told the present writer that many central ministries are beginning to provide data broken-down by religious affiliation.[7] Finally, as I have demonstrated in my book *Khaki and the Ethnic Violence in India*, even the composition of the armed forces, para-military forces, and the police is not exactly a secret. Given the widespread computerization of records since the 1990s, it would be much easier now than before to make such data available.

However, this is not to suggest that data is available for every economic activity involving all groups and for all years, nor is it suggested that it is necessarily delivered to interested parties just because it exists. For instance,. the National Commission for Minorities described one of its functions "is to serve as a national clearing house for information in respect of the conditions of the minorities."[8] But it inaccurately assumed that "unfortunately, not much information is available for the reasons that very little data, apart from non-official publications, exists on the condition of the minorities.[9] Confessing its inadequacies, it said in 1986, that: "The

Commission is not well-equipped to collect such data from the grass-roots. The State Governments have not shown much enthusiasm in collecting this information. The Commission, therefore decided that the Ministry of Welfare and Ministry of Home Affairs may be requested to direct the Registrar of Census Operations that in future, decennial census operations' data on economic indicators may be compiled community-wise to give an indication about the status of the various minorities...in employment, education, health, housing, income, agricultural holdings, industrial ownership and so on."[10] The NSSO survey of 1987-88 may partly be the result of pressure that Minorities Commission applied. The NSSO data has rightly emphasized the regional diversity but is not always broken down state-wise. Since the NSSO data is presently available only at the national level and not disaggregated at the state level, it is not used in the present study which focuses on state-wise details.[11] Ideally, the Census of India should take the lead in this direction by publishing the socio-economic figures at not merely the national level, but down to the smallest unit. So far the Census of India has not done so, since it will be a political decision.

Turning to the question of public availability of the data, let us consider the government-sponsored reports, such as the Gopal Singh Panel and the Minorities Commission's annual reports. The Government constituted the Gopal Singh Panel in May 1980, and the Panel submitted the Report in June 1983. However, the findings and the recommendations of the Report were presented in Lok Sabha only on 27 August 1990, a good seven years after its compilation and that too after persistent public pressure.[12] Leaving aside the government's rejection of most of the Panel's recommendations, it is surprising that even the National Minorities Commission was not given a copy in 1988 by the Ministry of Welfare when it asked for the Report though the Commission itself works directly under the same Ministry.[13] Other than the extracts published in *Muslim India*, the Report is not available, certainly not in any library as a search on *Worldcat*, an online database of libraries globally, revealed in October 2005. Nearly a quarter century after its compilation, the Gopal Singh Panel Report is now unknown to politicians as Asghar Ali Engineer remarked.[14] The National Minorities Commission has also gathered some data from various sources in its annual reports since 1978. However, these reports can be made public only when presented in the Lok Sabha and acted upon by the Government.[15] Since the Government has to also present an Action Taken Report, it often does not present these reports to the Lok Sabha. Therefore, the reports of the NCM have not been publicly available since 1996 as the Chairman informed the present writer.[16] Even more seriously, the NCM's own *Thirteenth Annual Report* covering the period 01.04.1989 to 31.03.1991, for instance, is not available even within the Commission's own office or its library.[17] What is true of the NCM is also true of the State Minorities Commissions in Andhra Pradesh, Bihar, and Uttar Pradesh. The states of Karnataka and Maharashtra have fortunately published their reports. There are variations in the kind of data on each state which become obvious as one looks at the situation of Muslims in the different states. Nevertheless, the data does allow for a reasonably accurate picture of the lived experience of Muslims with regard to employment and their role in the economy across the states covered in this book.

As previously stated, a country as large as India, with its immense regional diversity, demands a discussion of Muslims in the Indian economy that is broken down into manageable components, such as regions or sectors. Leaving aside Bengal and Punjab, whose major parts eventually became Pakistan and East Pakistan/Bangladesh in 1947 and 1971 respectively, and therefore have even greater specificities linked with partition of the states themselves, let us focus more deeply on Delhi and UP, then moving to Bihar, and finally to the southern states.

Notes

1 *The Times of India* 5 December 1949, as cited in Steven I. Wilkinson, *Votes and Violence* (Cambridge: Cambridge University Press, 2004), p. 40.

2 Asha Krishnakumar, "Caste and Census," *Frontline* 17, 18 (02-17 September 2000) Internet edition.

[3] Jawaharlal Nehru, *Letters to Chief Ministers*, III, edited by G. Parthsarathy (New Delhi: Oxford University Press, 1985), p.376.

[4] Cited in Omar Khalidi, *Khaki and the Ethnic Violence in India* (New Delhi: Three Essays Collective, 2003), p.11.

[5] *Sarvekshana* (September 1990), this is the Sanskrit name of the journal of the NSSO, though contents are in English; and http://mospi.nic.in/mospi_nsso_data.htm. Using NSSO data, several authors have analyzed the differing development of Hindus and Muslims, see Sudhanshu Ranade, "The Muslim Question: Whistling in the Dark," *The Hindu* (3 January 1992), idem, "The Muslim Question: And Now for the Facts," *The Hindu* (4 January 1992); Abu Saleh Shariff, *Some Socio-Economic and Demographic Aspects of Population According to Religion in India* (Bombay: Center for the Study of Society and Secularism, 1993); idem, "Socio-Economic and Demographic Differentials between Hindus and Muslims in India," *Economic and Political Weekly* (18 November 1995), pp. 2947-2953; idem, *India: Human Development Report: A Profile of the Indian States in the 1990s* (New Delhi: Oxford University Press, 1999).

[6] *Employment and Unemployment Situation among Religious Groups in India, Report no. 468 (55/1016 Survey Year 1999-2000* (New Delhi: NSSO, 2001); Abu Saleh Shariff, "On the Margins: Muslims in a State of Socio-Economic Decline," *The Times of India* (22 October 2004); electronic edition; Abu Saleh Shariff and Mehtabul Azam, *Economic Empowerment of Muslims in India* (New Delhi: Institute of Objective Studies, 2004); Garimella Subramaniam, "How the Muslims Figure," *The Hindu* (23 February 2001), Internet edition; C. Rammanohar Reddy, " Deprivation Affects Muslims More," *The Hindu* (12 September 2002), idem "The Gap Widened During the 1990s," *The Hindu* (13 September 2002) both on Internet; Azra Razzack and Anil Gumber, *Differentials in Human Development: A Case for Empowerment of Muslims in India* (New Delhi: National Council for Applied Economic Research, 2000).

[7] Personal email communication, 07 October , 2005.

[8] *Ninth Annual Report of the Minorities Commission for the Period from 1-4-1986 to 31-3-1987* (New Delhi: Ministry of Welfare, 1989),p. 42.

[9] Ibid.

[10] Ibid, pp. 42-43.

[11] Except Rijo M. John and Rohit Mutatkar, "Statewise Estimates of Poverty among Religious Groups in India," *Economic and Political Weekly* (26 March 2005): 1337-1345.

[12] "Gopal Singh Panel Report: Government Statement and Comments, Lok Sabha 24 August 1990," *Muslim India* (May 1991), pp. 225-227; *Muslim India* (June 1991), pp. 264-267; "Joint Letter to Prime Minister on Gopal Singh Panel Report, 3 August 1989," *Muslim India* (September 1989), p. 393, written by Syed Shahabuddin and others.

[13] *Tenth Annual Report of the Minorities Commission for the Period from 1-4-1987 to 31-3-1988* (New Delhi: Ministry of Welfare, 1990).

[14] Asghar Ali Engineer, "New Secular Government and Its Secular Tasks," *The Milli Gazette* (16-30 June 2004), p. 16. However Engineer is incorrect when he says that the report was not tabled in Lok Sabha, when in fact it was on 27 August 1990 when V.P. Singh was the Prime Minister.

[15] "Termites and the Reports," *Radiance* (12 June 1998), p. 2.

[16] Interview with the Chairman Tarlochan Singh, New Delhi 24 December 2004 and with NCM member Ahmad Rashid Shervani.

[17] I did not get a copy when I visited the Commission in December 2004, subsequent efforts through a journalist yielded the information that neither the Commission office nor its library owned copy!

MEDIEVAL AND COLONIAL INDIA

Coastal India and Arabia had been in maritime contact through centuries. Muslims in the form of Arab merchants first appeared on the Malabar[1] and Konkan[2] coasts during the 7th century C.E. not many years after the death of the Prophet Muhammad. Each year the sea brought a handful of traders, including Arabian and Persian horse dealers who settled in the west-coast ports. Over five centuries later, Central Asian Turkish invasions brought much of northern India under their sultanates based in Delhi. Except for the deep south much of the Deccan was also conquered by the late thirteenth century under the Bahmani sultanate. The Central Asian Turkish invaders and their camp followers included horse dealers. The Indian cavalry had always suffered from the inferior breed available in the country. In medieval times "horses remained the most expensive single item of import into India. Turkistan bred the finest stock, equal in quality to Arab thoroughbreds, and some of these trickled through the northwestern land routes during the intervals between the Mongol raids. But the sea was the more regular channel for the import of horses."[3] Except for these horse dealers and other merchants on the coast, the bulk of the fledging Muslim groups formed a military aristocracy thinly spread over the main population centers. The Muslim aristocracy was too busy soldiering and governing to undertake commercial activities. Its worldview on money did not stress wealth creation. The "elites of Mughal India regard money (whether as capital stock or as a means of exchange) as a respectable social phenomenon. But it is one respectable social phenomenon among several. Money is certainly not seen as expressing the highest value that a man should attain and can attain in his membership of the human society. It is a means of meeting basic needs, and the less time and effort a man spends in satisfying his basic needs, the closer he will be to fulfilling his 'real' nature."[4]

Gradually, certain castes and outcastes of the local population converted to Islam, mainly artisans and cultivators. Despite the rise and fall of various dynasties in the north and the south, the composition of the Muslim community did not change drastically. Thus the Muslim society as it evolved during the medieval and early modern era (c.1200-1800) fell into three broad categories: the aristocracy and nobility, both secular and religious, the artisans and the cultivators. During the Sultanate era (c.1200s-1520s), according to historian Romila Thapar, "elevation to the nobility was open to all, and many of the most exalted nobles had begun as retainers to the Sultan. Titles and offices were not hereditary and were dependent on the goodwill of the Sultan. In later years, when they came to be looked upon as hereditary, the nobility acquired elaborate genealogies to prove their aristocratic origins, and Indian converts began to assert a foreign ancestry...The nobles derived their income from the revenues of their *iqtas,* land-grant system, and those attached to the court from their offices at the court. Despite the obligation to maintain troops, the revenue from the *iqtas* was sufficient to allow of luxurious living...Functionally, the nobility was divided into two categories, described as "men of the sword," (*ahl-i saif*) and "men of the pen," (*ahl-i qalam*). The former were either the military commanders or those whose power was based on military strength. The latter were the religious leaders and the administrators. These were chiefly the *ulama* or theologians, of whom some were advisers to the sultanate and others occupied judicial offices...Theoretically, the religious category included the mystics or saints... The saints in some cases received endowments, which made life for them and their descendants both secure and comfortable...The Muslim population of the towns consisted mainly of artisans, with a floating population of traders. The latter were generally of Arab or Persian origin and were independent merchants. In addition to the artisans, the royal slaves working either at the court or in the royal workshops were large enough in number to form a considerable part of the urban Muslim population, both in the capital of the sultanates and other capital cities. The Muslim element in the peasant population grew in numbers toward the latter part of this period. The pattern of living of the cultivators, whether Hindu or Muslim, was almost identical in essentials."[5]

In the Mughal era *inams*, rent-free tenures of land, sometimes entire villages were gifted to Muslim divines as well as Brahmins as reward for public service or for the maintenance of charitable institutions, but the British revoked the system in the middle of the nineteenth century.[6] A few of the Muslim religious divines found no contradiction between earning a livelihood, *kasb*, and a devotional life, although characteristically other-worldly orientation led many Indian divines to discourage it. Many welcomed the royalty to the shrines, *dargahs*, and *khanqahs*, and accepted cash grants and lands, making many *dargahs* the foci of greed, power and, ultimately, of endless litigation among the Sufi descendants and shrine custodians.

Muslim peasants and cultivators, like their counterparts in other religions, remained economically active in agricultural production, fishing, herding and other manual work. Independent professionals among Muslims were few, except the traditional medical doctors or hakims.[7] In the post-Sultanate, Mughal period of history in northern India (1520s-1720s), the pattern of Muslim economic life did not change radically. The political authority and control on resources within the Mughal Empire tended to be concentrated in the hands of the Mughal ruling class, consisting of high *mansabdars*, office holders, not land holders. The *mansabdars* were military commanders, administrators and financial officers paid in cash. The Mughal ruling class did not include the vast Muslim pastoral or agricultural communities near the capital such as the Meos or the more distant tribes of the northwestern frontier. The Mughals and their contemporary regional sultans of the Deccan, such as the Adil Shahis and the Qutb Shahis, liberally recruited upper castes of martial reputations like the Rajputs, Khatris (Kshatriyas), even Marathas as soldiers, and Brahmans and Kayasthas as accountants in the revenue department and record keepers in the bureaucracy.[8] Outside the Mughal governing class, intelligentsia was one group of Muslims who enjoyed privileged positions in the high offices of *sadarat, diwani* and *buyutat.* Land ownership (as distinct from mere title to its produce) and inland trade remained a firm Hindu monopoly, as described by S.V. Desika Char from various sources.[9] Given the Hindu monopoly over land ownership, it is not surprising that the *zamindar* class was predominantly non-Muslim.[10] Thus it is abundantly clear that the various empires and kingdoms headed by Muslim dynasties did not make them Muslim states, certainly not in the sense that all Muslims regardless of class enjoyed the status and privileges associated with the royalty.[11] Even the privileged position of the Mughal *mansabdars* became precarious as the posts decreased, imperial authority began to shrink as a result of territorial losses to the Marathas, Rajputs, Sikhs and others inland and the European trading companies on the coasts in the early eighteenth century. The death of Emperor Awrangzib (1707) heralded the disintegration and fall of the Mughal Empire, and the emergence of regional kingdoms of Punjab, Rajputana, Awadh, Bengal, and Deccan. Little over a century after Awrangzib's death, the reigning Mughal emperor Bahadur Shah I had been reduced to the status of mayor of Red Fort in Delhi petitioning the British for stipend increment.[12] As opportunities decreased, numerous Persian and Urdu poets wrote *shahr ashobs*,[13] (literally, "the city's misfortune") lamenting the plight of the Mughal nobility and the intelligentsia everywhere in the country. They are eloquent testimonies to the declining fortunes of this class. Even a poet of Asadullah Khan Ghalib's (1797-1869) stature had to beseech the Emperor seeking regular pay:

Baske leta hoon, har mahine, qarz
Aur rahti hai sud ki takrar
Meri tankhwah main chaharum ka
Ho gaya hai sharik sahukar
Meri tankhwah kijiye mah ba mah
Ta na ho, mujh ko, zindagi dushwar

For the Mughal soldiers, officials, and the intelligentsia, employment choices narrowed as the authority of rebellious Rajputs, Sikhs, and Marathas spread wider. They could migrate to the newly established courts and armies of the regional political formations such as those of the Nawabs of Awadh and Rampur in the north, the Naib-Nazims of Bengal in the east, or the Nizams of Hyderabad in the Deccan. Or they could find employment with the foreign rulers, which some did, like the *munshis*, letter-writers, interpreters and counselors in the various towns.[14]

As the East India Company's authority grew in the Mughal territories, "the British at first retained the Muslim officials but from the time of [Lord] Cornwallis (1786-93) replaced them in their own favor. Their position in the law courts was steadily undermined as the British revised public law and introduced their own procedures in the courts. They were still the exponents of the official language of Persian. But this ceased to be of value when [Lord] Bentinck made English the language of official governmental and legal business in 1835. In the same year came the introduction of English education, which soon became a qualification for subordinate official career. Most Muslims were too conservative to learn English, many considering it the highway to infidelity. But the Hindu classes were not; they had learnt Persian for a livelihood, in the past, so why not English, and they soon monopolized the subordinate services. Muslims found themselves not only shut out from office, but also deprived of all hope of ever returning to it. The crowning disaster was the Mutiny of 1857, which, though commenced on caste grounds by Hindus, was blamed on the Muslim community as an anti-British revolt."[15] Barely a year earlier, in 1856, British annexed the Muslim kingdom of the Awadh nawabs based in Lucknow. The two events nearly completed the destruction and disintegration of the Muslim aristocracy in much of northern India, thus further curtailing the prospects of the soldiery, intelligentsia and the artisans dependent on feudal patronage. The Muslim peasantry remained unaffected by these major political upheavals. Distrusted by the state, divested of lands, deprived of employment, uneducated in modern science and technology through English, Muslim economic condition in the immediate post-Mutiny era is aptly versified by Mawlana Altaf Husain Hali (1837-1914), an eminent poet:

Na ahl-i hukumat ke hamraz hain ham
Na darbarion main sarfaraz hain ham
Na ilmon main shayan-i izzat hain ham
Na sanat main hirfat main mumtaz hain ham
Na rakhte hain kuch manzilat naukri main
Na hissa hamara ha saudagari main

We are not trusted by the government,
Nor are we among the prominent courtiers of the ruler
Neither are we among the educated elite
We have no share in trade or the industry
Nor do you find us in the civil services
Or in the businesses

For the Muslim soldiery and the intelligentsia, the only major center for employment now was the Nizam's Hyderabad, since the rulers of Arcot, Awadh, Bengal, and Mysore were all finished by 1857. As Insha Allah Khan Insha put it, they were ready to go wherever there was opportunity:

Kamar bandhe huwe chalne ko yan sab yar baithe hain
Bahut age gaye, baqi jo hain sab tayyar baithe hain
Najibon ka ajab kuch hal hai is daur main yaro
Jise dekho yehi kahte hain ham bekar baithe hain

We are all geared up and ready to leave
Many have moved, those left behind are ready too
The gentry in this age are not in good shape
Everyone says he is jobless.

No wonder that the last reigning Nizam, Mir Osman Ali Khan, put his perceived status as such in an oft-quoted lyric:

Salatin-i salaf ho chuke sab nazr-i ajal Osman[16]
Musalmanon ka teri saltanat se hai nishan baqi

The sultans of yesteryears are well past, O Osman!
Muslims' name and fame lives due to your kingdom.

The Lilliputian nawabs and begums of Bhopal, Rampur, Tonk, and a few other principalities were too small to offer much to a large number of employment seekers. In order to stem the tide of further economic loss, the Muslim elite which survived the catastrophic events of 1856-57 in upper India decided that the first order of business in the task of recovery was to come to terms with the British. Sayyid Ahmad Khan (1817-98) of Delhi, founder of the Aligarh movement, for example, took the opportunity to work closely with the British for political reconciliation between the new rulers and his co-religionists, and for securing modern education. In a letter to a friend he warned: "If the Muslims do not take to the system of education introduced by the British, they will not only remain a backward community but will sink lower until there will be no hope for recovery left to them."[17] Although the Aligarh movement's educational efforts were limited to the then North-Western Provinces, Oudh (i.e. modern UP), Bihar, Delhi and Punjab, he spoke in all-India terms. The Aligarh movement had no impact on the province with the single largest number of Muslims, Bengal. Nor did it have significant impact in the provinces of Bombay and Madras. Hyderabad State under the Nizam was of course a different category altogether. Educational advancement of millions of people in a vast country such as colonial India could hardly be managed by a single movement cutting across provincial boundaries, differing political and economic conditions. Given the large size of British India, its princely states and provinces, even a rapid survey of economic and educational condition of Indian Muslims in the colonial era is possible only when broken down first by employment in central government and then by provincial regions, to which we now turn.

Muslims in Government of India Employment During the Raj, 1857-1947

Colonial official and historian, William Wilson Hunter, published in 1871 an influential book *The Indian Musalmans: Are They Bound in Conscience To Rebel Against the Queen*?[18] Leaving aside other matters in the book, in the final chapter Hunter shows the near exclusion of Muslims from the officer ranks in the army, from the Revenue Department posts, and from civil employment.[19] Since only one Indian was in the Covenanted Civil Service[20] at that time, Hunter's book dealt with positions in the Uncovenanted Civil Service. According to him, the following distribution was in effect in 1871 in Bengal:

Table I

Holders of Gazetted Appointments in Bengal, 1871[21]

Groups	*Number*	*Percent*
Europeans	1338	63.3
Hindus	681	32.3
Musalmans	92	4.4
Total Gazetted Appointments	2111	100

The ratio of Hindus to Muslims in the number of Indians who were gazetted-appointment holders was 7.4 to 1.0. The ratio of Hindus to Muslims in the Indian population of Bengal was 3.1 to 1.0.[22] In other words, the Hindus of Bengal held slightly over 88 percent of the gazetted appointments held by Indians in Bengal, whereas they made up only 68 percent of the total population of the province. Hunter ascribed this uneven distribution of positions between Hindus and Muslims to the educational system in Bengal. He wrote: "The truth is, that our system of public instruction which has awakened the Hindus from the sleep of centuries, and quickened their inert masses with some noble impulses of a nation, is opposed to the traditions, unsuited to the requirements, and hateful to the religion of the Musalmans."[23] How was the system of public instruction in Lower Bengal opposed to the traditions of Muslims? The Muslim elite had the tradition of being conquerors of India. To be thrown into a school system with a "...people whom they hated as idolaters and despised as a servile race,"[24] was incomprehensible to them. The use of Bengali in the government schools of Lower Bengal along with employment of Hindus as instructors also repulsed some elite Muslims. Muslims also resented the absence of religious instruction in the government schools. Economic consequences also injured Muslim education in Bengal. The revenue free Muslim grants had been confiscated by the Raj. The British also misappropriated an estate that had been left for Muslim religious educational purposes by using a portion of the money from that estate to build an English college.[25]

Hunter proposed a revamped educational scheme for Muslims, with English taught in the Muslim schools, and periodical inspection to ensure implementation.[26] Hunter's contention was simply that the Muslims were not receiving the proper kind of education to ensure entrance into the public service. This is slightly different from the view that Muslims of Bengal were receiving no education. In this context, it should be remembered that with the victory of the Anglicists over the Orientalists in the 1830s, education in India came to mean English education.

How valid are Hunter's assertions? In some portions of his book, Hunter speaks of the adverse conditions concerning Muslim education in Lower Bengal, and in other places he refers to all of Bengal. In some sections of the book he neglects to mention the area of which he is speaking, giving the impression that he is talking about India in general. By hastily identifying Bengal (or Lower Bengal) with India, one is apt to get a faulty impression of Muslim education and Muslim representation in the public service. The following table shows the number of Hindus and Muslims appointed to the higher positions in the public service in India in 1871, broken down on a provincial basis.

Table II
Number of Hindus & Muslims Appointed to Positions in the Indian Public Service in 1871 Carrying a Monthly Stipend of at Least 150 Rupees[27]

Province	*Hindus*	*Muslims*	*Muslim %*
Bengal	88	11	11
Bombay	51	5	9
Sind	3	1	25
Madras	70	1	1
North Western Province	30	16	35
Punjab	51	31	38
Oudh	6	5	45
Central Provinces	4	2	33
Total	300	72	24

Source: Great Britain, *Parliamentary Papers*, Vol. LIV (Accounts and Papers) 63, 1875, Amended Return Showing the Number of Appointments in India, of No Less than 150 Rupees A Month, Filled During the Years 1867, 1868, 1869, 1870, and 1871, By the Appointment of Natives of India, Distinguishing Those Held by Hindoos From Those Held By the Mohammedans, p.1.

The above table shows that the situation was not the same in any two provinces. It also shows that eight Hindus were being appointed for every one Muslim in Bengal, which is quite close to Hunter's figure of 7·4 to 1 concerning the number of gazetted positions held in 1871. Hunter is correct, then, when he speaks of Bengal, but what of North Western India? The picture is not as dark there, concerning Muslim employment in the public services. When these figures are compared with population statistics from the various provinces (leaving aside for the moment large princely states like Hyderabad, and the smaller ones of Bhopal, Tonk and Rampur), another set of facts comes to light, especially concerning the North Western Provinces, and Oudh.

Table III
Percent of Muslims Appointed to the Public Services in 1871 Compared with Percent of Muslim Population

Province	*Total Population*	*Muslim Po pulation*	*% Muslim Population*	*% Muslim appointed in 1871*
Bengal	60,467,724	19,553,420	32	11
Bombay	16,349,206	2,528,344	15	9
Madras	31, 282,177	1,872,2141	6	1
N-W Province	30,781,204	4,188,751	14	35
Punjab	17,611,498	9,102, 488	52	38
Oudh	11,220,232	1,111, 290	10	45
Totals	**167,711,041**	**38,356,507**	**23**	**24**

Source: Report of the India Education Commission, (Calcutta: Superintendent of Printing, 1883),p. 484, as cited in Zafarul Islam and Raymond L. Jensen, "Indian Muslims and the Public Service, 1871-1915," *Asiatic Society of Pakistan Journal* 9 (June 1964), pp. 88-89.

The Muslims on a population basis were underrepresented in Bengal, Bombay, Madras, and the Punjab, they were over represented in the North Western Provinces and Oudh, although the statistics should be discounted, since so few persons were appointed in 1871. Considering India as whole, one sees that the Muslims are represented equitably in the public service in 1871, at least in so far as higher appointments are concerned. Even the population data needs breaking down to be really meaningful. First, it is probably not possible, even if desirable, that each community can be represented in each service or profession in exact or even near exact proportion to its population. We must know the class structure of the Muslim community in the various areas to make meaningful generalizations. Could the Muslims of the Ganges delta be considered candidates for the service? Were not many of these Muslims poor peasants? Were not Muslims the leading classes in the North Western Provinces and Oudh, at least until 1856, even though they constituted a minority? All persons could not aspire to positions in the public service in India in 1871. The problem, therefore, revolves around the question: who could aspire to positions in the public service and where did these aspirants live? Until the eligibility of the two major religious communities on a provincial basis can be determined, the supposed exclusion of Muslims from the public service cannot be verified.

On August 7, 1871, Lord Mayo's administration issued a resolution recommending:

> 1.That further encouragement should be given to the classical and vernacular languages of the Mohammadans in all government schools and colleges; 2. that in avowedly English schools established in Mohammadan districts, the appointment of qualified Mohammadan English teachers might, with advantage be encouraged; 3. that as in vernacular schools, so in avowedly English schools, assistance might justly be given to Mohammadans by grants-in-aid to create schools of their own; and 4. that greater encouragement should also be given to the creation of vernacular literature for Mohammadans.[28]

As we shall see in the survey of each province and state later on, Muslim elite in various parts of the country made efforts for the promotion of modern education. But with the appointment of the Indian Education Commission of 1882/83, headed by William W. Hunter, the author of the influential book cited earlier, the whole question came under official scrutiny again. After reviewing briefly the early efforts at imparting an English education to the Muslims, the Commission concluded that the aloofness, which the Muslims showed to English education, was "to be found in pride of race, a memory of bygone superiority, religious fears, and not an unnatural attachment to the teaching of Islam."[29] Regarding the investigations and attention that had been given the matter in 1871/73, the Commission concluded, "...that except in matter of higher education there had been a tendency to exaggerate the backwardness of the

Muhammadans."[30] The Commission did shed some light on why the percentage of Muslims in the public service was lower in the Punjab than in the North Western Provinces. By now the eligibility of persons for employment in the public service was directly linked to English education, and the one large group of non-English educated persons in the Punjab was Muslims—those who belonged to tribal groups in what became in 1901 the North-Western Frontier Province. The Commission noted that in the districts east of the Jhelum River, the Muslims were fairly well represented in the schools, as also in the districts of Delhi, Hissar, Ambala, and Amritsar Divisions, where the percentage of Muslims in the schools exceeded considerably the percentage of Muslims in the population. In the Derajat and Peshawar Division, however, where the Muslims made up over ninety percent of the population, there was but few Muslims in the school.[31] This goes to explain, why in the overall percentage of Punjab, the percentage of Muslims in 1871 was below the percentage in the population as was shown in Table III.

Responding to the agitation in Bengal regarding entrance to Indian Civil Service and other matters, the colonial administration appointed a Royal Commission under the chairmanship of C.U. Aitchison in 1886 to devise a scheme to enable Indians to be recruited to higher and more extensive levels of employment in public service. Among others, Sayyid Ahmad Khan of Delhi and Aligarh and Qazi Shahabuddin of Bombay were its members. The Aitchison Commission revealed data showing community-wise breakdown in 1886.

Table IV
Number of Persons Serving in the Statutory Service in 1886 arranged according to Province and Community

Province	*Hindus*	*Muslims*	*Parsis*	*Sikhs*	*Burmese*	*Total*
Madras	6	2				8
Bombay	5	2	2			9
Bengal	9	2				11

NW Provinces & Oudh	6	5				11
Punjab		3		2		5
Central Provinces	1	1				2
British Burma					2	2
Totals	**27**	**15**	**2**	**2**	**2**	**48**

Source: *Report of the India Education Commission,* (Calcutta: Superintendent of Printing, 1883),p. 484, as cited in Zafarul Islam and Raymond L. Jensen, "Indian Muslims and the Public Service, 1871-1915," *Asiatic Society of Pakistan Journal* 9 (June 1964), p.104.

When the data is transferred to a percentage basis and compared to the population on a provincial basis, it can be seen that the Muslims had more representation in the Statutory Service in every area than they had in the Uncovenanted Service,[32] and that the percentage of Muslims serving in the Statutory Service[33] exceeded the percentage of Muslims in the population in every province except Bengal.

Table V

Percentage of Muslims in India and Percentage of Muslims in the Statutory Service on a Provincial Basis in 1886

Province	*Muslim % in Population*	*Muslim % in Statutory Service*	*Muslim % in Executive & Judicial Services of the Un-covenanted Services*
Madras	6.2	25.0	4.0
Bombay	18.3	22.2	5.4
Bengal	31,2	18.2	8.5
N-W Province & Oudh	13.4	45.5	45.1
Punjab	51.3	60.0	39.3
Central Provinces	2.4	50.0	18.1
India	23.0	31.3	19.9

Source: *Report of the India Education Commission, (*Calcutta: Superintendent of Printing, 1883),p. 484, as cited in Zafarul Islam and Raymond L. Jensen, "Indian Muslims and the Public Service, 1871-1915," *Asiatic Society of Pakistan Journal* 9 (June 1964), p.105.

The Aitchison Commission commented briefly on Hindu and Muslim participation in the Executive and Judicial Services of the Uncovenanted Service.

Table VI

Percentage of Muslims in India and Percentage of Muslims in the Executive and Judicial Services of the Uncovenanted Service on a Provincial Basis

Area	*Muslim % in Population*	*% of Executive Positions held*	*% of Judicial Positions held*
Madras	6.2	5.4	1.6
Bombay & Sind	18.3	7.4	8
Bengal	31.2	12.9	3.1
N-W Provinces & Oudh	13.4	44.8	45.9
Punjab	51.3	41.8	33.6
Central Provinces	2.4	18.1	Exec. & Judicial combined
Hyderabad Assigned Dists.	7.0	16	Exec. & Judicial combined
Assam	26.9	.9	.9

Source: *Report of the India Education Commission,* (Calcutta: Superintendent of Printing, 1883),p. 484, as cited in Zafarul Islam and Raymond L. Jensen, "Indian Muslims and the Public Service, 1871-1915," *Asiatic Society of Pakistan Journal* 9 (June 1964), p.105.

The most striking feature in the above table is the difference between the percentage of Muslims employed in the Executive Service and those in the Judicial Service. The North Western Province and Oudh remains a stronghold of Muslim employment in the public service as in 1871. For the whole of British India, out of a total of 2,588 positions in the Executive and Judicial Services of the Uncovenanted Service, the Muslims held 514 positions or 20 percent, and made up 20 percent of the population. The Hindus held 1,866 positions for 72 percent of the total, whereas they made up 75 percent of the population.[34] In the Executive Service the Muslims held twenty-three percent of the appointments to the Hindus' 68 percent.[35] In the Judicial Service the Muslims were under-represented considerably, though equitably represented when the two Services are considered together in 1886.

The Government of India appointed a commission (known commonly as Islington Commission) on September 5, 1912 to examine the methods of recruitment, system of training, conditions of service, salary and related matters, as well as to recommend such changes as may seem expedient.[36] Around this time Syed Wazir Hasan, the officiating secretary of All India Muslim League wrote a detailed article on Muslim representation in the government service. Written in the context of the Commission's appointment, the article expresses the League's position and hoped to influence its findings. In his article,[37] Hasan admitted that Muslim education was improving, but complained that Muslims were not getting their fair share of employment. Even though he did not identify a method of determining a fair share, he seems to have taken the position that population proportions should govern the proportion of government employment held by any one religious community. As of 1912, he asserted that the Muslims were underrepresented. To prove his point, he included a table of employment statistics.

Table VII
Employment Statistics for Various Departments of Indian Administration, 1912

Departments	*Europeans*	*Hindus*	*Musulmans*	*Others*	*Total*
I.C.S.	1238	40	9	7	1294
Statutory Civilians		5	8	8	15
Provincial servants holding appointments reserved for ICS	7	26	11	3	47
Provincial Civil Service					

(Executive)	205	828	326	85	1444
Subordinate Judges	10	262	26	29	327
Munsifs	7	635	95	1	738
Provincial Forest Department	87	75	16	9	187
Salt Department	51	7	3		61
Customs	50	1		2	53
Post Office (Superintendents and Postmasters getting more than Rs. 200)	100	71	24	13	208
Telegraph Department Superintendents and Assistant and Deputy Superintendents	122	16	1	1	140
Accounts Dept.	68	20	2	4	94
Supdts. of Police	330	4	1	2	337
Deputy Superintendent of Police	58	93	72	24	247
Provincial Education Service	54	262	45	16	377
Indian Medical Service	387	13	2	4	406
Civil Assistant Surgeons	41	230	54	26	551
Public Works Department Imperial Engineers	538	51	3	6	598
Provincial Engineers	59	103	5	5	172

Source: Syed Wazir Hasan, "Mussalmans and the Public Service," *The Indian Nation* 14 (January 1913): 40-51.

One striking factor the Table brings out is the share of European involvement in the Indian administration. In order to verify the exclusion charge brought by Hasan, a comparison between Hindu and Muslim employment is made.

Table VIII

Share for Each Community of the Positions Held by Either Hindus and Muslims in 1912 (Computed from Table VII)

Department	*% of Positions held by Hindus of all positions*	*% of Positions held by Muslims of all positions*	*No. of Persons involved in computation*
I.C.S.	81.6	18.4	49
Statutory Civilians	38.5	61.5	13
Provincial servants holding appointments reserved for ICS	70.3	29.7	37
Subordinate judges	90.0	9.4	288
Munsifs	86.9	13.1	288
Provincial Forest Department	82.4	17.6	91
Salt Department	70.0	30.0	10
Post Office (Superintendents & Postmasters getting more than Rs. 200)	74.7	25.3	95
Telegraph Department (Assistant & Deputy Superintendent	94.1	5.9	17
Accounts Department	90.9	9.1	22
Superintendents of Police	80.0	20.0	22
Deputy Superintendents of Police	56.4	43.6	165
Provincial Education Service	85.3	14.7	307
Indian Medical Service	86.6	13.4	15
Civil Assistant Surgeon	80.9	19.1	284
Imperial Engineers	94.4	5.6	54
Provincial Engineers	95.4	4.6	108

% of Hindus in combined Hindu Muslim Populations 73.9

% of Muslims in combined Hindu Muslim Populations 26.1

Source: Zafarul Islam and Raymond L. Jensen, "Indian Muslims and the Public Service, 1871-1915," *Asiatic Society of Pakistan Journal* 9 (June 1964), pp. 121-122.

Excluding the princely states, Muslims and Hindus constituted 23.5 and 66.9 percent respectively of British India's population in 1911. These percentages are then used in Table V to arrive at the two population percentages in services. The above chart looks at the Hindus and Muslims in employment on the basis of the combined Hindu and Muslim populations.

When viewed against Hindu appointments, the Muslims lagged in thirteen departments out of eighteen. Again, as in 1886, the Muslims were under-represented in judicial appointments. It is further evident that Muslims trailed the Hindus in the proportion of certain technical appointments. The Muslims, however, more than held their own in the number of positions in the executive branch of the Provincial Civil Service. The relatively poorer number of Muslims in the technical appointments probably means that fewer Muslim boys enrolled in the arduous applied scientific and technical education courses. In his article Hasan observed that Muslims held only 2.6 percent of all positions carrying a stipend of at least Rs. 500 a month. The Hindus, on the other hand held 14.5 percent of such appointments. The Muslims were definitely under represented in the higher-paying positions. The Islington Commission report was published in 1917, but due to the First World War, it did not receive the attention it deserved as an exceptionally complete document for the public service just before the War on 1 April 1913 as shown here.

Table IX
Number of Persons Holding Civil Appointments Carrying a Monthly Salary of Rs. 200 or More Per Month on 1 April 1913

Number of Positions held	*% of positions held*	*Group Holding Positions*
Europeans	4898	44
Hindus	3199	29
Eurasians	1593	14

Muhammadans	771	7
Buddhists	198	2
Indian Christians	179	2
Parsis	159	1
Sikhs	67	1
Total	11064	100

Source: Zafarul Islam and Raymond L. Jensen, "Indian Muslims and the Public Service, 1871-1915," *Asiatic Society of Pakistan Journal* 9 (June 1964), p.125.

The ratio of Hindu to Muslim position holders was 4.1 to 1.0. The population ratio of Hindus to Muslims in British India (excluding princely states) was 2.8 to 1.0 in 1911. Expressed in another manner, whereas the Muslims made 26.1 percent of the combined Hindu-Muslim population, they occupied only 19.4 percent of the positions held by Hindus and Muslims. Compared to the Hindus, the Muslim position had apparently deteriorated since 1886, when the situation is viewed on the basis of population proportions. This may be partly due to the relatively greater increase in Muslim population compared to the Hindu population during the period. From 1881 to 1911, the Hindu population of India increased 15.3 percent, while the Muslim population increased 33.0 percent.[38] Thus, while the Muslims were getting more positions through the years, their growing numbers made their position in regard to government employment appear to worsen. The key question in this regard concerns the classes of Muslims who were increasing in number. If the peasants were responsible for this increase, then the number of Muslims eligible for government employment did not rise above the usual proportion, and in reality the position of the Muslims did not worsen. Only when we know both the figures for increase in population for the two communities as well as the increase in education, can we make the comparison meaningful.

As the most highly educated group of Indians, the upper caste Hindu Bengalis had been agitating to gain entrance in the elite Indian Civil Service, the ICS in 1885, hitherto a European monopoly. The ICS was the "steel frame" holding together the British Indian Empire since 1858. The Islington Commission also dealt with this question of throwing open the service to Indians. As a result, on October 12, 1887, there were twelve Indians in the ICS, all Hindus.[39] On April 1913, there were 49 Hindus in the ICS compared to 9 Muslims. While the Hindus obtained 29 positions during 1887-1913, the Muslims found 9 or about 23.7 percent of the total positions obtained by the Hindus and Muslims. From 1887-1913, the percentage of Muslims in ICS was very close to the Muslim community's percentage in the national population. The following Table shows ICS strength as of 1 April 1913:

Table X
ICS Strength on 1 April 1913

Community	*Numbers*
Europeans	1305
Eurasians	3
Hindus	41
Parsis	6
Muslims	9
Indian Christians	7
Total	1371

Source: Zafarul Islam and Raymond L. Jensen, "Indian Muslims and the Public Service, 1871-1915," *Asiatic Society of Pakistan Journal* 9 (June 1964), p. 133.

It is obvious how advanced the tiny minorities, Parsis and the Christians,[40] were, compared to Muslims. However, by the end of the British period, the Muslim presence in the ICS decreased. On 1 August 1947, the ICS had a strength of 955, of which 103 or only 10.79 percent were Muslims.[41] Of the 103, only 12 remained in India.[42]

Among other measures suggested for the improvement of Muslim share in the government employment, one suggestion was to "nominate" young men from influential families to the service for up to twenty five to thirty three percent of the available positions.[43] The other suggestion, coming mainly from the Muslim elite, was to fix percentages for various communities in the civil services. To this end they made representations to a commission consisting of representatives of various Indian communities and headed by Alexander Muddiman, established in 1924. The Muddiman Commission observed that "it is impossible to fix any percentage for the representation of the communities in the services by statutory rule, and the utmost action that is possible, is to arrive at some formula which will meet the point."[44] The formula it proposed recommended that: "the rules for recruitment for Government should provide that, with due regard to efficiency, *all communities should receive due representation in the public services.* That is, if a due representation of persons belonging to a particular community who have passed a prescribed efficiency bar can be obtained for each service, the community should receive due representations, if necessary by nomination, in each service."[45] The formula recommended by Muddiman Commission does not seem to have worked. Instead, an informal rule of reservation was in fact followed, though unsuccessfully as "the Government of India have carefully reviewed the results of the policy followed since 1925 of reserving a certain percentage of direct appointments to Government service for the redress of communal inequities. It has been represented that though this policy was adopted mainly with the object of securing increased representation for Muslims in the Public Services, it has failed to secure for them their due share of appointments, and it has been contended that this position cannot be remedied unless a fixed percentage of vacancies is reserved for Muslims. In particular, attention has been drawn to the small number of Muslims in the Railway Service, even on those railways which pass through areas in which Muslims form a high percentage of population."[46] Consequently, the Home Department resolved that: "Twenty-five percent of all vacancies to be filled by direct recruitment of Indians will be reserved for Muslims and 8 ½ percent for other minority communities."[47]

Muslim League leader Muhammad Ali Jinnah backed the government policy and specifically asked the Congress Party to support this measure. He demanded in 1929 that "Provision should be made in the Constitution giving Muslims an adequate share, along with the other Indians, in all Services of the State and in local self-governing bodies, having due regard to the requirements of efficiency."[48] To this demand, Jawaharlal Nehru gave a qualified answer: "The fixing of the Muslims' share in the State Services by statutory enactment necessarily involves the fixing of the shares of other groups and communities similarly. This would mean a rigid and compartmental State structure which will impede progress and development. At the same time it is generally admitted that State appointments should be fairly and adequately distributed and no community should have a cause to complain. It is far better to do this by convention and agreement. The Congress is fully alive to this issue and desires to meet the wishes of various groups in the fullest measure, so as to give to all minority communities...'an adequate share in all the Services of the State and in Local Self-Governing Bodies having due regard to the requirements of efficiency.' The State today is becoming more and more technical and demands expert knowledge in its various departments. It is right that, if a community is backward in this technical and expert knowledge, special efforts should be made to give it this education to bring it up to a higher level."[49]

However, even as the Congress came to power in various provinces in 1937, this reservation policy remained, as it was the prerogative of the Government of India. Muslims began to be represented in central government jobs often in proportion to their population, for example in the Labor Department of the Central Government. According to B.R. Ambedkar, then Member for Labor & Works, Viceroy's Executive Council, during 1939-1946 Muslims constituted between 23-24 percent of all gazetted posts in his department. Muslims represented a sizeable 21-32 percent of the Central Public Works Department personnel, also under Ambedkar's charge. A number of other institutions under the Labor Department, such as the Estate Office, Geological Survey, School of Mines, and training schemes showed a healthy Muslim presence.[50] Moreover, the Instrument of Instructions issued to the provincial Governors by the Viceroy in 1937 under the Government of India Act, 1935, contained the following specific direction:[51] "Our Governor shall interpret the ... responsibility as requiring him to secure a due proportion of appointments in Our Services to the several communities." These clear instructions were disregarded by some of the Congress ministries in some provinces when they were in power from 1937-1939, according to the Muslim League reports,[52] as this was not in keeping with the Congress view of the problem. In a practical sense it did not have much impact due to the strong position of Governors.

Notes

1 Stephen F. Dale, *Islamic Society on South Asian Frontier: The Mappilas of Malabar* (Oxford: Clarendon Press, 1980).

2 Omar Khalidi, "Konkani Muslims: An Introduction", *Islamic Culture* 74, no. 1 (January 2000): 127-53.

3 Romila Thapar, *A History of India,* I (Harmondsworth, Essex: Penguin Books, 1984), p. 297. Until the late nineteenth, early twentieth centuries, the lancers of the Nizam's cavalry obtained large number of remounts from the Arab horse marts of Bombay, see W. Tweedie, *The Arab Horse* (Los Angeles: Broden, 1961, reprint of 1894 edition). Since Thapar's work, more specialized books by Jos. J.L. Gommans, *The Rise of Indo-Afghan Empire, c. 1710-1780* (New Delhi: Oxford University Press, 1999) *and Mughal Warfare:Indian Frontiers and High Road to Empire, 1500-1700* (New York: Routledge, 2002) have vastly improved our knowledge about the horse breeders in South Asia.

4 Peter Hardy, "The Mughals and Money," pp.19-27, in *Urdu and Muslim South Asia,* edited by Christopher Shackle (London: School of Oriental & African Studies, 1989), citation on pp. 23-24.

5 Thapar, op. cit., pp.298-300. The endowments to the saints may have come with the understanding that the saint would direct popular loyalty toward the sultan.

6 However, the system remained unchanged in Hyderabad State until 1949 Jagirdari Abolition Act. To this day, many Brahmins' surname is Inamdar.

7 Most skills of a majority of these hakims were outdated compared to Europe, even as far back as 17th century, as indicated by the arrival of Dr. Peter de Laan, a Dutch surgeon based in the settlement at Masulipatnam to treat a Qutb Shahi princess in Golconda, who charged staggering sum of 800 pagodas as fee, see Francois Bernier, *Travels in the Mogul Empire, 1656-58, I,* edited by A. Constable (London: Constable, 1891), p. 301.

8 Athar Ali, *The Apparatus of Empire: Awards of Ranks, Titles, Offices to the Mughal Nobility, 1574-1658* (Oxford: Oxford University Press, 1985); Satish Chandra, *Parties and Politics*

at the Mughal Court, 1707-1740 (Oxford: Oxford University Press, 2002); B.B. Misra, *The Indian Middle Classes* (London: Oxford University Press, 1961), claims that Hindus almost exclusively manned Mughal revenue department, see p. 187. Names such as *Munshi* (letter, report writer), *Majumdar* (the Bengalized form of *majmuadar*, revenue official), *Talukdar* (*taluqadar*, or landlord) and *Chitnis* (*chitthi nawis*, letter, report writer) are obvious examples of the Mughal legacy.

9 S.V. Desika Char, *Hinduism and Islam in India: Caste, Religion, and Society from Antiquity to Early Modern Times* (Princeton, N.J.: Markus Wiener, 1997), p. 89.

10 Irfan Habib, "The Social Distribution of Landed Property in Pre-British India", *Enquiry* New Series II, 3 (Winter 1965): 62-64.

11 That the Mughal empire and its offshoots began to be perceived as Muslim empires by some Muslims as such is a different issue. In 1844 W.H. Sleeman reported that Muslims in general identified with the Mughal dynasty, longed for its restoration, and conceived of themselves as the former ruling class. "Whether they were really so matters not; they persuade themselves or their children that they were," cited in David Lelyveld, *Aligarh's First Generation: Muslim Solidarity in British India* (Princeton: Princeton University Press, 1978), pp. 32-33. Entertaining British guests at the palatial Hyderabad House in Delhi, around a century later, in June 1948, "Delhi," Begum Zain Yar Jang, wife of the Nizam's Agent General, sighed, "is not what it was, there are no Mughal Emperors now," according to Allen Campbell-Johnson, *Mission with Mountbatten* (London: Hale, 1951). The parliamentarian and wife of Muhammad Ikramullah, an ICS officer, Shaista Suhrawardy Ikramullah expressed similar sentiments, *From Purdah to Parliament* (Karachi: Oxford University Press, 1998), pp. 133-134, on the eve of Pakistan's creation.

12 Percival Spear, *Twilight of the Mughuls: Studies in Late Mughul Delhi* (Karachi: Oxford University Press, 1980), pp. 39-41. The emperor in question was Bahadur Shah I, who sent Raja Rammohan Roy to London requesting increase in his stipend. He is not to be confused with Bahadur Shah Zafar, the last emperor.

13 Carla R. Petievich, "Poetry of the Declining Mughals: The Shahr Ashob", *Journal of South Asian Literature* 25, 1 (1990): 99-110.

14 Muslims were a majority of the staff in the Persian department of the Residencies, the East India Company's quasi-diplomatic offices in the princely states throughout the 1770s-1850s, according to contemporary records, see Michael H. Fisher, *Indirect Rule in India: Residents and the Residency System, 1764-1858* (New Delhi: Oxford University Press, 1991), pp. 320-321.

15 Percival Spear, op.cit, pp. 223-224.

16 *Madah wa Qadah-i Dakan*, edited by Omar Khalidi and Muin al-Din Aqil (Hyderabad: Majlis-I Tarikh-I Deccan, 1993), p. 83.

17 Sayyid Ahmad Khan's letter to Mawlawi Tassaduq, cited in *Sources of Indian Tradition*, I, edited by William M. Theodore de Bary (New York: Columbia University Press,

1964),pp. 192-93. For extended accounts, see David Lelyveld, *Aligarh's First Generation: Muslim Solidarity in British India* (Princeton: Princeton University Press, 1978), and Hafeez Malik, *Sir Sayyid Ahmad Khan and Musilm Modernization in India and Pakistan* (New York: Columbia University Press, 1980)

18 First published in London by Trubner & Company, this book went through numerous reprints.

19 Hunter, op.cit.p. 162.

20 The East India Company required its personnel to sign a covenant or bond outlining rights, obligations, and conditions of the service, hence the term.

21 Hunter, op.cit., p. 166.

22 Computed from *Report of the Indian Education Commission (*Calcutta: Superintendent of Government Printing, 1883), p. 484, cited subsequently as *Hunter Commission Report*, Duke University Library Microfilms Collection of India Office Materials, named as Crane Collection hereafter)

23 Hunter, op.cit. 171.

24 Hunter op.cit. 176. Needless to say, Hunter ignores that a vast majority of Bengali Muslims were descendants of converts to Islam, and not those of the conquerors.

25 This was the Muhsin Waqf, established by an Iranian, Muhammad Muhsin of Hugli.

26 Nawab Sayyid Abdul-Latif Khan Bahadur (1828-93) had already initiated teaching of English in the Calcutta Madrasah.

27 Great Britain, *Parliamentary Papers*, Vol. LIV (Accounts and Papers) 63, 1875, Amended Return Showing the Number of Appointments in India, of No Less than 150 Rupees A Month, Filled During the Years 1867, 1868, 1869, 1870, and 1871, By the Appointment of Natives of India, Distinguishing Those Held by Hindoos From Those Held By the Mahomedans, p.1.

28 *Hunter Commission Report*, p.484.

29 Ibid, p. 483.

30 Ibid, p. 494.

31 Zafarul Islam, "National Central Muhammadan Association," *Pakistan History Conference Proceeding* 1959.

32 Uncovenanted Service was to differentiate it from Covenanted Service of the East India Company, cited earlier.

33 Statutory Civil Service was instituted in 1879 during Lord Lytton's viceroyalty as a device to recruit educated Indians desiring employment in the Government of India.

[34] Great Britain, *Parliamentary Papers, vol. XLVIII (Reports of Commissioners), C. 5327, 1888, Report of the Public Service Commission, 1886-87,)*, cited as *Aitchison Commission Report*, p. 37.

[35] Op.cit.p. 37.

[36] Great Britain, Parliamentary Papers, vol. VII (Report of Commissioners, vol. IV). Cd. 8382, 1917, *Royal Commission on the Public Services in India, Report of the Commissioners*, Volume I, p. 496, cited as Islington Commission Report.

[37] Syed Wazir Hasan, "Mussalmans and the Public Service," *The Indian Review* 14 (January 1913): 40-51.

[38] *Census Report*, 1911, p. 141.

[39] Zafarul Islam and Raymond L. Jensen, op.cit., p. 133. Beyond the executive branch of the government, the upper caste Hindu preponderance was true in the judicial branch as well, see S.M. Mitra, *Anglo-Indian Studies* (London: Longman, 1913), p. 316.

[40] It must however, be noted that only the upper caste Christian communities are highly educated, and most in North India are not according to a Christian leader, James Massey, *Minorities in a Democracy: The Indian Experience* (New Delhi: Manohar, 1999), p. 69.

[41] B.B.Misra, *The Government and Bureaucracy in India, 1947-1976* (New Delhi: Oxford University Press, 1986), p. 95; Ralph Braibanti, *Research on the Bureaucracy in Pakistan* (Durham, NC: Duke University Press, 1966), p. 116. For disadvantages Muslims faced in competition to the ICS exams, see Nadeem Shafiq Malik, "Indianization of the ICS and Muslim Representation in the Public Services," Part I, *Journal of the Research Society of Pakistan* 31, 2 (1994): 21-43; Part II *Journal of the Research Society of Pakistan* 31, 3 (1994): 33-50. A partial list of Muslim ICS officers from 1922 to 1947, is found in *Muslim India* (August 1989), p. 358.

[42] Those choosing India included Akhtaruzzaman; Sayyid Siddiq Hasan; Miyan Azim Husain; Hifazat Hussain of Arrah, Bihar, Khurshid Ahmad Khan of Aligarh, Ahmad Nazir Kidwai; Manzoor Alam Quraishi; M.Atiqur Rahman, Badruddin Tyabji; and Sayyid Hasan Zaheer, brother of the more famous Sayyid Ali Zaheer, a minister in the UP cabinet in the 1950s and 1960s. A full list of those opting for India among the Muslims is yet to be found. Khurshid Ahmad Khan died of a heart attack in 1951 when transferred from the important post of Chief Commissioner of Delhi in 1947 to an insiginificant position by Sardar Patel, see Maulana Abul Kalam Azad, *India Wins Freedom* (New York: Longmans, 1960), p. 249-250. Khurshid's brother Maj. Gen. Anis Ahmad Khan received no promotion to the next level despite qualification, see Omar Khalidi, *Khaki and the Ethnic Violence in India* (New Delhi: Three Essays Collective, 2003), p. 43.

[43] Nawab Abdul Lauteef Khan Bahadur, *The Present Condition of the Indian Mahomedans, and the Best Means for Its Improvement* (Calcutta: Muhammadan Literary Society, February 28, 1883), as cited in Zafarul Islam and Raymond L. Jensen, p. 108-109.

[44] *Report of Reforms Enquiry Committee,* headed by Alexander Muddiman, Cd. 2360 (London: HMSO, 1925), p. 87. The Muddiman commission membership included P.S. Sivaswami Iyer, M.A. Jinnah, Bijay Chand Mehta, R.P. Pranjpye, Tej Bahadur Sapru, and Muhammad Shafi.

[45] *Report of Reforms Enquiry Committee,* headed by Alexander Muddiman, Command. 2360 (London: HMSO, 1925), p. 114.

[46] "Reservation of Posts for Minorities and Backward Classes: Government of India, Home Department Resolution dated 4 July 1934," pp. 116-117, *in Speeches and Documents on the Indian Constitution, 1921-1947*, I, edited by Maurice Gwyer and A. Appadorai (Bombay: Oxford University Press, 1957). According to Misra, op.cit., the percentage reserved for Muslims was only13 1/3 , p. 118.

[47] Op.cit.

[48] Op.cit.pp. 246-247.

[49] Jawaharlal Nehru's letter to M.A. Jinnah, 6 April 1938, as reproduced on pp. 425-426, in *Speeches and Documents on the Indian Constitution, 19121-1947*, I, edited by Maurice Gwyer and A. Appadorai (Bombay: Oxford University Press, 1957).

[50] B. R. Ambedkar's speech in Central Legislature, New Delhi, 14 March 1946, as reported in *Muslim India* October 1989, pp. 456-457.

[51] *Speeches and Documents on the Indian Constitution 1921-47*, I, edited by Maurice Gwyer and A. Appadorai (Bombay: Oxford University Press, 1957), pp. 379-380.

[52] *Muslims under Congress Rule, 1937-1939: A Documentary Record*, edited by Khursheed Kamal Aziz (Islamabad: National Commission for Historical and Cultural Research, 1978)

INDEPENDENT INDIA

Enormous changes took place due to the major political events in India's history in middle of the twentieth century, independence, creation of Pakistan and the partition of Bengal and Punjab. These changes involved dislocations, large scale migration/transfer of populations, communal killings on both sides of the border and heightening of prejudice in the newly created nations of India and Pakistan, along with the joy of having achieved freedom from British rule. These were bound to effect the situation of the minorities in both countries. We deal here with the situation in India.

Central Government Services Around 1947

When Pakistan came into being on 14 August 1947, the party campaigning for its creation, the All India Muslim League desired all Muslim personnel in the government to opt for the new nation, even though a choice was given to choose between the two countries. The pogroms of Hindus and Sikhs in west Punjab and those of Muslims in Delhi, the east Punjab and its neighboring areas created panic among all the religious communities, resulting in a virtual exchange of remaining population. The government employees could not escape the pogroms or the population exchange either.

Moreover, according to Maulana Abul Kalam Azad, the Muslim League "incited all Muslim officials to opt for Pakistan and leave India. At that time, a large number of key positions in the Central Secretariat were held by Muslims.[1] The Muslim League pressed all of them to leave India. Those who did not readily agree were frightened by all kinds of reports as to what their fate would be once Congress came into undisputed power. As such, rumors were causing a certain amount of nervousness among Muslim employees. I pressed the government of India to issue a circular clarifying its stand. Lord Mountbatten and Jawaharlal Nehru supported me fully and a circular was actually issued reassuring men from Muslim and other communities that, if they remained to serve in India, not only would they be given their rights but they would be treated generously. The result of this circular was that a number of Muslim officers in the Central Secretariat regained their confidence and decided to stay on in India. When the League leaders came to know this, they started to canvass the officers who wished to remain. The action of the League in driving almost all the Muslim officers out of India was not only foolish but also harmful. In fact it was more harmful to the Muslims than to India as a whole. Now that partition had been accepted and Pakistan was being established, it was clear that the Muslims would get every advantage in the new State. If, in addition, some Muslims could have served in India, this would have been a great gain for the community as a whole. The presence of Muslims in some responsible positions would have given assurance to the community and allayed many unreasonable fears."[2]

Despite the reassuring words of the circular issued, there is evidence that it went unheeded, as shown in the Table noted below:

Table I
Employment of Persons Who Opted for Pakistan & Later Applied to Remain in India

1.	(a) Officers & subordinate staff who opted for Pakistan & applied to remain in India	23,233

	(b) Persons retained.	19,676
2.	(a) Muslims who opted for Pakistan, but did not join duty, applied to stay in India	16,090
	(b) Muslims reemployed	13,018

Source: Constituent Assembly of India, *Legislative Assembly Debates*, November-December 1949, p. 10.

The Muslim exodus from the general population and the government employment is confirmed in the contemporary accounts, such as the one by Richard Symonds, a relief worker who saw, "from Delhi alone twenty-five thousand government employees and their families, with sixty thousands tons of personal baggage, had to be moved to Karachi."[3] In spite of the circular referred to by Maulana Azad, those who opted for India were not always welcome to stay. Sardar Patel, as Home Minister, in fact removed Muslim officials who had opted to stay in India, according to S. Gopal.[4] Outside of Patel's control, a handful of Muslim officials clung to Maulana Azad's Ministry of Education, such as K.G. Saiyidain, 1904-71.[5] Reacting on the Maulana's refuge to a few frightened Muslim officials, Patel branded his colleague's Ministry a "miniature Pakistan", as recorded by J.N. Sahni, a contemporary journalist.[6] Inder Malhotra later wrote that "several of his cabinet colleagues used to say openly, "If you want to see Pakistan, you don't need a passport or a visa. Just go to the Ministry of Education in the North Block."[7] Far away from the scene of partition-related carnages, in distant Madras, a central government's tax officer Iqbal Masud found his Brahmin boss disapproving of his decision to remain in India.[8] Iqbal's case was indeed typical of thousands of others like him exemplified by the cases in Uttar Pradesh.[9] Men in state authority would look askance at those staying behind and those seeking employment were told to go to Pakistan.[10]

The demand to keep the reservation in place was made early on when the Constituent Assembly of India (the precursor of the national parliament) met for the first time on 9 December 1946. Sardar Patel headed the Advisory Committee on Fundamental Rights, Minorities, and Tribal and

Excluded Areas. The task of formulating constitutional rules on the matters of representation in the legislatures, reservation of seats in the cabinet, reservation in services and the establishment of administrative machinery for its implementation were entrusted to a Sub-Committee of the Advisory Committee on Minorities. After much deliberation it submitted a report on 27 February 1947.[11] The Sub-Committee "Agreed by a majority of votes (9 to 7) that there shall be reservation in the services for Muslims, among others."[12] However, on 8 August 1947, the same Advisory Committee seemingly withdrew the reservation recommendation. Instead it stated: "In the all-India and Provincial Services the claims of all the minorities shall be kept in view in making appointments to these services consistently with the consideration of efficiency of adminis-tration."[13] From the available literature, even this non-binding plea, "claims of all the minorities shall be kept in view in making appointments..." is absent in the subsequent draft constitution.[14] Like the reservation of seats for minorities in the legislatures, the Minorities Advisory Committee rejected a recommendation it proposed earlier.[15]

After Independence

Given these hostile circumstances, it is unsurprising that Nehru noted the drastic changes in Muslim employment in 1953, a mere six years after independence: "In the services, generally speaking, the representation of the minority communities is lessening. In some cases it is very poor indeed...looking through Central Secretariat figures, as well as some others, I am distressed to find that the position is very disadvantageous to them, chiefly to the Muslims and sometimes to others also. In our Defense Services, there are hardly any Muslims left. In the vast Central Secretariat of Delhi, there are very few Muslims."[16] In a subsequent communication to the Chief Ministers a year later in 1954, he noted "Muslims'...deep sense of frustration. They feel that the services are not really open to them in any marked degree, whether defense, police or civil."[17] The Government of India's 1958 Civil List, issued a decade after independence shows a massive reduction of already few Muslims. Out of several thousand strong staff, the following Table shows meager representation, especially when it is noteworthy that most officers were selected before 1947.

Table II
Muslim Representation in Union Ministries in 1958

Ministry	*Number of Muslims*
Community Development	04
Defense	09
Education	07
External Affairs	19
Finance	75
Food & Agriculture	16
Law	01
Railways	68
Rehabilitation	01
Scientific Research & Cultural Affairs	27
Steel	07
Works, Housing & Supply	12
Transportation	27
Health	02
Home	04
Information & Broadcasting	07
Irrigation & Power	07
Labor & Employment	12

Source: *All India Civil List, issued Half-Yearly* (Bombay: Printed & published under the Authority of the Govt. of India, January 1959).

Outside the ministries, the All India Civil List noted above gives the names of another 23 Muslims employed in various departments, but clearly, it is a dismal picture. Little wonder then that a Vice-Chancellor of Aligarh Muslim University discovered in early 1960s a "profound feeling of despondency and defeatism" on a campus where the largest concentration of Muslim students could be found.[18] Expressing his disbelief at the falling number of Muslims in a 1965 document, Inder Malhotra found "only six Muslim officers in the top two grades of the CSS [Central Secretariat Services] out of 681. In the next grade, there were only four Muslims out of 2000. As if this is not shocking enough, there were only 21 Muslims out of 9, 900 clerks."[19] According to American journalist Joseph Lelyveld, "a survey in [1968] showed that barely 2 percent of Government officials at the highest level were Moslems. But it also showed that this might have as much to do with the Moslem communities' demoralization as with outright discrimination...Outright discrimination is more clearly shown on the lower rungs of the bureaucracy. Moslems account for less than one-half of one percent of the clerks and messengers in the ministries of the central government here."[20] Answering a question about the total number of Muslims in the Central Secretariat in 1971, the then Minister of State for Home Affairs Ram Niwas Mirdha presented the following figure statistics:

Table III
Muslims in the Central Secretariat, in 1970 & on 1 May 1971

Central Secretariat Services	*Total 1971*	*Muslims*	*Total 1970*	*Muslims*
Selection Grade I	140	2	120	1
Grade I	395	5	392	2
Section Officers	1666	12	1599	11
Assistants	4507	19	4582	19
Central Secretariat Stenographic Service				
Selection Grade	130	0	1	
Grade I	195	0	129	0
Grade II	1954	7	2089	5
Grade III	1326	1		
Central Secretariat Clerical Service				
Upper Division Clerks	2511	9	2708	11
Lower Division Clerks	6585	30	7961	33
Class IV	5381	39	N/A	N/A

Source: Statement by Ram Niwas Mirdha, Minister of State for Home Affair's Statement in the Lok Sabha as noted in Kamlesh Kumar Wadhwa, *Minority Safeguards in India: Constitutional Provisions and Their Implementation* (Delhi: Thompson Press, 1975), p. 154; also cited earlier in *Secular Democracy* (December 1972).

Nearly a decade later Indira Gandhi administration appointed a High Power Panel to study the economic condition of Minorities, Scheduled Castes and Tribes on 10 May 1980, headed by Gopal Singh. The Report was presented to the Government on 14 June 1983. The Government spent Rs. 57.77 lakhs on the Panel, according to its own statement.[21] According to its member-secretary Rafiq Zakaria: "The Panel sent out 200 researchers to every state, to collect data on a sample survey basis, so as to assess the actual situation in every field—employment in government, in public sector undertakings, in the cooperative sectors, in local bodies and even in private industries and business. For almost four years they worked, traveling from one place to another. What they gathered proved an eye-opener: the economic condition of Indian Muslims was worse than that of the Scheduled Castes."[22] For instance it showed no improvement since the decade of 1970s [See Tables on the next two pages].

When the two volumes Report was submitted, Prime Minister Indira Gandhi did not want to make it public, even though the Panel was Government-appointed and worked on tax-payer's expense. Why? The Report, in the words of Zakaria, "sent shock waves through the corridors of South Block. Mrs. Gandhi thought it best to shelve its findings. She told me that a post-mortem never helped; it would be prudent to forget the past and plan for the future."[23] Indira's son and successor, Prime Minister Rajiv Gandhi, did nothing to change his mother's decision. Like many a Commission in India, it was yet another instance of a singular lack of accountability for the waste of public funds and shirking the responsibility of implementing its recommendations. The dejected Panel Chairman, Gopal Singh, died on 8 August 1990 complaining of Government indifference to his labor of love.[24] Finally, it required the defeat of Congress at the Center for the Government to reveal the Report. It was tabled before the Lok Sabha on 24 August 1990, with the comments of the new Government which amounted to the rejection of all the important recommendations.[25] The Report is not commonly available despite submission to the Parliament, though extracts have been published.[26]

Table IV

Share for Each Community of the Positions Held by Either Hindus and Muslims in 1912 (Computed from Table VII)

				Class 1			Class 2			Class 3			Class 4			
State	*Total*	*Muslims*	*%age*	*Total*	*Muslim*	*%age*	*Total*	*Muslim*	*%age*	*Total*	*Muslim*	*%age*	*Total*	*Muslim*	*%age*	*Pop. Prop.*
AP	258	27	10.5	8			10	2	20	187	19	10.2	53	6	11.3	26.45
Assam	3135	255	8.13	2			470	22	4.68	2205	192	8.71	458	41	8.95	36.72
Bihar	6617	359	5.43	28			995	27	2.71	3950	237	6	1644	95	5.78	
Gujarat	10361	494	4.77	371		0.27	477	5	1.05	6864	373	5.43	2649	115	4.34	8.48
Chandigarh	1479	8	0.54	33			28			1200	6	2.5	218	2	0.92	1.45
Haryana	897	6	0.67	27			28			750	4	0.53	147	2	1.36	33.62
Kerala	8898	337	3.79	1143	22	1.92	739	22	2.98	5609	224	3.99	1407	69	4.9	24.89
Madhya Pradesh	2811	179	6.37	20			69	8	11.8	1942	119	9.12	781 .	52	6.66	5.34
Maharashtra	4384	184	4.2	17	1	5.88	27			3230	121	3.74	1110	62	5.59	9.93
Orissa	13040	205	1.57	30			513	16	3.12	10031	160	1.6	2466	29	1.18	1.07
Rajasthan	6674	229	3.45	401			132	6	3.03	4821	199	4.14	1330	26	1.95	11.54
Tamilnadu	200	8	4	3	1	33.3	25	1	4	133	5	3.76	39	1	2.56	7.02
Uttar Pradesh	12307	929	7.55	134	11	8.21	335	15	4.48	7295	550	7.54	4543	353	7.77	17.29
West Bengal	4782	136	2.81	15			213			3740	85	2.25	814	51	6.26	26.22
Grand Total	75951	3346	4.41	2232	36	1.61	4060	122	3	52000	2294	4.41	17669	904	5.12	5.93

Source: Gopal Singh Panel Report on Minorities, Vol.II, as cited in *Muslim India* (January 1986), p. 30.

In addition to the depressing findings of a government-appointed commission such as the one headed by Gopal Singh, independent academic studies confirm the conclusions reached. For example, Suren Navlakha, in a study of the officers of Indian Administrative Staff (IAS), Indian Economic Service, Indian Statistical Service, and the Central Secretariat Service, found that there is proportionate representation all religious groups but Muslims and Buddhists![27] Besides Navlakha, numerous studies of the social background of IAS officers covering various decades and years show that Muslims represented less than four percent in the total cadre at any time since independence.[28]

The union government runs a large number of companies. Data gathered for 1981-82 reveals that out of hundreds of directors and senior employees of 82 companies only a handful were Muslims. More or less the same was true two years later: out of the hundreds of directors of 64 companies, only 5 were Muslims.[29] More or less the same was true of directors of public sector banks.[30]

At the dawn of the twenty-first century, the central government employed 37, 76, 666 civilians in four categories as seen below:

Table V
Employment in the Central Government, 2000 & Muslim Percentage

Group	*Estimated Strength*	*% of Total Strength*	*Muslim % in 1992*
A	77, 680	2.05	1.61
B	1,74, 675	4.63	3.00
C	23, 87, 625	63.22	4.41
D	11, 36, 686	30.09	5.12
Total	37,76, 666	100.00	

Source: http://persmin.nic..in/pq2001.htm. Source for Muslim percentage is *Economic Times* (21 December 1992)

Out of total, Muslims are clearly far fewer than their population percentage. There is also a clear, inverse relationship between higher posts and Muslims.

The following table shows Civil Service (Main) Examination Results from 1982-2003, i.e. of the last two decades.

Table VI

Successful Muslim Candidates in the Civil Service Exams, 1982-2005

Year	*Total Selected Candidates*	*Muslims*	*Muslim Percentage*	*Source*
1982-83	814	10	1.2	Rad.27.9.1992,p.12
1983-84	814	10	1.2	ditto
1984-85	790	11	1.2	ditto
1985-86	855	10	1.2	ditto
1986-87	817	14	1.7	ditto
1987-88		14		ditto
1988-89		15		ditto
1989-90		20		ditto
1990-91		25		ditto
1991-92	871	15	1.7	Ditto
1992-93	789	22		Rad. 3 July 1994 p. 11
1993-94	789	20		M1 July 94 p. 329
1994-95	703	24		Rad 2 July 1995, p. 10
1995-96	638	22		M1 July 1996 p. 317
1997-98	620	13		M1 July 1998, p. 320
1999-00	4	15		M1 July 200 p.316
2000-01	417	12		M1 Aug 2002 p. 326
2002-03	431	11		M1 July 2004 p. 769
2004-05	422	08		MG 1 June 2005,p.17

Abbreviations: Rad=*Radiance*; MI=*Muslim India*, MG=*Milli Gazette.*

It is obvious that the results are not satisfactory. Even though we do not have statistics for every year's successful candidates of all religions to compare with the successful Muslim candidates, the statistics available for the years do not show a marked long-term change.

Why So Few Muslims?

Why are there so few Muslims in the central government service? A worldwide phenomenon is the general decline of Muslims in modern scientific education and its offshoot the applied science and technology since the eighteenth century. Thus Arab Muslims are far behind Arabs of various Christian denominations, Turks and Iranians lag behind Armenians, Malays behind the Chinese, and Indian Muslims are far behind upper caste Hindus. Islam itself is certainly no impediment to education and critical inquiry. However, interpretations of Islam by certain vested groups can certainly be a roadblock to modern education, as I have dealt elsewhere.[31]

Leaving aside the universal problem of Muslim lag in modern education, let us consider the question about Muslim absence from government employment within the Indian conditions. The obvious explanations have centered around three major reasons: migration to Pakistan, discrimination and educational lag.

The "migration to Pakistan" theory is well documented, and true up to 1971. Until that year, Muslims with modern scientific education could easily qualify for legal migration by simply showing up at the Pakistan High Commission in New Delhi with technical education diplomas and receive immigration documents to relocate. The migration to Pakistan entailed more than the immediate loss of a qualified candidate who could have obtained employment in India itself. It also meant the loss of role models for other Muslims. Politicians unsympathetic to Muslims are fond of citing this reason by blandly stating that Hindus and Muslims simply traded jobs in the respective countries of India and Pakistan, and that was fair.[32] More than a quarter century has passed since that time, and "migration to Pakistan" theory is no longer valid now.

The second theory, of discrimination is plausible for some jobs, though it is hard to establish court-admissible evidence. Discrimination within the various castes is well known and the culture of patronage, wink and nod, is so well entrenched that the theory of discrimination—though not just against Muslims—is credible. The present writer asked former Prime Ministers V.P. Singh and I.K. Gujral about discrimination against Muslims in employment and allocation of public funds. Both agreed that obviously there is no discrimination in rules and regulations at the formal level, but admitted that there are instances of informal discrimination against Muslims.[33] Discrimination at the entry level is hard to establish, but there are instances where there is evidence for discrimination in promotion exemplified by a number of cases, for example of Justice Jaafar Imam in the Supreme Court[34] and of Maj. Gen. Enayat Habibullah and others in the Army.[35] The case of Mian Azim Husain, an IFS officer is the classic instance of discrimination. Unlike majority of the Punjabi Muslim ICS officers, he opted for India in 1947. In the mid 1960s, when "the post of Foreign Secretary was about to fall vacant, it was openly said in the corridors of the Foreign Office that Muslim officers in the highest echelons of the service were ruled out for selection to the top job."[36] Among the Muslim officers was of course Mian Azim Husain.[37] His junior in the same office, Salman Haider made history when he became India's first and so far only "Muslim" to become Foreign Secretary on 28 February 1995.[38] He was identified as "Muslim" despite the fact he himself declared not being as such, according to Mani Shankar Aiyar.[39] Haider's disassociation with his religion did not soften the BJP to give him a term extension when it came to power in 1998. Why? "The obvious explanation is Haider's name."[40] A newspaper headline "Muslim is Cabinet Secretary" aptly described Zafar Saifullah's promotion in the IAS to the highest post in civil service when he was appointed Cabinet Secretary in 1993, though he was continuously harassed by his colleagues for his religious affiliation.[41] The headline can be interpreted in many different ways: A Muslim is not expected to be appointed to this post. Or a Muslim's appointment to this post is newsworthy. Or religious affiliation is identified only when a non-Hindu is appointed to a high post, for such was the case when J.J. Singh became the Chief of the Army Staff on January 2005. In other words, appointment of Hindus is a matter of course, those of others is out of the ordinary. However, in one instance, in the late 1960s, a vacancy in the Delhi High Court needed to be filled, but all the competitors happened to be Sikh. Indira Gandhi wanted to find a Muslim to fill the position. No suitable Muslim could be found in Delhi and neighboring U.P. and Bihar. Upon her insistence, a suitable judge of Muslim background was located in Madras and appointed![42] Such are the vagaries of political will! Besides these well-known cases, there is some evidence confirming discrimination in the allocation of public goods to Muslims.[43] The examples cited here could be multiplied manifold.

The Union Public Service Commission (UPSC) conducts competitive exams for recruitment for better-paid jobs in the government, and the low pay jobs are filled through the Employment Exchange. There have been two Muslims who actually became chairmen of the UPSC —A.R. Kidwai (1973-79) and J.M. Quraishi (1998-2001), while there have been as many as ten who became members of the Commission.[44] They have uniformly rejected the theory of discrimination in promotion directed only against Muslims, while admitting the role of caste and regional lobbies in promotions and postings to desirable (lucrative?) departments and locations.[45] Instead, the Muslim members of the UPSC largely supported the theory of Muslim educational lag.[46] Lack of modern education is certainly an impediment for Muslim presence in the higher posts of the civil service, but it is true that lowest level jobs are distributed by politicians along caste or regional lines.[47] One explanation advanced is that Muslim politicians when they become ministers usually get insignificant cabinet portfolios and lack access to power; they are, therefore, unable to patronize the community's poor members in the manner done by others; and this explains the absence of Muslims from even the lowest rungs of the government jobs.[48]

In the foregoing section, let us consider the figures pertaining to the two largest employers in the public sector, the Railways and the Indian Armed Forces.

The Ministry of Railways: The Nation's Largest Civilian Employer

During the British raj, "attention [was] drawn to the small number of Muslims in the Railway Service, even on those railways which pass through areas in which Muslims form a high percentage of population."[49] At partition, Richard Symonds reported that "out of 925,000 railway employees, 73,000 had to be transferred from Pakistan to India, and 85,500 from India to Pakistan."[50] Less than twenty five years after that fateful event, former union minister Moinulhaq Chaudhuri disclosed in the Lok Sabha on 31 July 1973 that, "on March 31, 1971, out of 7000 Class I and Class II employees in the Railways, there were only 150 Muslims, forming a miserable 2.14 percent...Today the number of the officers has gone up from 7000 to 8216 but the percentage of the Muslims, as far as I know had gone down further from 2.14 percent."[51] Over two decades later, in 1990, Muslims constituted a mere 1.6 percent of Southern Railway's class I and class II officers.[52] With 1.65 million employees on its rolls, the Raiiways are the nation's single biggest employer.[53] Prime Minister Indira Gandhi agreed in 1983 to the representation of the SCs, STs and minority communities on selection committees for recruitment of the class IV employees.[54] In the 1990s and in early 2000s, many Muslims have risen to visible and top positions in the Railways such as Muhammad Shafi of Railway Recruitment Board, Muhammad Akhtar, Chairman Railway Recruitment Board South Central Railway (SCR), Mir Qudrat Ali Nasiri, Chairman of the SCR, and M.Z. Ansari, General Manager Western Railway, Muhammad Irshad, and M.S. Khan, directors of Railway Board. Yet by and large, Muslims are not in proportion to their population numbers in the Railways as a whole, according to a RRB official who pointed out that RRB continues to ask for religious affiliation of jobs applicants, thus making it possible to ascertain the number of railway staff according to religious groups.[55] In the related Ministry of Transport and Shipping, Muslims were found in 1983 to be less than one percent in certain jobs.[56] In November 2003, Railway Minister Nitish Kumar announced mass recruitment of 75,000 Group D employees (Class IV linemen, gang men, *khalasis,* cleaners) through an exam, leading to violence against "outsiders", i.e. Biharis in Assam, North Indians in Mumbai, and against the non-Biharis in Bihar.[57] A frightened Railway Ministry postponed the exam. What does this episode tell us? Job scarcity led Indians to target fellow countrymen outside their region thus showing that discrimination in employment is by no means directed against Muslims alone.

The Indian Armed Forces and the Central Paramilitary Forces

In the Raj's army, though not all Muslims from every part of the country were recruited, yet they constituted as much as 30-36 percent of the forces, as I have shown elsewhere.[58] Similarly Muslims were found in good numbers in the Imperial Police. Of the total 1,711 recruited between 1861-1947 as many as 97 were Muslims, or 5.67 % according to an official record.[59] The percentage may appear small compared to the community's population percentage (23 %) in British India, but it should not be forgotten that the IP included European officers as well. When only Indian percentage is computed, the Muslim percentage goes way high. Except in a few princely such states such as Jammu and Kashmir, Muslims did well in various provincial police departments.[60]

Major changes have taken place in the armed forces and central police forces since independence. Migration to Pakistan, real or perceived discrimination and poor education are again responsible for less than 3 percent Muslims in the 1.5 million strong armed forces at the beginning of the twenty first century. The same is true of the Central Paramilitary Forces.[61]

One of the major issues for Muslims in the first decade of independence was the harassment by the Custodian of Evacuee Property, to which we now turn.

Evacuee Property

The partition of India caused enormous hardship not merely to the residents of two divided provinces of Bengal and Punjab. Its consequences were felt far beyond the borders of the affected provinces extending all over India.

One such consequence was the Evacuee Property Act passed soon after independence. This Law provided "that no intending Muslim evacuee would be allowed to sell his property in India. This had the beneficial effect of arresting the course of Muslim emigration but it did great damage to Muslim businessmen, because, according to the general social pattern in India, the Muslim families had generally joint properties and business establishments and it was not customary to divide them. Now under the Evacuee Property Act, if a single member of a family migrated to Pakistan the whole property was put in charge of the official custodian and the remaining members of that family could neither sell their shares of the property nor raise loan on them. Besides, the term 'intending evacuee' was so widely interpreted that at one stage almost all Muslims were covered by it and their properties declared unsaleable. Obviously, this put many people to great difficulty, but for the business classes of Muslims, it was simply disastrous, because it became impossible for them to borrow money in time of need, and this often sounded the death-knell of their business."[62]

Prime Minister Nehru admonished his own cabinet minister for Rehabilitation, Mohanlal Saxena, who had ordered the sealing of Muslim shops in 1949 in Delhi and U.P.[63] Beyond Delhi and U.P. the law was applied even as distant in the south as Hyderabad, where Muslims similarly suffered.[64] Nehru admitted this in 1954: "The Evacuee Property Laws, which unfortunately continue even though they are not applied frequently, bear down upon them and restrict their opportunities."[65] The laws were directed not merely against powerless shopkeepers of Delhi alone, even properties belonging to Muslims of impeccable credentials such as the freedom fighter Mukhtar Ahmad Ansari, educator K.G. Sayidain, filmmaker K.A. Abbas, were seized.[66] Like Saxena, N.B. Gadgil, the minister succeeding him, justified the draconian law against Muslims in his autobiography.[67] According to Nehru's biographer S. Gopal, the laws were "repealed in 1956, but the pending exceptions ran into many thousands and the custodians continued to exercise their inquisitional powers in a manner which looked to Nehru as a vendetta against a large section of the Indian citizens."[68] This was certainly the case with an Agra shoe manufacturer, dramatically portrayed by Balraj Sahni in the 1974 movie *Garm Hawa*, or hot wind, a reference to the anti-Muslim environment of the 1950s. Banks did not consider Muslims credit-worthy; they were deemed high-risk customers for a decade. Less than a decade after the scrapping of the Act, the India-Pakistan war of 1965 resulted in the Enemy Property Act (EPA), which is still in place according to a former Congress member of parliament Jitendra Prasada.[69] No one could believe Prasada when he casually cited the possible invocation of the EPA in 1983, until nearly a decade later in 1998 when Delhi Muslims received a notice asking them to prove their nationality. Despite representations by the National Commission for Minorities, the Act has not been scrapped yet.[70]

This is not to say however, that the going has been all negative for the Muslims. The Government has brought forth a number of central schemes aimed at benefiting the minorities, which are listed in the Appendix to the volume. No doubt, greater say of democratic forces in government will increase such schemes.

Notes

1 Khalid B. Sayeed, *Pakistan: The Formative Phase, 2nd edition* (London: Oxford University Press, 1968), Appendix I.pp. 301-305, compiled from The Indian Year Book 33 (1946-47),published in Bombay by Bennett & Coleman, shows Muslims in the civil and military services of central government.

2 Maulana Abulkalam Azad, *India Wins Freedom* (New York: Longman, 1960), pp. 238-39. Besides the ICS officers who chose to remain in India, Mohammad Hidayatullah, then a judge at Nagpur, "resisted the blandishments held out to me..." See the former chief justice of India's biography, *My Own Boswell* (New Delhi: Arnold Heinemann, 1980), chapter 18. Hidayatullah, 1906-92, Chief Justice of India 1968-70. His brother Mohammad Ikramullah, chose to move to Pakistan becoming the foreign secretary in the Ministry of Foreign Affairs. There are many such cases, for example, Mian Azim Husain, ICS chose India while his brother in law Mian Arshad Husain chose Pakistan. The close relatives even signed the Kutch border dispute agreement, "Kutch: A Political Award," *The Illustrated Weekly of India* (03 March 1968), shows a picture showing the relatives on the opposite sides!

3 Richard Symonds, *The Making of Pakistan* (London: Faber & Faber, 1950),p.79.

4 S. Gopal, *Jawaharlal Nehru: A Biography*, II, 1947-1956 (Delhi: Oxford University Press, 1976-1984), pp. 15-16.

5 *All India Civil List, issued Half-Yearly* (Bombay: Printed & published under the Authority of the Govt. of India, January 1959), lists exactly 7 Muslims in 1958, the year the Maulana died. They were Nizamuddin Ahmad, N.A. Ansari, Mahdi Baqir, the two brothers with identical names M.N. Masud, Miss S. Rahman and K.G. Saiyidain!

6 J.N. Sahni, *The Lid Off: Fifty Years of Indian Politics, 1921-1971* (Bombay: Allied Publishers, 1971), p. 366.

7 Inder Malhotra, "How Prejudice Speaks," *The Illustrated Weekly of India* (22 April 1973), p. 11.

8 Iqbal Masud, *Dream Merchants, Politicians, and Partition: Memoirs of an Indian Muslim* (New Delhi: Harper Collins, 1997), p. 48.

9 Shamsurrahman Faruqi, "Sayyid Hamid," *Kitab Numa* (October 199): pp. 27-30.

10 As late as 1966, P.V. Narasimha Rao, then Minister of Education in AP told Mirza Jamil Ahmad Baig, a lawyer, to go Pakistan., when he sought employment. Conversation with Baig, Hyderabad, 1972.

11 *The Framing of India's Constitution: Select Documents*, II, edited by B. Shiva Rao,(New Delhi: Indian Institute of Public Administration, 1967), p. 396.

12 Op.cit. 399.

13 Op. cit., p. 418. The same words were inserted into the first draft constitution dated October 1947, see *The Framing of India's Constitution: Select Documents*, III, edited by B. Shiva Rao,(New Delhi: Indian Institute of Public Administration, 1967),p. 94.

14 I mined the five-volume work *The Framing of India's Constitution: Select Documents*: *The Framing of India's Constitution: Select Documents*, II, edited by B. Shiva Rao. The revised draft constitution of November 1949 did not mention minorities in the services at all, see the section on this subject in *The Framing of India's Constitution: Select Documents*, IV, edited by B. Shiva Rao,(New Delhi: Indian Institute of Public Administration, 1967),pp.859-861. In the final V volume of this book, p. 758, merely recapitulates earlier discussion on the subject.

15 An exact date on which the Constituent Assembly or one of its Committees decided to do so is unclear.

16 Jawaharlal Nehru, *Letters to the Chief Ministers*, III, edited by G. Parthasarathy (New Delhi: Oxford University Press, 1985), p.376.

17 Ibid, p. 535.

18 Badruddin Tyabji, *More Memoirs of an Egoist* (New Delhi: Har-Anand, 1994), p. 147. Tyabji was the Aligarh Vice-Chancellor from 1962-1964.

19 Inder Malhotra, "What Ails Indian Muslims," *The Illustrated Weekly of India* (22 April 1973), p. 9.

[20] Joseph Lelyveld, "India's 55 Million Moslems Living in Rejection and Isolation," *The New York Times* 28 October 1968, p. 20.

[21] "Government Statement on Gopal Singh Panel Report on Minorities," *Muslim India* (April 1989), p. 150. The statement was made in the Lok Sabha.

[22] Rafiq Zakaria, *The Widening Divide: An Insight into Hindu-Muslim Relations* (New Delhi: Viking, 1995),p. 163.

[23] Ibid, p. 163.

[24] Gopal Singh, "The Muslim Question," *The Hindustan Times* Sunday Magazine 27 May 1990, p. 4. "Gopal Singh R.I.P. (1917-1990)", *Muslim India* (September 1990), p. 424.

[25] "Gopal Singh Report: Government Statement and Comments, Lok Sabha 24 August 1990-I-," *Muslim India* (May 1991), pp. 225-227 and "Gopal Singh Report: Government Statement and Comments, Lok Sabha 24 August 1990-II-," *Muslim India* (June 1991): 264267.

[26] "The Forgotten Recommendations of the Gopal Singh Panel-I on Educational Development," *Muslim India* (May 1984): 212215; "The Forgotten Report of the Gopal Singh Panel-II," *Muslim India* (June 1984) 261-263; 267; "The Forgotten Report of the Gopal Singh Panel-III", *Muslim India* (October 1984): 465-468; "The Forgotten Report of the Gopal Singh Panel-IV," *Muslim India* (November 1984): 522-525; "The Forgotten Report of the Gopal Singh Panel-V," *Muslim India* (December 1984): 571-574; "The Forgotten Report of the Gopal Singh Panel-VI," *Muslim India* (March 1985): 117-119. "The Forgotten Report of the Gopal Singh Panel-VII," *Muslim India* (April 1985 "The Forgotten Report of the Gopal Singh Panel-VII," *Muslim India* (April 1985): 165-167.

[27] "Religion, Language and Caste," pp. 57-67, in his *Elite and Change: A Study of Elite Formation in India* (New Delhi: Sage, 1989).

[28] The latest list of the IAS officers on http://demotemp117.nic.in/webexp/BrowseCL.asp confirms Muslim percentage. For earlier years see in reverse chronological order, Santosh Goyal, "Social Background of Officers in the Indian Administrative Service," pp. 426-433, in *Dominance and State Power in Modern India,* I, edited by Francine R. Franckel and M.S.A. Rao (New Delhi: Oxford University Press, 1989); V. Subramaniam,*Social Background of India's Administrators: A Socio-Economic Study of the Higher Civil Services of India* (New Delhi: Publications Division, Ministry of Information & Broadcasting, 1971).

[29] "Muslim Directors in Public Sector," *Muslim India* (October 1984): p. 410.

[30] "Board of Directors of Public Sector Banks," *Muslim India* (January 1983), p. 30.

[31] Omar Khalidi, *Indian Muslims Since Independence* (New Delhi: Vikas, 1996), Chapter IV, The Problem of Muslim Educational Backwardness.

[32] K.R. Malkani, "Muslim Representation in the Services," *Organiser* (4 August 1978). p.8.

33 Conversation with V.P. Singh 26 June 1995 at MIT, Cambridge, Mass; with I.K. Gujral, 24 December 2004 at his residence in New Delhi.

34 See "The Case of Justice Jaafar Imam," pp.117-119, by K.L. Gauba, *Passive Voices: A Penetrating Study of Muslims in India* (New Delhi: Sterling, 1973), in which Justice Imam was denied promotion as chief justice in 1955. In the same book Gauba cites "The Case of Dr.M.K. Durrany Shastri," pp. 41-42, was hired as a lecturer in Sanskrit at Shivaji College in Delhi in 1964 on the mistaken belief that he was a Sindhi Hindu, given that many Sindhi names end in *ni*, as in Advani! When the College found out he was a Muslim, Durrany Shastri was dismissed from service, according to *Hindustan Times* (19 December 1970).

35 Omar Khalidi, *Khaki and the Ethnic Violence*, pp. 36-37.

36 Inder Malhotra, "What Ails the Indian Muslims?" *The Illustrated Weekly of India* (22 April 1973), p. 10.

37 According to Mian Azim Husain, his promotion was blocked by fellow officer, T.N. Kaul (1913-2000), email communication via Shahid Qadir, dated 17 January 2004, in which he calls Kaul "a shoe-licking stooge of the then PM Indira Gandhi." Salman Haider, IFS, and Foreign Secretary confirmed Kaul's part in this matter, interview with Haider, New Delhi 18 December 2004.

38 "Salman Haider is New Foreign Secretary," *India Abroad* (10 March 1995), p.12.

39 Haider filled "none" in the column "Religion" on his IFS application form, Mani Shankar Aiyar, "Sacking Salman the Wise," *India Today* (30 July 1998), p.17.

40 Ibid.

41 "Muslim is Cabinet Secretary," *India Abroad* (16 July 1993), p. 4. Muhammad Vaziruddin, "Saifullah Harassed by Indian Bureaucrats," *Arab News* (Jeddah 19 August 1994), p. 6.

42 K.L. Gauba, *Passive Voices: A Penetrating Study of Muslims in India* (New Delhi: Sterling, 1973) pp. 349-50. Since the 1960s, only two Muslims Malik Sharifuddin and Muhammad Shamim were appointed judges in Delhi in 1983 and 1991 respectively.

43 Roger Battencourt and Suzanne Gleason, "The Allocation of Publicly Provided Goods to Rural Households in India: On Some Consequences of Caste, Religion and Democracy," *World Development* 28, 12 (2000): 2169-2182.

44 "UPSC: Muslim Members Since 1947," *Muslim* India (April 1983), p. 179. This list includes Sayyid Hasan Zaheer, ICS.

45 Conversation with A.R. Kidwai, Dallas, September 26, 2003.

46 Prof. Naseem Zaidi, emeritus Department of Economics, Aligarh Muslim University, in his article, "Muslims in Public Service: A Case Study of AMU Alumni," *Economic and Political Weekly* (22 September 2001):pp. 3592-3595. supports this view, though one of

his reasons, lack of motivation among Muslims, is rightly questioned by Mahmood Alam Raz, "Muslims in Public Service: A Comment," *Economic and Political Weekly* (9 March 2002), p. 983.

47 Zafar Jung, "Evidence of Bias Against Muslims," *The Times of India* (New Delhi, 25 September 1993) op ed page.

48 "Muslim Ministers in the Union Cabinet: Half a Century of Distrust or Lack of Power," *Radiance* 11-17 February 2001): 14-15.

49 "Reservation of Posts for Minorities and Backward Classes: Government of India, Home Department Resolution dated 4 July 1934," pp. 116-117, *in Speeches and Documents on the Indian Constitution, 1921-1947*, I, edited by Maurice Gwyer and A. Appadorai (Bombay: Oxford University Press, 1957).

50 Symonds, op.cit., p. 78.

51 Moinulhaq Chaudhuri in Lok Sabha Proceedings, 1973.

52 "Muslim Representation in Southern Railway," *Muslim India* (August 1991),p. 363.

53 "Indian Railways: Wheels of a Nation," *India Today* (19 August 2002), p. 29.

54 "Railways: Selection Committees to Have Minorities Representation," *Muslim India* (June 1983), p. 261.

55 Mir Qudrat Ali Nasiri, interview Bangalore 2 June 1999. An RRB, Secunderabad, Employment Notice number 4/1991, published on October 27 1991, in *Indian Express,* confirms Nasiri's remark.

56 "Muslim Representation in the Central Ministry of Shipping & Transport," *Muslim India* (December 1983), p. 540.

57 Sandeep Dikshit, "Battle for the Shrunken Pie," *The Hindu* (22 November 2003), internet edition.

58 Omar Khalidi, *Khaki and the Ethnic Violence in India.*

59 *Roll of Indian Police Officers, 1861-1947*, compiled from records in the India Office collection in the British Library by an IP officer Basil B.E. La Bouchardiere (Horsham, Sussex, 1985). I am grateful to Theon Wilkinson of British Association for Cemeteries in South Asia (BACSA) for supplying me with this handy list.

60 Omar Khalidi, *Khaki and the Ethnic Violence in India.*

61 Ibid.

62 Syed Abid Husain, *The Destiny of Indian Muslims* (Bombay: Asia Publishing House, 1965), pp. 131-132.

[63] S. Gopal, *Jawaharlal Nehru: A Biography*, II (Cambridge, Mass: Harvard University Press, 1979), p. 77.

[64] Sri Kishan, *Forty-Five Years a Rebel* (Hyderabad, 1952),pp. 44-45, where the author cites the case of several victims. More light came about the Hyderabad cases during a scandal, see V. Krishna Ananth, "A Controversy in Hyderabad," *Frontline* 20, 8 (2003) electronic edition, citing the office of the Chief Commissioner for Land Administration.

[65] Jawaharlal Nehru, *Letters to Chief Ministers*, III,1947-1964, edited by G. Parthasarathy (New Delhi: Oxford University Press, 1987), p. 535.

[66] According to Ansar Harvani, former member of parliament, see his letter in *The Pioneer* 28 November 1995, as reproduced in *Muslim India* (January 1996), p. 26.

[67] N.B. Gadgil, *Government from Inside* (Meerut: Meenakshi Prakashan, 1968).

[68] S. Gopal, op. cit., pp. 206-207.

[69] Late Jitendra Prasada who passed away in January 2001, presented a paper translated into Urdu as "Dushman Mulk ke Bashindon ki Jaydad ka Qanun," *Siyasat* (30 October 1983). The Custodian of Enemy Properties, under the Department of Export Insurance and Enemy Property is within the Union Ministry of Commerce, New Delhi. It controls property worth Rs. 3000 crores, besides generating an annual income of Rs. 50 crores to the Indian exchequer since the 1965 war.

[70] *National Commission for Minorities Annual Report for 2000-2001* (New Delhi: NCM, 2001),p. 53-55.

DELHI

As the seat of the sultans and emperors, Delhi has been the capital city since the thirteenth century. Despite intervals of temporary shifts of the capital elsewhere, Delhi remains in public imagination as the preeminent symbol of Muslim urban life in India and a center of literary and artistic creativity besides being the political and military hub. The sultans and the Mughal emperors were able to attract a large number of the literati, artists, architects, soldiers and Sufis from all parts of the world.[1] However, the East India Company, moving from its coastal enclaves on the eastern and western coasts gradually penetrated the hinterland after the death of Awrangzib in 1707. At the dawn of the nineteenth century, it captured Delhi in 1803, rendering the incumbent emperor a mere figurehead.

Then came the anti-British uprising of 1857. With the suppression of the uprising, the British inflicted probably the most drastic alteration in the character of the city since its sack by Nadir Shah in the seventeenth century. Presuming all Muslims to be rebels, and therefore criminals, the British expelled them from the city, executing all who could be construed as having roles in the uprising. The British confiscated considerable amount of property as a punitive measure. They noted "as the bulk of the Prize was taken from the houses of Musulmans and their owners being excluded from the Town as Outlaws, they have no opportunity of claiming their property."[2] Emperor Bahadur Shah Zafar was exiled to distant Rangoon, and his two sons were executed in his presence. Members of the royal family and the nobility dispersed helter-skelter, many reduced to appalling poverty in exile in different parts of the country.[3] The misery inflicted on the Muslim inhabitants of Delhi moved Ghalib to pen one of his famous lines:

> *Bas ke faal ma yurid hai aaj*
> *Har silahshur Inglistan ka*
> *Shahr-i Dihli ka zarrah zarrah-yi khak*
> *Tishna khun hai Musalman ka*
>
> Surely today every English Tommy is Almighty God
> Now every man going from house to the bazaar is panic-stricken
> The marketplace has become a slaughterhouse, and the house looks a prison
> The very particles of dust in Delhi thirst for the blood of Muslims.

Delhi's literati, so far living under the precarious and uncertain patronage of the royalty fled to Rampur, Tonk, and distant Hyderabad. This is exemplified in a couplet famously attributed to Mir Taqi Mir:

> *Kya bud-o-bash pucho ho purab ke sakino*
> *Ham ko Gharib jaan ke hans-hans pukaar ke*
> *Dilli jo ek shahr tha 'aalam men intikhab*
> *Baste the muntakhab hi jahan rozgar ke*
> *Usko falak ne loot ke wiran kar diya*
> *Ham rahne-wale hain usi ujre dayaar ke.*
>
> The easterners ask us of our native place
> Thinking and ridiculing us as strangers
> Delhi was a chosen city of the world
> Where only the select lived
> The cruel fate looted and ruined it
> We are the natives of that ruined city.

The lowest rung of the Muslim community, the *karkhanedars,* laborers in small workshops, craftsmen, artisans, bricklayers, masons and other manual workers survived the upheaval of 1857 and took refuge in the walled city quarters named after each avocation. Some decades after 'the Mutiny', when the Hindu commercial and upper classes became assertive, the British began an even-handed policy toward the two communities, a policy that was thus far anti-Muslim. A madrasa, founded originally by Nawab Ghaziuddin Khan Firuz Jang in 1792, a son of the Nizam of Hyderabad, reopened under the British auspices as the Delhi College in 1825 though the Mughal royalty and nobility shunned it.[4] Nonetheless, some Muslims did become its famous alumni and faculty, such as Mawlawi Zakaullah and Mawlawi Nadhir Ahmad.[5] At the turn of the twentieth century, the Muslim community constituted 32.5 percent of the total population. Educational condition began to improve. According to one report, Muslim pupils constituted 30 percent of the total student population, which was certainly close to the community's percentage in the population as a whole.[6] Yet the community largely consisted of artisans, petty shopkeepers and the unskilled laborers. The traditional Muslim leadership represented by the ulema and physicians trained in Yunani medicine, led by Hakim Ajmal Khan,[7] regained self-confidence lost after the fateful event of 1857. But this was not to last. A decade before the centenary of 1857, there occurred the catastrophic partition of India in August 1947.

Since Independence

Large pogroms in and around Delhi, destruction and seizure of property, left the community shattered. Nearly all Muslim police officers left for Pakistan.[8] A decade after independence, the 1958 civil list indicates no Muslim officer at all in the police force of several thousand, and a mere four Muslims in the rest of the civil service.[9] In mid 1960s, this tiny number of Muslims in the civil service told journalist Taya Zinkin what it felt to be marooned at home.[10] From a population of 304, 971 in 1941, Muslim numbers came down in 1951 census to a mere 99, 501, a drastic reduction by any standard.[11] The following table shows Muslim population over time.

Table I
Muslim Population in Delhi, 1941-2001

Year	*Muslim Population*	*%Muslim of Total Popn.*	*Muslim Lit. % in 2001*	*Urdu Pop. %*
1941	304, 971			
1951	99, 501	5.71		
1961	155, 543	5.85		
1971	263,019	6.47		
1981	461,802	7.75		
1991	889.641	9.4		5.45
2001	1,623,520	11.7	66	

Source: Census of India

Fundamental changes took place in ownership of immovable properties and businesses. "Thousands of houses and places of property changed ownership in the first years after partition. Illegal takeovers and allocation of Evacuee Properties through the Ministry of Relief and Rehabilitation offered the quickest solution to the acute housing crisis. The less needy also took advantage of this easy opportunity to gain their "own" property. Tenants took over the houses of landlords who had fled; neighbors claimed adjacent plots and dealers the businesses of competitors who left. The numerous nontransferable properties in formerly Muslim quarters found new "owners".[12] According to official records, Delhi Muslims left 20,198 acres of agricultural land, and 10,212 houses and industrial premises.[13] A large number of mosques, cemeteries and other religious institutional property was illegally occupied and remains so despite protest.[14] Bereft of political power after the catastrophic events of partition, Muslims were unable to evict land and property-grabbers by state action. The Evacuee Property Act was replaced after the 1965 India-Pakistan war by the Enemy Property Act, under which Muslims continue to be harassed to this day.[15] Spatially, Muslims were now confined to Old Delhi, some even afraid to venture into New Delhi to seek fresh opportunities as late as 1968 according to an American journalist Joseph Lelyveld.[16] The journalist's observations are confirmed by an academic who found old Delhi Muslims inhabiting Suiwalan and Matia Mahal to be predominantly small factory workers and stall owners, many unwilling to step outside the familiar groves of the walled city.[17]

Labor, Commerce and Industry

A comprehensive survey of Muslims' economic and educational condition after independence is lacking. The Delhi State Minorities Commission, formed in 2000, is indeed interested in sponsoring a survey but handicapped due to lack of funds, according to its Chairman Abu Bakr.[18] Such Muslims as were left in Delhi belonged to the lower economic and unemployed classes of the society,[19] like *Dafali* (drum makers), *Dhobi* (washer men), *Gadheri* (brick layers), *Ghosi* (milk men), *Teli* (oil pressers), *Kamelia* (ear cleaners), *Qasai/Qasab* (butchers), *Mirasi* (folk singers), *Momin* (cotton cleaners), *Naalband* (horse-shoe makers), *Saqqa/Bihishti* (water carriers).[20] *Halal-Khwor*, also known as *Lalbegi*, *Mehtar* and *Bhangi*, are night soil removers; some profess Islam, while others do not.[21] The state-appointed G.C. Jain Commission identified some of these Muslim groups as eligible for reservation,[22] though it is not clear if the recommendation translated into action, as the Delhi Minorities Commission was going to adopt a resolution for action to happen.[23] Anthropological studies of occupational categories such as *Zardoz*,[24] makers of gold-embroidered clothes, and Telis show groups that have remained stagnant.[25] As many as 35,000 Muslim women are reported to be involved in various stages of *zardozi* work.[26] Contrary to popular perceptions, Muslim women are involved in economic activities, especially those of the working class.[27] A socio-economic profile of the Delhi Muslims describes a community largely of poverty-ridden, illiterate slum-dwellers, like the community everywhere else.[28] A small group of petty shopkeepers such as the Punjabi Saudagaran[29] and Pirachas comes from the merchant class.[30] Even this small class of Muslim merchants of Delhi was adversely affected by the actions of Prime Minister Indira Gandhi and her son Sanjay Gandhi. Under the guise of beautification of the Jama Masjid area they deployed armed thugs against civilian population to force eviction. In November 1975 the entire market area around Jama Masjid was "cleared" by bulldozers after a forced eviction ordered by the Delhi Development Authority, under its then Vice-Chairman Jagmohan (now with RSS).[31] He was reported to have said that he would not allow another Pakistan in Delhi, a reference to the concentrated Muslim population around the Jama Masjid.[32] Since the infamous era of 1975-77 Emergency, the Jama Masjid area bazaars and attendant economic interests is the constant battleground between the Shahi Imam, the Waqf Board and the various civic authorities, leading mostly to the loss of the Muslim masses.[33] Besides the Jama Masjid area, Muslims in the highly congested Nizamuddin Dargah area are mainly unemployed or daily wage earners, while the custodians of the shrine pocket donations from the pilgrims.[34] According to the Delhi Waqf Board Survey Commissioner, the daily offering at the Nizamuddin Dargah approximates Rupees 7000-10,000, whereas the Pirzadas, the saint's descendants claim a lower sum.[35] Regardless of the exact sums, the Dargah authorities have not spent any funds on public good in the poor neighbourhood. In fact, when the Delhi High Court directed the Central Waqf Council and the State Waqf Board to ensure proper accounts of the collection, the two organizations were simply unable to act due to the power of the Pirzadas.[36]

Labor, Commerce and Industry

Since the 1970s, Delhi Muslim population is now dispersed in the Old City, in Basti Nizamuddin, Okhla and Seelampur in East Delhi. In Seelampur, a large number of Muslim-owned workshops have sprung up, inviting the wrath of the Hindutva brigade in 1992 leading to large-scale destruction.[37] Given the decline of vegetarianism among affluent upper caste Hindus, and the large number of upscale hotels and restaurants, the meat market, a near-Muslim monopoly has expanded, though there are still a large number, an estimated 30,000 Muslim butchers, often affected by policies unfriendly to them.[38] Undeterred by the hostile environment, a handful of Muslims have prospered exemplified by the cases of meat export businesses,[39] real estate,[40] and other businesses such as pharmaceuticals. In pharmaceuticals, Yunani herbal medical products have long been a Muslim monopoly and remain so exemplified by the success of Hamdard Laboratories products, though even this family business is in trouble due to infighting.[41] Himalaya Drugs, a Muslim-owned company has entered the manufacture of Ayurvedic, health care products, hitherto associated with upper caste Hindus.[42] Similar to the herbal medicine is a line of cosmetics and beauty parlor franchise established by Shahnaz Hussain, popularly called the "Helena Rubenstein of Asia".[43] As the only prominent Muslim businesswoman she is certainly a role model for many. A new generation of Muslim entrepreneurs is emerging exemplified by the case of Taab Siddiqi and her husband Adil Hassan of Harvest Gold bread[44] and Arif Sheikh of Sabka Bazaar, a grocery chain.[45] These examples illustrate Theodore P. Wright's observation that "there is a beginning of self-employed Muslim business class in the interior North...but its growth has been obscured by the highly visible and articulate Muslim middle and upper-middle class (*ashraf*) politicians and professionals.[46] Wright quotes approvingly of Edward Shil's anti-bureaucratic and anti-political analysis written decades ago: "The creativity of the successful business enterprise is as unattractive to the political and intellectual elite of the underdeveloped countries as it is to the intellectuals of the Western countries...There is no logical necessity for the self-sustaining, self-developing economic system to be a capitalistic economy...It is, however, most unlikely that it would be a centrally planned economy, run by government departments which monopolizes all initiative at their higher levels...because they seek efficiency without basing it on...the specifically economic form of ambition-economizing activity...For a self-developing economy to emerge, there must be dispersion of charisma from the sphere of political authority into...the economic sphere...A host of tiny shops...and a large number of small firms...do not themselves constitute economic progress...Both of these are, however, indispensable for economic development (for) they provide...the recruiting ground and the atmosphere from which can come forward more vigorous, more farsighted, more creative entrepreneurial types."[47]

Education and the Tertiary Sector

The most recent study of Muslim girls' education in Delhi confirms a popular perception: girls' education is hampered by the parents' fear that a highly educated girl is unlikely to find a husband given widespread illiteracy among Muslims.[48] Yet, contrary to these assumptions, a survey in the Hazrat Nizamuddin area also shows concern for female education, a precondition for upward economic mobility.[49] Similarly, a field study demonstrated that the school system's shortcomings may be responsible for its lack of appeal for some slum dwellers, which flies in the face of conventional wisdom that sees poverty as the major factor for lack of interest in education.[50] Studies after studies have documented the educational poverty of Muslims at the base levels of primary through higher secondary.[51] A psycho-social examination of slum-dwelling Hindus and Muslims showed no difference regarding positive attitude toward education, which proves that it is mostly poverty that prevents access to modern, high quality education.[52] The imposition of upper caste Hindu cultural material in the curriculum further diminishes the appeal of government schools to Muslims.[53] Most Muslim-managed institutions suffer from poor finances whether as government grants or community donations.[54] Muslims run four English-medium senior secondary schools in the capital.[55]

Delhi has 158 Muslim-managed educational, religious and welfare organi-zations in 1995, many of them madrasas.[56] The Madrasa graduates do not enter the competitive examinations leading to public employment, thus adding to the dismal picture of the educational situation of Muslims. Here and there, there are examples of success stories, a reminder that the picture is not totally gloomy.[57]

Higher Education

Though primary through higher secondary education is poor among Muslims in the state, yet Delhi is also home to prestigious colleges and universities. The Delhi College remained shut for nearly a year after partition, the college building taken over by the Custodian of Evacuee Property. It required the tireless efforts of Zakir Husain to get it back.[58] Now fully 300-year old, the College is renamed after its rescuer and obtained the status of a minority institution. The Jamia Millia Islamia, founded in 1920 by rebellious students of Aligarh Muslim University angry at the pro-government policy of the establishment, is a major institution. In 1947, it also became victim of the partition and was forced to move from its campus in Karol Bagh to Okhla.[59] In an institution founded by such luminaries of India as Maulana Muhammad Ali Jauhar and Maulana Mahmud al-Hasan, it is not surprising that one of its longest-tenured Vice Chancellors, Muhammad Mujib (1948-73), refused the request of a parliament member seeking religion-wise statistics on the students at Jamia. He is reported to have said that at Jamia, *students* are enrolled not *Hindus and Muslims*![60] The university authorities informed an American scholar that Muslims in the 1960s and 1970s constituted a mere 40 percent of the student population.[61] The Muslim percentage among the students increased to around 45 percent according to two Vice-Chancellors who held the office in the 1990s.[62] Muslim percentage however goes down when enrollment in the faculties of natural sciences, engineering and technology are examined, a fairly national phenomenon in India.[63]

The Central government took over Jamia gradually. In 1988, the government introduced legislation in the parliament taking over its management, guaranteeing funds but removing its distinction as a Muslim institution much to the anguish of many members of the community.[64] Jamia's official website http://jmi.in/HistoryofJamia.htm translates the first two elements of its name Jamia Millia but omits "Islamia" completely, showing discomfort with its own name! Evidently the National Minorities Commission recommended to the government of India in 1997 that it declare Jamia a minority institution, but nothing has happened since then.[65] Like other universities, student indiscipline and factional politics among faculty and staff is endemic, sometimes leading to violence among its 12,000 students, exemplified by the cases in 1992 and 2000.[66] Until 1988, Jamia was merely a "deemed university", i.e. it lacked the status of a university as recognized by the state, and more importantly it did not receive the large amount of money it now does as a central government-funded institution. The biggest problem Jamia faces is how to excel and compete while in the shadow of the two giant institutions: Delhi University and Jawaharlal Nehru University.[67] Within Jamia, there are bright spots; its Mass Communication Research Center has gained good reputation, with its alumni staffing electronic and print media in the nation's leading TV stations and newspapers. The Mass Communication Center's success partly stems from the absence of competition as there are no comparable centers at its rival universities in the Capital.

The newest Muslim institution is Hamdard University, founded on August 1, 1989, by Hakim Abdul Hamid (1908-99), a scion of a family of Yunani hakims noted for promotion of traditional medicine in India and Pakistan. Fifteen years after its foundation, the government declared it a minority institution in early 2004 through a letter issued by the Ministry of Human Resource Development.[68] It effectively means that the University can reserve 50 percent admission seats for Muslim students. Outside these minority institutions, Muslims are not found in good numbers at the two other universities in the national capital, Delhi University and Jawaharlal Nehru University, beyond the familiar groves of Arabic, Persian, and Urdu departments.[69] The poor state of Muslim education is naturally reflected in poorer numbers in professional positions such as university professorships.

Muslim Waqf Board

Delhi has had rich endowments consisting of mosques, cemeteries, lands and other immovable property. However, much of it was lost in the upheaval of partition and occupied by illegal owners. Added to the illegal occupation is the unlawful sale and transfer by those in charge of the religious properties such as the *mutawallis* or custodians. In 1987, the Waqf Board had as many as 1886 properties as inventoried by the Waqf Commissioner.[70] The Waqf Board, formally in charge of the protection and promotion of the endowments, has never been able to perform its duties due both to the lack of executive powers and a hostile bureaucracy, a direct consequence of the state policy of indifference toward Muslim issues. In fact, over 200 endowed properties and government institutions such as the Delhi Development Authority, Central government offices, police stations, and five star hotels such as Oberoi occupy Waqf land pieces.[71] Even the government-sponsored Sahitya (literary) Academy building is built on land seized from the Waqfs.[72] As far back as April 1983, Muslim MPs submitted a memorandum to the government seeking removal of government-occupied Waqf properties, but nothing has happened.[73] When the state itself treats the Waqf properties in an unfair manner, it is understandable why there is such disorder within the Board and outside. Reports have been published, committees have been established, and inquiries have been held,[74] yet the state of affairs remain where they were since independence, partly because of the Waqf Board itself. According to Siraj Piracha, Waqf Board Chairman in 1995: "There is no system in the Waqf Board office. No one is willing to work. No one knows even the basics of filing!"[75] Nearly 15 years later, there is no improvement.[76] The illegal occupation of Muslim endowments by government agencies is a clear cut, court-admissible evidence of gross discrimination against the Muslim community.[77] Whether in Delhi or elsewhere, if properly documented and released from illegal occupation, the Waqf properties can be utilized for the economic betterment of the community. This is where government intervention is needed to uplift the community. Self-help is possible in some, but not in all areas.

Notes

1 For a superb account of economy of Delhi see, Stephen Blake, *Shahjahanabad: The Sovereign City in Mughal India, 1639-1739* (Cambridge: Cambridge University Press, 1991), Chapter 4, Economy, and for later period, see Shama Mitra Chenoy, *Shahjahanabad: A City of Delhi, 1638-1857* (New Delhi: Munshiram Manoharlal, 1998).

2 Home Public Proceedings, No. 97 of 14 May 1858, available in the National Archives of India, New Delhi, as cited in Warren Fuslfeld, "Communal Conflict in Delhi, 1803-1930," *The Indian Economic and Social History Review* 19, 2 (April-June 1982): 181-200, citation on p.192.

3 Accounts of Bahadur Shah Zafar's descendants living in miserable condition appear from time to time seeking government pension, see for example, "Prince Bedar Bakht," p. 56 in *Autobiography of a Princess*, compiled by James Ivory (New York: Harper & Row, 1975); "Wisps of Memory," *National Geographic* (April 1985), pp. 468-469; "Surviving Mughals: Disputed Inheritance," *Muslim India* (January 1983), p. 39; Shadab Bakht and Kiran Raivadera, "Direct Descendants of Bahadur Shah Zafar ... Living in Slums," *The Telegraph* 14 May 1989, as reproduced in *Muslim India* (July 1989), p. 325; Arijit Gupta, *The Living Mughals*, a documentary made in August 2002; see Amarnath K. Menon, The Last Mughals, *India Today* (October 14, 2002), p. 27 about the former royal family members in Hyderabad, one of them opened a restaurant Ziyafat-I Deccan, in Chennai, see Padma Ramnath, "Mughal Delights," *Business India* (March 29-April 11, 2004), p. 148.

4 Mawlawi Abd al-Haq, *Marhum Dehli Kalij* (Delhi: Anjuman-I Tarraqi-yi Urdu, 1944).

5 Gail Minault, "Sayyid Ahmad Dehlavi and the 'Delhi Renaissance,'" pp. 287-298, *in Delhi Through the Ages,* edited by R.E. Frykenberg (Delhi: Oxford University Press, 1986).

6 *Progress of Education in India 1927-32,* II, Table 99 (B) as cited in Ratna Naidu, *Communal Edge to Plural Societies* (New Delhi: Vikas, 1980), p. 35.

7 Barbara D. Metcalf, "Hakim Ajmal Khan: Rais of Delhi and Muslim Leader," pp. 299-315, *in Delhi Through the Ages,* edited by R.E. Frykenberg (Delhi: Oxford University Press, 1986).

8 Omar Khalidi, *Khaki and the Ethnic Violence in India,* op.cit., pp. 77-79.

9 *All India Civil List,* Issued Half Yearly (Bombay: Printed & Published under the Authority of the Govt. of India, January 1959), pp. 306-308.

10 Taya Zinkin, *Challenges in India* (New York: Walker, 1966), see the two chapters, Death and the Pendulum, and Muslim Mood.

11 *Census of India, 1951,* Chapter I, Section 2 (New Delhi, 1952), p. 29. By the next decennial census, the Muslim population rose to 155, 534, according to *Delhi Census Handbook,*

1961, as cited in *Delhi Through the Ages,* edited by R.E. Frykenberg (Delhi: Oxford University Press, 1986), p. 451. And in 1981, the population rose to 481, 802, nearly (97 percent) all urban.

[12] Thomas Krafft, "Contemporary Old Delhi: Transformation of an Historical Place," pp. 65-91, in *Shahjahanabad/Old Delhi,* edited by Eckart Ehlers and Thomas Krafft (Stuttgart: Franz Steiner, 1993), citation on p. 67.

[13] *Constituent Assembly of India, Legislative Debates,* November-December 1949 (Delhi: Manager of Publications, 1949), p. 4, slightly different figures on p. 16 of this document,

[14] See the well-documented study of Ataurrahman Qasimi, *Dilli ki Tarikhi Masajid,* 2 vols. (Delhi: Mawlana Azad Academy, 1997)

[15] It may seem incredible that such would be the case, but see "Minorities Harassed," *Radiance* (26 December 1999), p. 9, and the *Annual Report of the National Minorities Commission, 1999* (New Delhi: National Minorities Commission, 1999), p.; A.B. Masood, "Old Delhi Muslims' Harassment Unabated," *Islamic Voice* (March 1999) internet edition.

[16] Joseph Lelyveld, "India's 55 Million Moslems Living in Rejection and Isolation," *The New York Times* 28 October 1968, p. 20.

[17] Violette Graff, "Communal Relations in Indian Politics: A Case Study of Chandni Chowk (1967-1977), pp. 397-409, *Asie du Sud: Traditions et changements,* edited by Marc Gaborieu (Paris: CNRS, 1984).

[18] Interview with Abu Bakr, New Delhi, 19 December 2004. There are no reports or any literature that the Commission produced in five years.

[19] Sabiha Qureshi, Unemployment of Muslims in Old Delhi Since 1980, Mphil dissertation, Aligarh Muslim University, 1988.

[20] Short accounts of these occupational groups are in *Delhi, People of India Series, XX,* edited by T.K. Ghosh and Surendra Nath (New Delhi: Anthropological Survey of India, 1996).

[21] Khwaja Hasan Nizami, *Halal Khwor* (Delhi: Mashayikh Book Depot, 1924), and a modern account by Vijay Prashad, "The Killing of Bala Shah and the Birth of Valmiki: Hinduisation and the Politics of Religion", *The Indian Economic and Social History Review* 32, 3 (July-September 1995): 287-325.

[22] "53 OBCs in Delhi On Mandal List," *Radiance* (6-12 November 1994), p. 4.

[23] "Reservation for Backward Minorities in Govt Jobs Soon," *The Pioneer* (25 August 2004) electronic edition.

[24] Charu S. Gupta, Subhadra Mitra Channa, "Caste Among the Muslim Zardoz of Delhi: A Study of Occupational Culture and Subgroup Identity," *Man in India* 76, 2 (June

1996):103-114; and Charu S. Gupta, *Zardozi: Glittering Gold Embroidery* (New Delhi: Abhinav, 1996).

25 Ragini Sahay, "Dowry and Dower in Muslim Marriage: A Study Among Muslim Telis of Delhi," *Indian Anthropologist* 26, 1 (June 1996): 47-52.

26 *Eighth Annual Report of the Minorities Commission for the Period from 1-4-1985 to 31-3-1986* (New Delhi: Ministry of Welfare, 1989), p. 196. Deepti and Pushpa Mehta, "Behind the Glitter: Zardozi Workers in Delhi," *Manushi* (September-October 1984).

27 Sunbul Rizvi, "Lower Class Working Women in the Traditional Muslim Belts of Delhi: A Recent Survey Report," *Islamic and Comparative Law Quarterly* 8 (1988): 244-247.

28 K.G. Munshi, *Socio-Economic Profile of Indian Muslims: A Case Study of Delhi* (New Delhi: Institute of Objective Studies, 1997).

29 Neelam Malhotra, "The Punjabi Muslim Community in Delhi: Its Growth and Development, 1912-1927," *Indian Journal of Secularism* 2, 3 (October-December 1998): 17-35.

30 *Delhi, People of India Series* and Special issue of *Afkar-I Milli* on the Delhi Saudagaran (October 1996).

31 John Dayal and Ajoy Bose, *Delhi under Emergency* (New Delhi: Orient, 1977); Emmat Tarlo, *Unsettling Memories: Narratives of the Emergency in Delhi* (London: Hurst, 2003).

32 Tavleen Singh, "Turkman Gate Incidents: A Critical Analysis of Defamation Ruling," *Indian Express* (2 August 1992), p. 6. Jagmohan hauled *The Indian Express* correspondent Jawid Laiq to the court.

33 Khurshid Alam, "Shopping Complex aur Jama Masjid ki Siyasat," *Afkar-i Milli* (August 1994): 19-21; Abdurrahman Abid, "Ilaqa-yi Jama Masjid...aur Market..." *Afkar-i Milli* (October 1991): 49-51.

34 "Marital Practices and Demographic Patterns Among Muslims and How it is Affected by Family Income", *Progressive Perspective* 1, 5 (November 1995): 1-5; the Delhi High Court directed the Delhi Waqf Board's Survey Commissioner to report on the collection at the Dargah, according to a UNI news published in *Siyasat*, 08 April 2004, electronic edition.

35 "Dargah Authorities to Give Accounts," *The Milli Gazette* (16-31 October 2004), p. 20.

36 *Munsif Daily*, online edition, 11 April 2005.

37 A.U. Asif, "Old Seelampur Disturbances: Muslim Economy Main Target," *Radiance* (7-13 June 1992): 12; M. Ahsan Siddiqi, "Seelampur: Fasad ke Baad," *Afkar-I Milli* (May 1993): 18-19; M. Ahsan Siddiqi, "Jaafarabad: Mashriqi Dilli ka Manchester," *Afkar-I Milli* (August 1993): 57-60.

[38] Gill Tudor, "Butchers Sell Family Jewels to Survive Delhi Strike," India West (20 May 1994), p. 10; "High Court Order Turns 30,000 Jobless", *Radiance* (12-18 February 1995), p. 10; Muhammad Faheem, "Abattoir Closure Hits Poor Muslims," *Radiance* (15-21 December 1996), p. 12; Directory of Qureshi Biradari, published in *Qureshi Express*, New Delhi, June 2002; *All India Jamiatul Quresh Conference* brochure (Hyderabad: al-Quersh Secretariat, 1990).

[39] The Hind Agro Industries Limited owned by Samar Qureshi is one example out of many, see Mamuni Das and Harish Damodaran, "Buffalo Meat Exporters Bullish as Saudi Lifts Ban," *Business Line* (02 August 2004) Internet edition; "Qureshi Community Facing Great Difficulties," *The Milli Gazette* (16-31 October 2005), p. 3. The various state governments have banned cow slaughter in the name of animal protection, a mask for pandering to the sentiments of some upper caste Hindus; see "Court Upholds Ban on Slaughter of Bulls, Bullocks," *The Hindu* (27 October 2005), Internet edition.

[40] See the autobiography of a real estate czar and founder of the Abulfazl Enclave, Muhammad Abulfazl Faruqi, *Nashib-o Faraz: Swanih Hayat* (New Delhi: Applied Publishers, 2001).

[41] "Hamdard in Family Knot," *Tehelka: The Popular Paper* (21 July 2005), Internet edition.

[42] See the company profile on http://www.himalayahealthcare.com/abouthimalaya/index.htm. Himalaya is in stiff competition with its old rival Dabur..

[43] Madhu Jain, "Shahnaz Hussain: No Biz Like Shah Biz," *India Today* (15 May 1993): pp. 58-59.

[44] "Better off Than Dad," *India Today* (9 February 2001), p. 37; Manjari Raman, "Harvest Gold: Key to a Well-Bread Campaign", *The Indian Express* (23 February 1998) internet edition.

[45] S. Ubaidur Rahman, " Hard Labor Always Pays," *The Milli Gazette* 1-51 November 2003, p. 8.

[46] Theodore P. Wright, Jr. "The New Muslim Businessmen of India," pp. 37-46, *in Changing South Asia: Development and Welfare*, edited by Kenneth Ballhatchet and David Taylor (London: School of Oriental & African Studies, 1984), citation on p. 37.

[47] Wright, Jr. op. cit., p. 37.

[48] Zoya Hasan and Ritu Menon, *Educating Muslim Girls: A Comparison of Five Cities* (New Delhi: Kali For Women, 2005).

[49] Conducted for UNICEF by Ali Baqir, see the news item, "Survey of Basti Nizamuddin Shows Monogamy and Concern for Female Education," *Muslim India* (April 1984): 167.

[50] Rukmini Banerji, "Poverty and Primary Schooling: Field Studies from Mumbai and Delhi," *Economic and Political Weekly* (4 March 2000): 795-802.

51 Aijazuddin Ahmad, *Muslims in India: Their Educational, Demographic and Socio-Economic Status with Indicators for Hindus, Sikhs, Christians, and Other Communities, Based on a Singular and Systematic Field Survey, 1990-1993*, 4 vols. (New Delhi: Inter-India Publications, 1993-96), v. 3 is on Delhi and the most comprehensive; "Delhi's Muslim Schools: Saga of Truancy, Apathy and Negligence," *Islamic Voice* (September 1992):1-2; Firoz "Why Muslim Girls Stay Away from Schools?" *Communalism Combat* (June 1994):10; Firoz Bakht Ahmad "56 Year Old Urdu School Faces Closure," *The Milli Gazette* (16-31 July 2004):5.

52 M.G. Husain, *Psycho-Social and Demographic Profiles of Hindu Muslim Slum Dwellers in Delhi* (New Delhi: Institute of Objective Studies, 2004).

53 "Ramayana and Mahabharat in Schools…Efforts at Assimilation of Religious and Cultural Minorities," *Radiance* (7-13 May 1989): 41; "Saffronising Education in Delhi," *Radiance* (4-10 October 1998): 10.

54 M. Ansar Alam, "A Case Study of Two Muslim-Managed Schools of Delhi," *Journal of Objective Studies* 6, 2 (July 1994): 131-138.

55 Nusrat & Ahmad Rashid Shervani, " Muslim Managed English Medium Schools in Delhi," *The Milli Gazette* (1-15 August 2005),p. 6.

56 Mohammed Qamar Ishaq, *Directory of Muslim Educational, Religious & Welfare Organizations in India* (New Delhi: Institute of Objective Studies, 1995), pp. 47-54; updated by Rahat Abrar and Mohammed Qamar Ishaque, *Directory of Muslim Educational Institutions in India* (New Delhi: Institute of Objective Studies, 2002), pp. 122-27.

57 Marcus F. Franda, "Education for Young Muslims: the Crescent School of Old Delhi," *American Universities Field Staff Report*, 23, 1979; S. Ubaidur Rahman, "Safinatul Hidaya's Services to Education," *The Milli Gazette* (1-15 June 2001),p. 24.

58 Rana Tahseen, *Education and Modernization of Muslims in India* (New Delhi: Deep & Deep, 1993), p.112.

59 An excellent account is by Shamsurrahman Muhsini, *Hindustani Musalmanon ki Qawmi Taalimi Tahrik* (New Delhi: Maktabah-I Jamia, 1988).

60 Razi Ahmad Nadwi, "Aslaf ki Qurbaniyon ka Samra," *Kitab Numa* (November 2005), p. 31.

61 Richard A. Schermerhorn, *Ethnic Plurality in India* (Tucson: University of Arizona Press, 1978), p. 175.

62 Interview with Syed Shahid Mahdi, Vice-Chancellor from March 2000 to June 2004; New Delhi, 16 December 2004. and with Lt. Gen. M.A. Zaki, Vice-Chancellor from 1997-2000, Hyderabad, December 29, 2004.

63 Interview with Vice Chancellor Mushirul Hasan, December 17, 2004.

[64] "Jamia Bill Disowns Jamia Past," *Radiance* (18-24 September 1988),pp. 6-8; Syed Shahabuddin, "Jamia Loses it Purpose, Character," *Radiance* (16-22 October 1988), pp. 6-8.

[65] "Minority Character to Jamia Millia Islamia Urged," *Radiance* (20-26 June 2004), p. 11.

[66] Rajeev Ranjan Roy, " An Institution on the Brink," *Meantime* (11 November 1999): 36-38. A.B. Masood, "Barbaric Police Attack on Jamia Millia Students," *Islamic Voice* (May 2000) Internet edition.

[67] Conversations with Prof. Seema Alavi, JMI History Department on flight from Boston to London, 1 July 2005.

[68] "Hamdard Wins Minority Status," *The Milli Gazette* (16-28 February 2004),p.1.

[69] "Muslim Representation in Delhi University," *Muslim India* (January 1987).

[70] Hasanuddin Ahmad and Ahmedulla Khan, *Strategies to Develop Waqf Administration in India* (Jeddah: Islamic Research and Training Institute, Islamic Development Bank, Research Paper no. 50, 1998), p. 138.

[71] Ibid, p. 141.

[72] Suhayl Anjum, "Waqf Imlak ki Hifazat Kayse Ho? *Afkar-i Milli* (October 1997): 14-18.

[73] "Memorandum to the Sethi Committee by the Muslim Congress (I) MPs in April 1983", *Muslim India* (July 1983):309-311.

[74] "Transfer of 123 Wakf Properties Approved in 1984, Not Yet Effected," *Muslim India* (October 1988), pp. 459-461; "Wakf Properties Under Dispute in Delhi," *Radiance* (28 January-03 February 1990), pp. 15-16; and in the same issue of *Radiance*, "Recommendations of the Burney Committee Report".

[75] Shahnawaz Siddiqi, "Siraj Piracha se Guftgo," *Afkar-i Milli* (August 1995): 17-18; Khurshid Alam, "Dilli Waqf Board Afratafri ka Shikar," *Afkar-i Milli* (June 1993): 32-34.

[76] Andalib Akhtar, "Delhi Waqf Board in Doldrums," *Islamic Voice* (August 2004) Internet edition.

[77] "Mosque Encroached Upon under UPA's Nose," *The Milli Gazette* (1-15 November 2004), p.1.

UTTAR PRADESH

Uttar Pradesh, formerly known as the United Provinces or simply U.P., is the most populous state in India. It was created out of various territories the British conquered in the late eighteenth and mid nineteenth centuries, comprising the regions of Agra, Doab, Rohilkhand, Oudh, and Bundelkhand. Muslim population in the state from 1881 to 2001 as given in the census may be seen in the Table below:

Table I
Muslim Population in U.P., 1881-2001

Year	*Muslim Population*	*Muslim % Popn.*	*% Rural Muslim*	*%Urban Muslim*	*Muslim. Lit. %*	*% Urdu Pop.*
1881	6,162,900	13.74				
1891	6,346,651	13.53				
1901	6,731,034	13.84				
1911	6,658, 373	13.82				
1921	6,481,032	13.88				
1931	7,181, 927	14.42				
1941	8,722,864	15.43				
1951	9,027,207	14.28				

1961	10,788,089	14.62	25.7	74.3		
1971	13, 76,533	15.48				
1981	17,657,735	15.93				
1991	24,109,684	17.3	35.65	65.35		8.98
2001	30,740,158	18.5			66.6	

Source: Census of India.

Agriculture and Land Ownership

The process of post–Mutiny punishment of rebels by confiscation[1] in the North Western Provinces in 1858 and 1859 official policy was "community blind"; both Muslims and Hindus suffered equally.[2] While the Mughal Emperor's pauperized descendants dispersed in various directions, the descendants and dependents of the Oudh Court were luckier. These dependents received a *wasiqa*, or certificate entitling them to receive small pensions through a trust made for them. In 1913, there were 1661 *wasiqadars* in Lucknow, a figure that must have increased later.[3] The *wasiqadars* "made little or no effort to change circumstances that befell them, considered it derogatory to earn their own living, and rather than do so sold what little land they possessed, and became increasingly indebted to the Rastogi money-lenders by pawning their jewelry."[4] Gradually the *wasiqa* money became a mere pittance.[5] As the wounds of the Mutiny healed, the government restored the lands by providing *sanads* or ownership and revenue collection documents to a group of landlords called *zamindars, pattidars and taluqdars.* The last ones were most influential and numbered 272, of which 76 were Muslims or roughly 28 percent.[6] At the dawn of the twentieth century, "Muslims held approximately one-fifth of the land in the province. They tended to hold particularly large amounts around former centers of Muslim power such as Jaunpur, Allahabad, and Fatehpur, Bareilly and Moradabad, Lucknow and Bara Banki…In Agra [sub] province, just as there were few large landlords, so were few large Muslim landlords…Further west, where Muslims were more numerous and Muslim influence had been greater, their situation was better. In one area, the districts of Aligarh and Bulandshahr, where the estates of Lalkhani Rajputs and Sherwani Pathans were situated, there was a very powerful concentration of Muslim landlords."[7]

Post-Independence Era

Next only to Bengal, Delhi, and Punjab, U.P. was drastically affected by the partition of India. Large number of Muslims migrated from the U.P. districts bordering Punjab to Pakistan. According to official statistics, Muslims left as many as 14, 221 *bighas* (portions) of land, which were acquired by the Custodian of Evacuee Property.[8] The havoc it caused has gone beyond official statistics to fictional prose, indicating large-scale hardship to Muslims, given the hostility of the Custodians.[9]

One of the most well publicized achievements in the Indian agricultural economy in the early days of independence was the land reform in the various states. In U.P, a Zamindari Abolition Committee was appointed even before independence in 1946, and its report formed the basis of legislation enacted in 1951, meant to strip the large landlords of the bulk of their estates and award the land to the cultivators. The purpose of the land reforms was of course to improve the lot of the cultivators and enhance agricultural productivity. Half a century since the abolition, in the academic scholarship on the enactment there is near consensus that neither of the purposes was achieved. Most of the debate on the *zamindari* abolition has focused on the village society and agricultural productivity. Less attention has been paid to the *differential* impact of land reforms upon the *zamindars*. Nor has much attention gone into the question of Muslim women's right to inherit agricultural land.[10]

Despite some opposition, the *taluqdars* were unable to prevent the passing of the Zamindari Abolition Act of 1951, which took effect on July 1, 1952. As a result of the legislation, the *taluqdars* found themselves deprived of all their land holdings except that which they had kept unlet as "home farms" (*sir* and *khudkasht*) or as grove (*bagh*) land. To cushion the blow, the Government gave compensation in the form of a non-negotiable government bond to all *zamindars* at the rate of eight times their net assets. As a group accustomed to support themselves from the rental income of their extensive holdings, the process of adjustment was difficult for most. In addition to their immediate and some times extended family, the landlords supported a large number of servants, menials, artisans, and a smaller number of accountants, teachers, and other dependants, for whom the abolition had immediate negative consequences leading to unemployment and penury. In the words of Attia Hosain, "Hundreds of thousands of families were faced with the necessity of changing habits of mind and living conditioned by centuries, hundreds of thousands of landowners and the hangers-on who had lived on their largess, their weaknesses and their follies. Faced by prospects of poverty, by the actual loss of privilege, there were many who lost their balance of mind when their world cracked apart. Others retired to the anonymity of their villages."[11]

In addition to coping with the consequences of the land reforms, the Muslim *taluqdars* were confronted with another problem: facing the stigma of having supported the creation of Pakistan. Many of them were active in the Muslim League, the party spearheading the campaign for the creation of a separate state, exemplified by the cases of Rajas of Jahangirbad, Kotwara, [12] Mahmudabad,[13] Nanpara, Pirpur, Salempur and women like Begum Qudsiya Aizaz Rasul.[14] According to one observer, "The abolition of zamindari was a signal for another transfer of property from the old elite to the neo-rich. This prompted the real exodus of Avadhi Muslims to Pakistan. *Much after 1947* (italics added), Lucknow now saw families leave for reasons related to changes in class and economic positions. The Muslim aristocracy understood that besides taking away their land, the abolition had also done something more fundamental—it had cut-off their link with the peasantry, their *watan* (country) and soil. Thereafter, the Raja of Kotwara was never able to win an election. He was defeated in 1952 [election] in a totally changed atmosphere where he suddenly became a Muslim zamindar while his opponents turned up as patriotic patrons of the peasantry. This was something the Raja found difficult to handle as an individual. His family was a trustee of the ancient Hindu shrine of Gola Gokaran Nath in Lakhimpur Kheri."[15] The stigma of association with Muslim League prevented access to the centers of political power and influence. Unlike Hindu *zamindars*, Muslim *zamindars*, deprived both of lands and access to power, left for Pakistan, illustrated by the cases of Raja of Mahmudabad.[16] The dependants and hangers on of the *zamindars* can now be found inhabiting the slums of Lucknow, by definition living in poor circumstances.[17] Some are even forced to sell body parts, such as kidneys to survive.[18]

Among the *taluqdars* who were able to successfully adapt to the new circumstances were the middle size landlords. These middle size landlords were invariably educated, therefore able to evade certain provisions of the land reforms. Some even began shifting cultivated land into mango groves and orchards, and converted tenant holdings to *sir/khudkasht* cultivated by hired labor. Others were able to invest their savings into profitable businesses through access to the political leadership of the Congress Party. Thus we can divide the differing fortunes of the Muslim *taluqdars* into three groups.

The first group comprised the urban Muslim *taluqdars*, whose members were essentially absentee landlords maintaining a marginal or tenuous link with their *zamindaris* through a series of intermediaries who were directly responsible for collecting agricultural rents from the cultivating tenants. The dealings of the intermediaries of such city-based Muslim aristocratic families with the cultivating tenants were by and large exploitative and they were not able to anticipate the impending changes that came with abolition of the *zamindari* system. Even when they were able to foresee the legislative measures they were unable to do very much about it. In the case of such families, the impact of *zamindari* abolition was much more sudden and direct than on other categories. Muslim aristocratic families in this category found their real estates slipping out of their hands and they were unable to prevent losses given the lack of an alternative income source. Since many of their residential properties were located in the older, depressed parts of the towns, such real estate was sold at depreciated value.

The deprivation caused by the land reforms would have been less severe on this class were they prepared to take up gainful employment. The feudal ethos of high spending, low or no savings, conspicuous consumption, and luxurious living further depleted their wealth. Some of the families of this class had substantial movable effects such as jewelry, expensive clothes, and furniture, which could have been sold and invested in profit making ventures. In many instances, the *zamindars* lost their landed properties as a result of long drown-out and expensive litigation, bureaucratic hostility, illegal occupation by gangsters, and the like. The Zamindari Abolition Act provided for compensation to be paid to the affected landlords. The compensation money paid was spread over a number of years and installment amounts were rapidly consumed leaving no savings. In sum, this class of the *taluqdars* was most negatively affected.

The second group of the classes affected by the zamindari abolition consisted of the small landlords. Unlike the middle size landlords, some of whom had gained some administrative experience, they lacked even that limited advantage, and were thus forced to face a sudden change in fortunes. According to sociologist Zarina Bhatty, "lacking power, their maneuverability was limited and consequently they lost a good part of their lands to the tenants who acquired legal rights over the lands that they were cultivating. Also lacking means, they were not able to buy Bhumidari rights. The economic condition of these small landlords, has, therefore deteriorated."[19] Gradually this segment of the Muslim landed aristocracy has been edged out of the rural economy or forced to join the ranks of the peasants.

The third group consisted of those Muslim families who in addition to possessing land in the rural areas also participated in the economy of the urban areas. Many members of these families obtained higher education and secured jobs in the cities while rooted in the rural social structure. Active in the state politics during the freedom movement as members of the Congress Party, they were able to anticipate political and economic changes and prepared accordingly. Such families survived the affects of zamindari abolition. The survival was achieved through two strategies. On the one hand, members of this segment ensured that the land, which was leased out, was protected from legal transfer to the cultivators. Zarina Bhatty provides an example of the strategy employed towards this end by the Kidwai clan of Oudh. "Anticipating the *zamindari* abolition bill, the dominant Kidwai lineage was able to retain (as many did), substantial area of land under their control by a series of manipulations. The land was re-distributed within the joint family and each owner was shown as a cultivator. In practice, they continued to let out land on an arrangement, which described the tenant as a hired laborer. The latter accepted this system on account of his inherent weakness and his inability or unwillingness to take advantage of the law. If a tenant was expected to cause difficulties, he was not allowed to cultivate the same plot of land for more than two years. This led to a well-managed reshuffling of tenants every two years. Simultaneously, the dominant lineage began to cultivate relatively large farms directly with the help of the hired labor drawn from the landless labor classes."[20]

In addition to agriculture, members of this group secured their position through economic diversification. They strengthened the trend for employment. Those among the educated members of the group who did not want to go for employment entered trade and commerce. Many opened restaurants, transportation companies, rice, flour, and saw mills. As many members of this group were politically active, it was easy for some to obtain permits and licenses for their businesses. Thus according to Bhatty: "They aligned themselves with the dominant political party and using earlier and new associations, secured nomination for state assembly seats. It was easy to win election from the home constituency."[21] Indian Air Force Wing Commander Riazurrahman Kidwai gives the example of an entrepreneurial relative of his clan, Nasirurahman Kidwai, who introduced a tractor and tube well on his own farm, bought a Gobar Gas Plant, introduced sugar cane cultivation, and held a series of appointments on Sugar Control Board, Cooperatives Banks, Planning Commission and so forth.[22] In fact according to Elizabeth Whitcombe, the *zamindari* abolition was a boon to some landholders. According to her ... "Q. Sahib," in the post-abolition period, "emerged with exclusive rights to his *sir*, and his mango-grove, and compensation for the lost *zamindari* with which to embellish them. Two decades after the abolition, the thirty-acre ex-*sir* was a showpiece: Nanpara, amply fertilized and ablaze with hybrid vigor. Reduced in size but not in circumstances, the ex-estate, no more than a tenth of the old *zamindari*, brought in an estimated net annual income of Rs. 6,000, ten times of the best years in Q. Sahib's father's time."[23]

Compared to the Awadh *taluqdars*, the *zamindars* of western UP, such as the Nawab of Chattari, fared better, partly because the area as a whole came under the green revolution of the 1960s. In one instance, a Muslim female farmer successfully overcame impediments for upward mobility in a rural area of Saharanpur.[24] Elsewhere in the state, Muslim peasants in Badayun, Bulandshahr, Mathura, Moradabad, and Muzaffarnagar, were found to be significantly behind others in a survey of farming communities in Uttar Pradesh, done by the Giri Institute of Development Studies.[25]

In some ways akin to the landed gentry, is the large number of the religious aristocracy represented by the descendants of the mystical saints—the *pirs*, *sajjadanashins*, *murshids*, *mashayikh*—who presided over a number of large and small *dargahs* or shrines dotting the entire state. Many of these shrines own substantial lands, commercial real estate, besides donations offered in cash and kind on special occasions. They were entirely unaffected by the political changes of the last fifty years.[26]

Muslim Peasantry

The NSSO's 1987 survey data on socio-economic information of various segments of Indian population is available only at the national level, as state-wise data has not yet been released. In the absence of large-scale statewide data, we have to depend on sample surveys such as available.

Not all Muslims living in the rural areas are agriculturalists. In fact in the 1921 government statistics Muslims represented a small segment of those engaged in agriculture, forestry and fishing. For instance, only 3.35 percent of "Ordinary cultivators" were reported to be Muslim.[27] A large number are artisans and menials, who do participate in agricultural activities during the busy portion of the agricultural season and occasionally own land, which they cultivate, but their main occupation is non-agricultural. Like other segments of the Muslim society, the Muslim peasantry falls into different categories according to the size of landholding, the area of habitation, and the general characteristics of the agricultural production of the area since independence. So far as one can generalize about a group so vast and dispersed, it does not seem that the economic condition of the Muslim peasantry has improved greatly in half a century since independence, above or below the improvement or impoverishment that has accrued to the general rural population in the country, or at least that is the impression one gets from village and town-level studies in Uttar Pradesh.[28] Like the rest of the Indian peasants, most Muslim peasants are engaged in subsistence agriculture with small land holdings, some are tenants, and the remainder laborers without land, and thus without access to credit, modern technology, electrical power, in short all the requirements of commercial farming.

A number of factors have affected the agricultural sector since independence. These include better strains of seeds, chemical fertilizers, improved irrigation, tube wells, and some mechanization, e.g. the introduction of tractors in the areas of Green Revolution. The Green Revolution in India heralded a radical change in agricultural productivity and transformed a section of peasants into capitalist farmers. However, the Revolution has had little positive impact on the Muslim peasantry outside western Uttar Pradesh,[29] as is the case of the majority of the peasantry in general we may add. The Green Revolution is largely the outcome of a breakthrough in wheat cultivation, confined to some areas in Punjab and Haryana. The Muslim peasantry is largely confined to the rice-growing areas dominated by the traditional methods of agriculture. Should a breakthrough achieved in wheat-growing areas be extended to the rice-cultivation areas, it is reasonable to expect that Muslim peasantry would also benefit.[30] Some Muslim orchard owners, for instance, the mango-growers of Malihabad, near Lucknow, are quite successful in growing and marketing India's signature fruit of many varieties.[31]

Labor, Commerce and Industry

In contrast to landlords and pensioners, who did not earn their own living, the vast majority of Muslims remained landless laborers or engaged in various forms of manual, semi-skilled or skilled labor as artisans. The most obvious occupational groups were, and remain so, *julaha* or weavers, *dhunya* or cotton carders, *darzi* or tailors, *Faqir*, or religious mendicants, *Qassab/Qasai* or butchers, *Nai* or barbers, *Kabariya* or waste sellers, *Kunjra* or green grocers, *Kumhar* or potters, *Mirasi* or folk musicians, *Teli* or oil pressers, *Dhobi* or washer men, *Gaddi* or grazers,[32] *Bhangi* or sweepers and scavengers, and *Chamar* or tanners.[33]

In commerce Muslims certainly did not lag behind others, contrary to the popular and governmental perception. "Twenty-two per cent of those earning a living from commerce were Muslims...Muslims dominated the trades in clothing, transport, hides, perfumes and luxury articles, and played a large part in food trade and others, though in spite of this they do not appear to have made much money. Apart from one or two trading and money lending communities, such as the Pathans of Shahjahanpur and Syeds of Jansath, nearly all the middling and all the big trading and banking concerns in the province were Hindu owned. Muslims were mainly peddlers, stall holders and shopkeepers—a minor section of the commercial community."[34] This was because, since the 17th century, the Hindu merchant castes dominated commerce, in the United Provinces as elsewhere.[35] The 1921 Census figures showing occupation by religion for selected occupations reveal a picture not dramatically different than shown in the 1911 census.[36]

Unskilled Muslim labor is indistinguishable from the similar classes of other communities, which is hardly surprising.[37] For instance, the *bidi* rollers of Allahabad are mostly Muslim women, while in Tamilnadu, they are mostly scheduled caste women, and the issues facing them are identical.[38] However there are certain artisans of Muslim origin who specialize in certain fields to the near exclusion of others. Like artisans everywhere, the U.P. craftsmen knit, weave, mould and carve to produce work of superior workmanship.[39] It is in the field of handicrafts that Muslims have done best.[40] A 1991 survey gives the following figures for Muslim employment in various handicrafts: art metal ware (76 %), embroidery (87.5 %), cotton rugs (67 %), *zari*, gold thread/brocade and *zari* goods (89 %), cotton rugs (67 %), wood wares (72 %).[41] Muslims' specialization in these crafts is exemplified by the cases of Master Weavers such as Pir Muhammad and Abdus Samad in Varanasi.[42] Varanasi is noted for its silk saris, silk embroidery,[43] and *zari*, gold embroidery.[44] Bhadohi[45] and Mirzapur[46] are known for carpets and rugs, durries, bed sheets. *Kargha* and handloom cloth are made in Mau. These weaving centers are the near-monopoly of Muslim *julaha* (weavers) based, besides Varanasi, in parts of eastern UP such as Azamgarh, Mubarakpur, and Barabanki.[47] Hand printed textiles are made in Farrukhabad. The famed *chikan,* embroidered clothes, are associated with Lucknow.[48] *Jamdani*, muslin manufacture is centered in Faizabad, and *zardozi, kalabattun*, gold threads in Tanda. The *julaha* are also known as Momins/Ansaris.[49] In addition to weaving, there are other textile-related occupations in which Muslims predominate: *Dhuniya* (cotton cleaners); *Rangrez* (dyers, tailors); *Naddaf* (fluffers), whose work is to rejuvenate the contents of quilts, pillows, and mattresses.[50]

Muslims are in large numbers either as workers or owner-manufacturers in crafts such as brassware in Moradabad;[51] woodwork based in Saharanpur[52]; and pottery manufacturing in Khurja.[53]

Occupational groups such as *Rain* (green grocers), butchers, and the like have been clamoring for inclusion in the official category of "Other Backward Classes", which will entitle them to reservation in educational institutions and employment opportunities.[54] A high percentage of workers and owners of small-scale industries such as locks and glass are to be found in Aligarh and Firozabad respectively. [55]Aligarh is among the largest producers of locks in India.[56] The lock manufacturing is mostly small-scale. Both Muslims and Hindus are owners and manufacturers. There are an estimated 80, 000 to 90,000 workers involved directly or indirectly in the lock industry.[57] Many employ child labor—as much as 10, 000—locking them into a drudgery from which an escape is exceptional.[58]

Transition from Master Weavers, Master Craftsmen to Business Owners

Muslims excel in craftsmanship; what they lack is the ability to organize and plan the enterprise on modern lines. With access to credit and marketing guidance, they are likely to succeed more than they do now. Since the 1970s a few Muslim entrepreneurs have begun to make inroads into traditionally Hindu-dominated businesses.[59] Not surprisingly, the businesses Muslim entrepreneurs enter are disproportionately in those industries in which Muslims already constitute a large share of the workforce, such as textiles, handicrafts, transport, auto and appliance mechanics. In Mau, for example, a major handloom center in eastern U.P., Muslim subcontractors began in late 1970s to try to edge out the Hindu middlemen who control the business. And in Varanasi, Muslims, of whom there were only handfuls in the wholesale silk trade in the 1970s, now account for one *Kothidar/Gaddidar* (merchant) in five.[60] Besides in Varanasi, some 200,000 Muslims work making saris to supply to the city's huge export industry. The *Kothidar/Gaddidar*'s success in moving up from weavers to middlemen has been resented by some of the Hindu competitors, particularly among the less established merchants.[61] According to Muhammad Salih Ansari, a prosperous *kothidar*, "The Hindus don't like their grip slackening and that often gives rise to communal tensions."[62] Year after year, Muslim master weavers and craftsmen have won accolade and government-endowed titles like the Padma Shri, an indication that discrimination cannot be practiced in the face of such excellence.[63] In

Meerut, skilled Muslim craftsmen, roughly 2000, monopolize musical instruments' manufacture.[64] The scissor and razor industry is completely dominated in Meerut by Muslim workers, numbering about 10,000 in 2004. In this industry, about a thousand Hindus and Muslims are traders and suppliers. Few Muslims have become major traders, who are mostly Hindu.[65] In Rampur, the famed knives industry has fallen on bad times due to obsolescence of the weapon.[66] What is surprising is that the metal workers and owners in Meerut and Rampur have not moved up as did the Sikhs in similar industries in Punjab as recorded by Minu Tewari.[67]

There has been a miniscule group of entrepreneurs in the community, for instance the Shervanis of Allahabad. Undaunted by the anti-Muslim environment of the late 1940s, Mustafa Rashid Shervani (1921-81), launched the Great Eastern Electroplates Limited, subsequently renamed GEEP. Evidently "the first bank manager he approached disdainfully dismissed him as a "high risk" person due to the likelihood of his going away to Pakistan."[68] But the politically well-connected Shervani did not give up, and ran a successful company of his times. Since then his descendants have branched out into other businesses after selling their dry cell and batteries enterprise.[69] But a majority of U.P. Muslim businessmen are actually retailers, not big businessmen or industrialists.[70] In Lucknow, in 1994, for instance, Muslim firms formed barely 1.53 percent of the total industrial firms.[71] The new and most spectacular example of Muslim entrepreneurship has come from Moradabad, where many brassware artisans have turned owner-manufacturers. Several reasons account for the Muslims' rapid progress against established competitors in handicrafts business. First, because the new Muslim entrepreneurs are themselves skilled craftsmen, they do not need to employ additional personnel—as do the Hindu merchants—to deal with their contract weavers or perform quality check on the goods they buy. Second, because it is easier for the contract weavers to complain about arbitrary deductions by the wholesaler when they are both of the same religion, some Muslim craftsmen seem to prefer to work for their co-religionists. Many Muslims are involved in the leather trade. This is not surprising. Leatherwork is considered an "unclean" occupation by some upper caste Hindus.[72] Many Muslims own tanneries in Kanpur,[73] just as many Muslims owned shoe factories in Agra before they were ruined by the Partition-related events. A few Muslims have even graduated into national level companies, exemplified by the case of Mirza Tanneries—the largest exporter of leather footwear.[74] However, research has established that most Muslim leather-goods businessmen make less profit than their Hindu and lower caste competitors due to better access to political power.[75] In the absence of access to political power, Muslim owned businesses in Kanpur have become target of destruction, as seen during the 1992 demolition of Babri Masjid.[76]

Economist Tahir Beg suggested "promotion of Muslim entrepreneurship under state support" to overcome constraints such as finance and marketing.[77] Such an enterprise is already in the charter of U.P. Minority Financial Development Corporation (UPMFDC). It was established in 1984 with a share capital of 5 crores.[78] UPMFDC started a scheme of Margin Money Loan, under which a loan not exceeding 75% of a given project up to Rs. 200,000 is given bearing 7.5 percent interest. In 1985/86 it advanced a total sum of Rs. 8.24 lakhs to 47 units under this scheme.[79] At its instance, the Punjab National Bank advanced loans totaling Rs. 11 lakhs to 173 units engaged in footwear trade.[80] What has been the performance of UPMFDC in the two decades since its inception? Evidence so far suggests less than satisfactory work. In 1991, for instance, wood craftsmen in Saharanpur told Minorities Commission member, M. Varadarajan, that Margin Money was not coming from the UPMFDC.[81] In 2000-2001, the Corporation claims to have given term loans to 5419 individuals with an amount of Rs. 1062.33 lakhs, Margin Money Loans to 1213 individuals amounting to Rs. 26.97 lakhs, Interest Free Loans to 100 individuals amounting to Rs. 42.28 lakhs, Industrial & Technical Training to 985 individuals amounting to Rs. 25.00 lakhs, and a Coaching Scheme costing the same amount i.e., Rs. 25.00 lakhs.[82] The UPMFDC has not made available its performance through publicly available reports to enable an informed evaluation.

As far as the community's own self-help finance schemes are concerned, there is great potential for financial institutions to do so in India's new liberalized economy.[83] There are a number of successfully run local institutions in Deoband, Faizabad, and Najibabad with potential for growth.[84]

A detailed survey of all major industries may reveal a world of prosperous small businesses owned by Muslims, if they are not destroyed or looted by the Sangh Parivar gangs as has happened all over India, but particularly in places where Muslims have either made inroads into or displaced Hindu businesses. As long as the Hindu-Muslim relationship in businesses remains asymmetrical—moneyed Hindu middlemen versus impoverished Muslim workers, as in the *chikan* craft of Lucknow, peace tends to prevail. Where Muslims enter the market as competitors the dynamics change, sometimes resulting in violence and destruction of Muslim businesses as has happened in Moradabad, Varanasi, and Aligarh, unless the state fulfills its primary duty—protection of the life and property of its citizens regardless of religious affiliation. Sometimes the government itself has segregated Muslim artisans from the mainstream of business at international fairs—such as the 2001 International Trade Fair in Delhi, leading to charges of discrimination.[85] This is a pointer that an impartial bureaucracy is needed for the promotion of artisans.

Education and the Tertiary Sector

Despite the real and perceived educational handicaps, with regard to public services in North India, Muslims, as a legacy of former Mughal rule, retained a sizeable comparative advantage. The administrative system of North India did not have the integrated pattern that the established presidencies of Bengal, Bombay, and Madras had from the beginning of the nineteenth century. The East India Company annexed Oudh only in 1856. Six years prior to the Oudh annexation, Muslims made up 72 percent of the judiciary.[86] The predominantly Muslim administration of Oudh remained and change came gradually. In fact in the whole area of North Western

Provinces and Oudh, the Muslims enjoyed greater percentage of the judicial and executive jobs than their numbers warranted. In 1882, Muslims held nearly thirty-five percent of all government posts.[87] But their share of all influential posts was greater. Thirty years after the Oudh annexation, in 1886, for example, Muslims held 45.1 percent of the total number of posts in the judicial and executive services of the North Western Provinces and Oudh. The Hindus held only 50.2 percent of these posts, although they constituted 86.2 percent of the total population.[88] Even though Persian was abolished as the language of revenue administration and law courts in the British-held territories, Urdu took its place in much of North India except in the large Bengal province, which included Bihar until 1912.[89] A glance at the number of persons serving the statutory service in 1886 in the North Western Provinces and Oudh showed that out of 11, 5 were Muslims.[90] Thus as far as the traditional sector of government employment—civil service and judiciary were concerned—-Muslims were doing well.

But what of the modern sector of government employment requiring technical and applied scientific education? The picture here is not bright, as Sarojini Ganju has shown: "They took hardly any advantage of the employment opportunities offered by the post office, telephone and telegraph services, and had little to do with the construction of roads and railways, though in the railway and administrative services they were represented, and in fact recruitment took place on the basis of communal ratios."[91] In the professional categories Muslims outnumbered the Hindus in the categories of medicine [traditional hakims?] and instruction…in Lucknow until 1911."[92]

Educational Policy and Its Impact on Employment

Up to the middle of the nineteenth century, British educational policy had limited impact in the North-Western Provinces. But thereafter the government established schools in various towns and cities resulting in rapid expansion of education. With this expansion of education there came several changes of emphasis in the curriculum: English was emphasized whereas oriental learning was de-emphasized. For Muslim landowners the change did not matter as they were not interested in modern education, whereas the poor Muslim cultivators could not send their children to schools as they were needed on the land or at the workshop. The most directly affected Muslims came from the service class. As noted earlier, to begin with, the Muslim service class and the gentry had held aloof from modern education, for reasons of pride as self-perceived former rulers, religious taboos, fear of identity loss and the like. After an initial reluctance, Muslims did take to modern education, spurred by the efforts of Sayyid Ahmad Khan and his colleagues at Aligarh. His efforts culminated in the founding in 1875 of Mahomedan Anglo-Oriental College, the precursor of the Muslim University founded in 1920. A major impetus for establishing the college was the changing criteria for government employment and modern professions, based on modern scientific education imparted through English. Thus Aligarh heralded the entry of Muslims into colonial employment.

By the late 1860s, the proportion of Muslims in the government primary and secondary schools was as large as their percentage in the population, and their percentage in higher education increased similarly by 1890s.[93] The initial hesitation in seeking modern education caused a lag: Hindus became better educated than Muslims. Bureaucratic reform initiated in the closing decade of the nineteenth century by the U.P. Lieutenant Governor Anthony MacDonnell resulted in adverse consequences for the Muslim elite. MacDonnell, "unlike his predecessors, who had treated Muslim landlords and government servants as pillars of British rule...developed a remarkable prejudice against them. He invariably described them as 'fanatical' and in times of Muslim agitation was sure that Muslim officers did not pull their weight. Muslims were a danger to security and their strong position in government service had to be reduced as far as was politically possible. To achieve this end MacDonnell used the methods that had been employed before. He applied the principle of fixing communal quotas for employment in the government service to Muslims:

they were appointed in the ratio of three to five Hindu—an arrangement which he thought very liberal."[94] Another measure that MacDonnell took was the [Deva] Nagri resolution of 1900. This resolution, in addition to allowing acceptance of petitions to the government in Devanagri letters, required that clerical appointments henceforward would require ability to read both Persian and Devanagri script. Since Muslims did not normally read the Devanagri script, the new measure was bound to hurt Muslim interests. Though it did take time, through its bureaucratic reforms, "in the long run, government did succeed in changing the caste and communal composition of its services."[95]

Table II
Hindus & Muslims in the Subordinate Judicial & Executive Services in UP 1857-1913

Year/%	*1857*	*%*	*1886-7*	*%*	*1913*	*%*
Total	316	100	521	100	378	100
Muslims	202	63.9	235	45.1	131	34.7
Hindus	76	24.1	262	50.3	227	60

Source: Modified from the original table in Francis Robinson, *Separatism among Indian Muslims* (Cambridge: Cambridge University Press, 1974), and p. 46.

His table shows that between 1886-87 and 1913, the position of Muslims, and to a lesser extent Kayasthas and Rajputs, deteriorated, while that of Brahmins, Banias and other Hindus improved. It also shows that from 1857 to 1913 Muslims lost their dominant position and Hindus gained a much larger share of appointments.[96] Yet, it is clear from the table noted below that Muslims still exceeded their population percentage in almost all fields of economic activity other than as ordinary cultivators and in land rent collection.

Table III
Occupation by Religion for Selected Occupations in UP, 1921

Total Population	*Hindu %*	*Muslim %*
100 %	84.48	14.28
Agriculture & related occupations	93.44	6.01
Cultivators	96.18	3.35
Income from Land rent	69.61	27.58
Agents, managers of landed estates, clerks	82.02	15.54
Other	81.04	18.30
Exploitation of Minerals	51.54	44.13
Industry	54.07	43.50
Transport	51.42	46.60
Trade	55.71	40.40
Bank managers, money lenders and changers, etc.	43.73	45.36
Brokers, commission agents etc.	44.63	49.42
Trade in piece goods	45.28	47.82
Grain & Pulse dealers	58.07	35.45
Public Force	50.41	46.00
Army	52.51	38.36
Police	48.98	49.79
Village Watchmen	50.08	49.04
Public Administration	57.99	37.49
Service of the State	47.37	47.67
Municipal & Local Service	52.12	43.22
Professions & Liberal Arts	76.63	18.42
Lawyers	63.49	28.07
Medical Practitioners	51.17	39.83
Instruction	67.64	22.47
Letters, Arts & Science	48.46	49.23

Source: Census of India, 1921, vol. XVI, pt. II, pp. 396-407, as cited in Paul Brass, *Language, Religion and Politics in North India* (Cambridge: Cambridge University Press, 1974), p. 152. I have modified the table to make it simpler.

Muslim education condition also improved. In fact, in 1927 Muslim students constituted 18.1 percent of the total enrolled, though Muslim population in UP at the time was only 15.5 percent.[97] Further progress is evident "throughout the 1930s. Among the various literate categories, Muslims increased their proportion steadily, until 1931, they comprised more than 15 percent of the literate population of the province, more than 28 percent of the urban literate population and more than 22 percent of that tiny but politically crucial population—the urban English educated class."[98]

As Muslim education improved in the U.P., Muslim representation in the provincial civil service became proportionate to their population, sometimes even exceeded it. Thus Pandit Govind Ballabh Pant, the first elected Prime Minister—as the chief ministers were then called—-told a press committee on 11 January 1939 that the UP Civil List stood as described in the Table noted below.

Table IV
Community-Wise Composition of the UP Civil Service in 1939

Service Category	*Hindus*	*Muslims*
Provincial Executive Service	52.5	39.6
Tahsildars	54.9	43.6
Naib Tahsildars	55.9	41.4
Provincial Judicial Service	72.0	25.0
Deputy Superintendent of Police	56.0	28.0
Police Inspectors	54.2	43.8
Head Constables	35.3	64.4
UP Agriculture Service Class I	64.0	21.0
UP Agriculture Service Class II	73.0	25.0
Veterinary Inspectors	24.0	52.0
Subordinate Agriculture Service	73.0	25.0
Gazetted Co-Operative Officers	62.5	37.5
UP Forest Service	57.0	19.0
Assistant Excise Inspectors	65.0	31.0
UP Educational Service Class I	75.0	25.0

Source: "Position of Muslims in U.P. Services Before Partition," *Muslim India* (September 1994).

In light of the employment statistics, Pant "claim [ed] that what we have done is not only just but even generous."[99]

Post-Independence Era

However, barely eight years later, even before the British departure from India, the Muslim fear of discrimination in post independence era began to come true. Sardar Patel directed the UP administration to stop employing Muslims until the Muslim employment percentage is reduced to the community's population percentage.[100] In response, the Congress government led by Pandit Pant dutifully obliged. Pant informed Vallabbhai Patel on 28 May 1947 that "According to the present practice and rule, 60 percent of the posts are reserved for Hindus, 30 for Muslims and 10 for others. In the lower grades, especially of the police service, Muslims have been recruited in still larger numbers. As a result they preponderate specially in civil police. For the future, we propose that the recruitment of Muslims for non-competitive posts should be on a population basis, which will come to about 15 percent. For competitive posts, all recruitment should be purely on the basis of merit and fitness, regardless of communal considerations."[101] Pant continued, "the present structure and composition of the services is the outcome of the policy that has been followed for several decades. Certain sections are over-represented with the result that inevitably others have been denied a ratable share. It is necessary to change the rules on the subject and we are going to revise them, but nevertheless the present composition cannot be altered forthwith and we may have to face a crisis at once."[102]

The U.P. Hindu Mahasabha presented a list of ten demands to the state government, threatening direct action from August 1, 1947, if they were not accepted. The demands included that "armed police and home guards be manned exclusively by Hindus, that key posts in government be removed from Muslim control and given to Hindus. In his reply to the Mahasabha, Pant reassured that "as far as recruitment to government service was concerned...where selection is made otherwise than by competitive test, recruitment of different communities will be on the basis of population."[103] "The implementation of this policy," wrote Pant, "would remove anomalies,"[104] an euphemism for Muslim over representation. In a similarly euphemistic passage Pant conveyed his government's intentions in the matter of armed police: "We have already initiated some scheme of strengthening the Military Police which has a Muslim proportion of about 37 percent so far. We have formed a number of new companies and are recruiting some more ...to strengthen... our civil defense. Loyalty to the state will be a fundamental condition of service...[105] Regarding the demand for a Hindu monopoly over important jobs, Pant wrote that despite the inability of the government to discriminate between its officers on communal grounds, matters were moving in the desired direction. English officers were going back and many Muslim officers had opted for Pakistan.[106] "In the result there will be considerable reshuffling and most of the important posts will be filled by Hindu officers."[107] Chaudhri Khaliquzzaman, who complained to Nehru about the matter, confirmed Pant's hostile policy toward Muslim recruitment in the police.[108] In November 1947, the U.P. government announced that all jobs would henceforth be available on "merit", which was a cloak to debar Muslims less proficient in Hindi, the newly declared official language.[109] Verbal instructions were given to police officers not to recruit Muslims at all, according to Keki Daruwala, an IPS officer then posted in the province. "... in the late 1950s, it was common knowledge that a secret Government order discouraging the recruitment of Muslims to the Police had been issued by the Government when Govind Ballabh Pant was the chief minister."[110] In 1958 Muslim employment in the U.P. civil service was reduced to a mere 6 percent, according to official statistics.[111]

In addition to the negative measures of the hostile administration, developments within the Muslim community certainly contributed to the worsening picture in the civil service. One is the large-scale migration of educated, qualified men to Pakistan. The second is the reluctance of

Muslims to come forward and enter the competitive world of employment market. According to an Aligarh Vice-Chancellor Badruddin Tyabji, in his time at the Muslim University (1962-65), "there was a profound feeling of despondence and defeatism about these [employment] matters among the Muslim students in particular. Often without reason they considered it useless to apply for a job, being convinced in advance that they would not be selected. In addition, many of them had a complex about serving in parts of India where they knew no one, or where there was no society of fellow Muslims. They suffered from all kinds of inhibitions, lacking altogether a spirit of adventure and self-confidence for venturing outside their sadly shrunken world."[112] Nearly three decades later, journalist Tavleen Singh echoed Tyabji, discovering a "frightening atmosphere of discrimination... grievance" on campus.[113]

An *All India Civil List* for 1958 shows only 78 Muslim names, even though Nafisul Hasan was the Chairman of the UP Public Service Commission at the time.[114] The Civil List for 1964 found Muslims to be a bare 7.7 in government employment, far below their proportion in the population.[115] Chaudhri Charan Singh, Chief Minister of U.P. (between 1967-68, 1970), told Dr. A.J. Faridi that he wanted Muslim percentage in the police to come down, as it was too high before independence.[116] N.S. Saxena, UP Police Chief in 1970-71, verified the official statistics on the subject.[117] The 1969 statistics for certain departments of UP provincial service showed Muslims to be between 3 to 10 percent of the total strength.[118] The 1980 UP Civil List shows no improvement: minorities, which could include Christians and Sikhs, formed 7.47 percent of the total, with an inverse relationship between higher posts and the minorities number. [119] Muslims represented in 1981 a meager 5.59 percent of the state judicial service.[120] In 1983, the UP State Public Service Examination results showed that only 2.46 percent were Muslims among the successful candidates.[121] One study finds the Muslim pupils' aspiration levels significantly lower than those of Hindus.[122] The lower aspirations of Muslims may partly explain poor performance in 1979-80 competitive exams as documented.[123] In 1993, figures show that only four percent Muslims were found in Provincial Armed Constabulary.[124]

What happens to those Muslims who do make it into the police service? One answer is "the Muslim officers' basic grievance is that they are not given charge of substantive post—posts of districts and ranges."[125]

The UP administration has taken some measures in the 1980s to increase Muslim presence in the government employment, for instance, by holding employment information camps in minority concentration districts and minority educational institutions, by registering minority candidates in employment exchanges, by including a minority representative in selection committees for recruitment,[126] and by establishing coaching classes to prepare candidates for civil service examinations.[127]

Some Muslim groups in U.P., frustrated with the results of the open competition for admission to educational institutions and jobs hoped to be named "Other Backward Class", especially since the government decided to accept the recommendations of the B.P. Mandal Commission in 1990. In 1994/95, the demand for reservations was made forcefully with the support of the Congress Party, no doubt encouraged by the rise of political parties in UP based on lower caste support such as the Bahujan Samaj Party (led by Mayawati and Kanshi Ram) and Mulayam Singh's Samajwadi Party.[128] However, some groups within the larger Muslim community would like the reservations to be restricted to what they call "lower caste Muslims."[129] Secular, leftist intellectuals (journalists, academics, social activists) generally oppose reservation for Muslims as a community—though not for segments within it. However, it is significant that when Andhra Pradesh became the first state to legislate—as distinct from mere government order or governor's ordinance—reservation for the entire community, the CPI and CPM members of the AP Legislature supported the government bill when it was passed on 5 October 2005.

Educational Status

In the absence of thorough, official statistical documentation covering all levels of education and at various times, one has to depend on sample survey data that is available.[130] The Hamdard Education Society's survey done in 1983 indicates that Muslims' standard within their own institutions is far from rosy.[131] By far the most detailed survey by Aijazuddin Ahmad shows a dismal picture: Muslims' literacy rate is a mere 27 percent.[132] A sample survey conducted by Brij Raj Chauhan in 1992 in both urban and rural regions of Meerut found that the "educational level of the members [Muslim community] is not commensurate with their economic attainments and greater attention to the need for education has to be given for these groups."[133] This is a conclusion reached similarly in roughly the same geographic area by Nasim Aijaz in her dissertation.[134] The Union Ministry of Home Affairs sponsored a survey in 1981 of 45 districts in 12 states with a large Muslim population, including U.P. It showed that Muslim enrollment and successes in elementary, secondary, and high schools was poor. Similar was the case with Muslim enrollment in engineering and medical schools.[135] A.R. and Nusrat Shervani's data and efforts for Muslim education in various districts spread over two decades have shown mixed results.[136] Nita Kumar's work among the artisans of Varanasi shows an educationally depressed Muslim community, with little interest in modern education.[137] The U.P. Rabita Committee's 1992 survey of education in Aligarh discovered rampant illiteracy among the Muslim villagers of the district.[138] Female education is even lower than men's as seen by the cases of Aligarh[139] and Bijnor.[140] The low standard of Muslim pupils in the Aligarh district shows that a simple expansion of education alone is not enough to guarantee Muslim entry into high-paying jobs and professions, as researched by Naseem A. Zaidi of AMU.[141] Before Zaidi's research in the 1990s, a 1970 report about on the UPSC showed that out of 6,700 university graduates appearing for the exams, less than 50 belonged to AMU.[142] The graduates of *madrasas* probably do not even enter the competitive exams offered by the UPSC. The Madrasa graduates, with appropriate training in English, Mathematics, and Hindi can successfully compete if prepared through coaching.[143] Their number is way too large to be left out of the employment market. For example in UP there are as many 2315 such institutions. Even leaving aside non-madrasas, this is a number too large to be ignored.[144] Muslim female literacy is low as everyone recognizes, and some effort has now gone into improving this situation.[145]

Aligarh Muslim University and other Institutions

According to Rahat Abrar, the Public Relations Officer of Aligarh Muslim University, in 1996 there were 15 Muslim-managed degree colleges in Uttar Pradesh.[146] Like other U.P. institutions, many are stagnant, some in decline.[147] Some, like Shibli National College in Azamgarh[148] have become the target of the Hindutva brigade, beating up students and faculty.[149] On 26 January 2000, RSS members attacked students and faculty who refused to sing *Vande Mataram*. A new breed of professional colleges is springing up thanks to the economic liberalization unleashed since the 1990s. Invariably such institutions charge capitation fee or donations. Invariably, the beneficiaries of these institutions are the children of the wealthy, off springs of the non-resident Indians working abroad in the Middle East or elsewhere.[150]

Leaving aside these institutions of local significance, the role and performance of Aligarh Muslim University deserves some attention due to its significance and influence. Under the leadership of Zakir Husain (1948-56), B.H. Zaidi (1956-62), and then from 1962-65 under the Vice-Chancellorship of Badruddin Tyabji, the University survived the challenge posed by the hostile environment of post-1947 Uttar Pradesh administration, which was firmly in the grip of the anti-Muslim faction of the Congress Party.

Let us focus on the issue of Muslim representation in its various faculties. The post-independence survival of AMU began to be marred by declining Muslim numbers in the Engineering College due to the poor performance of Muslim candidates seeking admission. In order to stem the tide of Muslim decline, the AMU Academic Council decided to reserve 60 percent of the seats for the "internal" candidates coming from within the University, raising it from the existing 40 percent reservation.[151] During the time of Tyabji's successor Nawab Ali Yawar Jang (1965-68), a student riot in 1965 shut down the University and invited Central government interference, as the financial provider. "The immediate precipitant of the fracas was a proposal to reduce the percentage of admissions to medical and engineering colleges which were reserved for internal students from 75 to 50 percent."[152] What happened in 1965 is clearly relevant despite the passage of time. The Supreme Court ruled that "when it came into existence in 1920, the University was established by the Central Legislature by the 1920 Act. It may be that the 1920 Act was passed as a result of efforts of the Muslim minority. But that does not mean that the Aligarh Muslim University was...established by the Muslim minority."[153] The purpose of the University as described by Tyabji, was "an all-India teaching and residential Muslim university for the study and teaching of the religion and culture of Islam along with modern science and technology..."[154] This goal, according to the AMU Old Boys Association, could only be accomplished when "the majority of students, teachers, staff and office bearers be Muslims."[155] This did not happen until the University formally acquired a minority status in 1981 through legislation.[156] In AMU's engineering, medical, and other professional schools, Muslim students are in a slim majority due to the minority character, though officially there is no reservation of seats for students along religious affiliation.[157] For example the 1984-1987 statistics show:[158]

Table V
Admissions to Aligarh Muslim University

Academic Session	*Muslims*	*Others*	*Total*
1984-85	2040	743	2783
1985-86	3314	1271	4583
1986-87	3466	1355	4821

Table VI

Academic Session	Science	Engineering	Medical	
			MBBS	MD/MS
1984-85	72%	62%	68%	32%
1985-86	67%	64%	53%	29%
1986-87	66%	64%	48%	44%

Source: *Tenth Annual Report of the Minorities Commission for the Period from 1-14 1987 to 31-3-1988* (New Delhi: Ministry of Welfare, 1990), p. 260.

Since the mid 1980s, the Registrar of the University unofficially told me that the in 2005, the Muslim percentage is roughly 55 percent in the faculties of agriculture, engineering, life sciences, dentistry, medicine, science, and management.[159] The internal quota system gives advantage to those who get admitted to the AMU from the school of higher secondary stage, or who live in and around Aligarh district and other regions of Bihar and U.P.[160]

In April 2005, a newspaper reported the decision of the AMU Executive Council to reserve fifty percent of seats in MD, MS and some post-graduate courses for Muslim students from all parts of the country, the rest of the fifty percent to be divided by 25 percent for "all India quota", and the rest for AMU's internal students.[161] Endorsed by the Union Ministry of Human Resource Development, AMU faculty and students' union, some Muslim organizations predictably hailed the decision, while the Sangh Parivar also predictably opposed it.[162] Saiyid Hamid, a former VC and a long time promoter of education, supported the move.[163] Outside AMU, the Vice Chancellor of Hamdard University Muhammad Iqbal supported the move.[164] CPI-M associated faculty members like Professors Irfan Habib and Shireen Moosvi opposed it on grounds that it would not be good for the university in terms of maintaining standards, and would also create discrimination on basis of religious affiliation within the University among its students.[165] A number of faculty members, present and past also opposed the reservation, calling it discrimination on religious grounds, privileging one community over the other, lowering the prestige of the degrees, and "vitiating the atmosphere".[166] The CPM called the move an "inadvisable step", preferring the solution to Muslim backwardness by means other than reservation.[167] Discussion among Aligarh alumni on the Internet showed a majority favoring reservation while a minority opposed it.

Amidst the continuing controversy about the reservation policy, Justice Arjun Tandon of Allahabad High Court quashed the minority status of AMU (legislated by Lok Sabha in 1981) in a judgment on 4 October 2005. In the same judgment, the Justice held the reservation notice of 25 February 2005 issued by the Ministry of Human Resource Development as invalid.[168] The 2005 judgment reiterated that it was the Government of India, which established the University.

Let us now consider the quality of education in other faculties as measured against Aligarh students in the UPSC examinations. Evidently very few AMU students even enter the examination, either because they do not meet the basic criteria for entering the exams or do not feel confident to do so.[169]

In 1985-86, the total enrolment of students at AMU was 11,671; it goes up to 17,421 if school students are included.[170] In 2005, the University's official website boasts of "about 28,000 students" on its rolls.[171] Leaving aside quantity, a glance at the quality of education in Aligarh Muslim University shows an unsatisfactory picture, marked by occasional violence. Given these conditions at Aligarh, the AMU has lost the centrality that it had among the middle and upper middle class Muslims of North India in general and UP in particular.

This is evidenced by the establishment in 1996 of the Institute of Integral Technology in Lucknow, which acquired the status of a University after a decade.[172] It began as a controversial project as its purpose was perceived as catering to the children of Non-Resident Indian parents.[173] Just outside Lucknow, the renovated colonial-style palace of a *taluqdar* is now home to Jahangirabad Institute of Technology, a project funded by

Indian Muslims in the United States since 2000. These two new initiatives are likely to have a positive impact on UP Muslims' educational condition.

A major Muslim grievance about state-run educational institutions relates to school textbooks distorting Indian history and presenting Indian culture as essentially Hindu.[174] A related matter is the enforcement of Hindu prayers such as Vande Mataram on Muslim pupils. The BJP administration forced the issue in December 1998 when it ordered the compulsory singing of *Vande Mataram.* However, the government withdrew the order in the face of determined opposition.

Given the poor performance of Muslim students in schools, it is not surprising that Muslim institutions of higher education are not doing well either. A related question is the teaching of Urdu in government schools of Uttar Pradesh. Before independence, Urdu was the language of instruction in a number of schools and was taught as one of the subjects in schools where the medium of instruction was English. Since the early 1950s, Urdu has been edged out of government schools through what is called the Three Language Formula: state language, English, and another modern Indian language. In UP it could have worked for Urdu speaking children if Sanskrit was not imposed instead of mother tongue Urdu. But the successive Congress administrations in the state adopted an anti-Urdu policy rivaled only by the Sangh Parivar. Matters have come to such a stage that in 2002, there is a not a single government school in the entire state where Urdu is taught as a subject at any level, according to the reports of I.K. Gujral and Ali Sardar Jaafri. Urdu literacy in UP is now confined to young pupils schooled in the madrasas or among the older people above 70. Urdu literacy among non-Muslims is exceptional.[175] The absence of a critical mass of Urdu-literate students has not prevented the cynical politicians from approving the formation of an Urdu university in the state in 2005, a palpably political gimmickry.[176]

Muslim Waqf Board

One of the most talked about but least implemented scheme is the utilization of endowed lands, properties and assets of the Waqf.[177] In 1988, there were a total of 16, 099 waqfs registered with the U.P. Board.[178] The condition of the UP Waqfs is not different from other parts of the country, and urgently calls for remedial steps.[179] The government established on 27 April 1987, the Waqf Vikas Nigam (Waqf Development Corporation Limited) with an authorized share capital of 5 crore rupees.[180] What is unclear is the performance of the Waqf Corporation to date,[181] except that it has not met the expectations.[182]

Conclusions

What does the half a century of Muslim experience in educational and economic development tell us? Three major patterns can be seen. First, the experience of Muslim peasantry and landlords to the changing agrarian relations in rural India is mixed and uneven. Some have done well while others have not; in this respect their experience is analogous to other Indians irrespective of their religious affiliation. Muslims are educationally poorer at the dawn of the 21st century compared to their position in 1947, at both national levels as well as in Uttar Pradesh. A direct consequence of poor education is reflected in their poor numbers in civil and military service and professions. A qualitative improvement in Muslim education is a necessary prerequisite for entry into civil service. The state needs to be active in preventing discrimination. Some Muslim artisans and workers have become owners of small to medium businesses, while the industrialists among Muslims remain confined to the historically rich Bohras, Khojas, and Memons, barring a handful of exceptions.

Notes

1 Some Oudh land owners, both Muslim and Hindu "proved to be strenuous and determined rebels. Confiscation of their lands was declared as the general penalty," see S.H.S. Cunningham, *Earl of Canning* (Oxford: Oxford University Press, 1892), pp. 155-56; 159.

[2] Peter Hardy, *The Muslims in British India* (Cambridge: Cambridge University Press, 1972) p. 71.

[3] Sarojini Ganju, op.cit., p. 286.

[4] Ibid. On the eve of independence, the Oudh Wasiqadars and Political Pensioners Association passed a resolution in Lucknow on 13 July 1947, seeking restoration of Oudh to the descendants of the Nawab, prompting a sharp response from the provincial prime minister G.B. Bant, see *Selected Works of Govind Ballabh Pant*, edited by B.R. Nanda (New Delhi: Oxford University Press, 1993), p. 287.

[5] Deepak Goswami, " A Pittance from the Past," *India Today* (31 October 1993), p. 13.

[6] Francis Robinson, op.cit. p. 20.

[7] Ibid.

[8] Constituent Assembly of India, *Legislative Debates*, November-December 1949,(New Delhi: Manager of Publications, 1947-50) p. 16.

[9] Attia Hosain, *Sunlight on a Broken Column* (New York: Penguin-Brooks Virago Press, 1989, first published in 1961), pp. 278-279.

[10] Faizan Mustafa, "Muslim Woman's Right to Inherit Agricultural Land" *Radiance* (14-20 April 1996), pp.14-15, with reference to U.P.

[11] Attia Hosain, op. cit. p. 277.

[12] Interview with Muzaffar Ali, filmmaker, music composer, and a descendant of the Raja of Kotwara, New Delhi, September 10, 2000.

[13] V.S. Naipaul, *India: A Million Mutinies* (New York: Viking, 1990), p. 371.India pressured the Nawab, who was on pilgrimage to the Shiite shrines in Karbala and Najaf, Iraq in mid 1947, to issue a statement condemning the Nizam of Hyderabad's refusal to accede to the Indian Union, failing which he was to be denied return, according to Naipaul. After a 32-year legal battle, Muhammad Khan, the Raja's only son won back his ancestral property from the Custodian, see "Indian Royal Wins Back Property," *BBC News* (25 October 2005) Internet edition.

[14] Omar Khalidi, "Begum Qudsiya Aizaz Rasool: An Extraordinary Career," *Radiance* 9-15 December 2001, pp. 15-17; her own posthumous autobiography *From Purdah to Parliament* (New Delhi: Ajanta, 2001).

[15] Amaresh Misra, *Lucknow: The Fire of Grace* (New Delhi: Harper Collins, 1998), p. 248.

[16] Oddly the Raja did not reflect on his migration to Pakistan in "Some Memories," he wrote on pp. 390-405, in *The Partition of India: Policies and Perspectives, 1935-1947*, edited by C.H. Philips and Mary D. Wainwright (Cambridge: MIT Press, 1970).

[17] S.S.A. Jafari, *Socio-Economic Condition of Downtrodden Minorities in Lucknow Metropolis* (Lucknow: Giri Institute of Development Studies, 2004).

[18] Akram Raza Khan, *They Stole My Kidney* (New Delhi: Media House, 2005).

[19] Zarina Bhatty, "Status and Power in a Muslim-Dominated Village of Uttar Pradesh," p. 98, in *Caste and Social Stratification Among the Muslims in India*, edited by Imtiaz Ahmad (New Delhi: Monohar, 1973).

[20] Ibid., pp. 87-98.

[21] Ibid., pp. 100-101.

[22] Riaz-ur-Rahman Kidwai, *Biographical Sketch of Kidwais of Avadh* (Aligarh: Kitab Ghar, 1987), pp. 147-150.

[23] Whitcombe, op. cit. p. 159.

[24] V.B. Rawat, "Rehana's Fight for the Struggle of Her Life," *The Milli Gazette* (16-31 January 2005), p. 8.

[25] Manjari Mishra, "Muslims Ranked Lowest on Development Index" *Indian Express* (30 November 2003) internet edition.

[26] Elizabeth A. Mann, "Religion, Money and Status: Competition for Resources at the Shrine of Shah Jamal, Aligarh," pp. 145-171, in *Muslim Shrines in India*, edited by Christian W. Troll (New Delhi: Oxford University Press, 1989).

[27] *Census of India,* 1921, 31, Part II, pp. 396-407, as reproduced in Paul Brass, *Language, Religion and Politics in North India* (Cambridge: Cambridge University Press, 1974), p. 152.

[28] S.P. Jain, "Religion and Social Differentiation: A Town in Uttar Pradesh," *Economic and Political Weekly* 20 January 1968, pp. 201-202; ibid, "Social Mobility in a Town: An Intergenerational Analysis," *Economic and Political Weekly* 25 October 1969, pp. 1703-1710.

[29] Majid Husain, "Diffusion of New Agricultural Technology and Its Impact on the Economy and Society of Muslim Cultivators: A Case Study, pp. 127-138, in *Muslims in India Since Independence: A Regional Perspective,* edited by M.H. Qureshi (New Delhi: Institute of Objective Studies, 1998).

[30] Ajit K Danda, *A Rural Community in Transition: The Case Study of Gandhar, Saharanpur, U.P.* (New Delhi: Inter-India, 1987).

[31] Preeti Verma Lal, "Mango Mania," *India Currents* (August 2005): 12-18.

[32] Parvez Abbasi, Social Inequality among Indian Muslims (Udaipur: A.C. Brothers, 1990), shows that some Gaddis have done well in recent years.

[33] Ghaus Ansari, *Muslim Castes in Uttar Pradesh* (Lucknow: Ethnographic and Folk Culture Society, 1960).

[34] *1911 Census, UP*, Part I, p. 333, as cited in Francis Robinson, *Separatism Among Indian Muslims: the Politics of the United Provinces Muslims 1860-1923* (New Delhi: Oxford University Press, 1993, reprint of 1974), pp. 14-15.

[35] C.A. Bayly, *Rulers, Townsmen and Bazaars: North Indian Society in the Age of British Expansion, 1770-1870* (Oxford: Oxford University Press, 1992), pp. 449-57, in which the author contrasts the prosperity of the Hindu-dominated *gunj* or market as opposed to the *qasbas* or small towns where the Muslim gentry declined.

[36] *Census of India,* 1921, Vol. XX!, part II, pp. 396-407, as cited in Paul R. Brass, *Language, Religion and Politics in North India* (Cambridge: Cambridge University Press, 1974), p. 152.

[37] Gerard Heuz, "Les rapports entre la classe ouvriere et al communaute musulmane en Inde du Nord: une dialectique comlexe et actuelle," pp. 127-134, in *Islam et societe en Asie du Sud,* edited by Marc Gaborieau (Paris: Edition de l'Ecole des Hautes Etudes en Science Sociales, Collection Purusartha, 1986).

[38] Zarina Bhatty, *The Economic Role and Status of Women in Bidi Industry in Allahabad* (Geneva: International Labor Organization, 1981); idem, "Economic Contribution of Women to the Household Budget: A Case Study of the Bidi Industry," pp. 35-5-, in *Invisible Hands in House-Based Production,* edited by Andrea M. Singh and Anita K. Viitanen (New Delhi: Sage, 1987).

[39] L.C. Jain, "A Heritage to Keep: The Handicrafts Industry, 1955-85," *Economic and Political Weekly* 17 May 1986, pp. 873-887.

[40] *Crafting Traditions: Documenting Trades and Crafts in Early 19th Century India,* by Ghulam Yahya, edited, translated with an introduction by Mehr Afshan Farooqi (New Delhi: Indira Gandhi National Center for Arts and the Aryan Books, 2005).

[41] S. Vijayagopalan, *Economic Status of Handicraft Artisans* (New Delhi: National Council for Applied Economic Research, 1993), p.9.

[42] Vidya Srinivas, "Rugs to Riches," *Business India* (22-24 November 2002),pp. 94-96.

[43] M. Showeb, *Silk Handloom Industry of Varanasi: A Study of Socio-Economic Problems of Weavers* (Varanasi: Ganga Kaveri Publishing House, 1994).

[44] M. Showeb, *Muslim Handloom Weavers in Varanasi: Problems and Remedial Measures* (Varanasi: Gandhian Institute of Social Studies, 1993).

[45] R.K. Ram, R.K. Singh, and Chandan Gopal, *Handicraft Survey Report: Bhadohi Carpet Industry* (New Delhi: Controller of Publications, 1988).

[46] Sheobahal Singh, "Organization of the Carpet Industry of Bhadohi," *Economic and Political Weekly* , May 1979, pp. M-69-M71; S. Vijayagopalan, *Child Labour in the Carpet Industry: A Status Report* (New Delhi: National Council for Applied Economic Research, 1993).

[47] Deepak Mehta, *Work, Ritual, Biography: A Muslim Community in North India* (Delhi: Oxford University Press, 1997).

[48] Claire M. Wilkinson Weber, *Embroidering Lives: Women's Work and Skill in the Lucknow Embroidery Industry* (Albany: State University of New York Press, 1999).

[49] Gyanendra Pandey, "The Bigoted Julaha," *Economic and Political Weekly* January 1983, pp. PE-19-PE28; "The Colonial Dislocation: Muslim Weavers and Their Industry in Colonial North India," pp. 370-421, in *Urbanism in Islam: The Proceedings of the International Conference on Urbanism in Islam* (Tokyo: Institute of Oriental Culture, University of Tokyo, 1989); Nabi Ahmad, Educational Opportunity and Socio-Economic Change among the Muslim Backwards and Scheduled Castes of Faizabad District During the Post-Independence Period: A Comparative Study, Ph.D. dissertation, Aligarh Muslim University, 1980; Syed Matanat Husain Zaidi, A Socio-Economic Study of the Ansaris of Bijnore. Ph.D. dissertation, Aligarh Muslim University, 1988.

[50] Armanullah, A Study of Problems and Performance of Muslim Entrepreneurs in Handloom Industry of Gorakhpur, unpublished M.Phil thesis, Aligarh Muslim University, 1992.

[51] M. Akbar, *Entrepreneurship and Indian Muslims* (New Delhi: Manak, 1990); Kishwar Shabbir Khan, *Brassware Industry of Moradabad and its Muslim Artisans* (Aligarh: Interdisciplinary Centre of Development Studies, Aligarh Muslim University, 1991). For an earlier time, see Tirthankar Roy, "Home Market and the Artisans in Colonial India: A Study of Brass-Ware," *Modern Asian Studies* 30, 2 (1996): 357-383.

[52] Kishwar Shabbir Khan, *Woodcraft Industry of Saharanpur and its Muslim Artisans* (Aligarh: Interdisciplinary Centre of Development Studies, Aligarh Muslim University, 1992). Quality wood is reported to scarce leading to unemployment in this industry, see *Fourteenth Annual Report of National Commission for Minorities for the Period from 1-4-1991 to 31-3-1992* (New Delhi: Controller of Publications, 1995),p. 106.

[53] Geeta Jayaram, "The Muslim Traditional Potters of Khurja: History, Identity and General Features," *Islam and the Modern Age* 26, ii-iii (May-August 1995): 85-136.

[54] Omar Khalidi, "OBCs Among Indian Muslims," op.cit., and Theodore P. Wright Jr., "A New Demand for Muslim Reservation in India," *Asian Survey* 37,9 (1997): 852-858; Laura D. Jenkins, "Becoming Backward: Preferential Policies and Religious Minorities in India," *Commonwealth and Comparative Politics* 39, 1 (July 2001): 32-50.

[55] Neera Burra, "Glass Factories of Firozabad," *Economic and Political Weekly* 15 November 1986, pp. 1983-1985; and part two in the same journal dated 23 November 1986, pp. 2033-2036.

56 Elizabeth A. Mann, *Boundaries and Identities: Muslims, Work and Status in Aligarh* (New Delhi: Sage, 1992), is the best work on the world of small businessmen, hitherto ignored in studies of Aligarh.

57 Baharul Islam Laskar, "Social Stratification and Child Labor among Muslims: An Exploratory Study," pp. 203-213, in *Indian Muslims: Precepts and Practices,* edited by Noor Mohammad (Jaipur: Rawat, 1999), citation on p. 208.

58 Baharul Islam Laskar, op. cit. and Neera Burra, *Born to Work: Child Labor in India* (New Delhi: Oxford University Press, 1995), and Mohammed Izhar Ahmed, "Unorganized Muslim Manufacturing Enterprise in an Indian City," *Journal Institute of Muslim Minority Affairs* 7, 1 (January 1986): 261-267; Agha M.A. Siddiqui, "Lock Industry: A Household Business in Aligarh, U.P." *Indian Journal of Regional Sciences* 23, 1 (1991): 17-25; Baharul Islam Laskar, "Child Labour in Aligarh Lock Industry," *Economic and Political Weekly* 12 February 2000, pp. 510-513.

59 Mariola Offredi, "The Muslim Weavers of Banaras and Mau in the Seventies," *Eurasiaica* 40 (1996): 303-336.

60 Sudeep Chakravarti estimates that Hindus represent 70 percent of the merchant class while the rest are Muslim, see his "Money Talks," *India Today (*31 January 1993), p. 40.

61 M. Showeb, *Silk Handloom Industry*, pp. 1-2.

62 Sanjeev Verma, "A Matter of Pride," *Business India* (February 28-March 13, 1994) p. 261. See also Ramesh Menon, "Zari Weavers: The Doomed Looms: Riots in Varanasi Ruin Traditional Industry," *India Today* 15 July 1991, p. 72; "Mubarakpur Riots Destroy the Banarasi Sari Industry," *The Milli Gazette* 1-15 December 2000.

63 See the painstaking documentation in *Muslim India* (July 1983), p. 332; *Muslim India* (April 1984),p. 177; *Muslim India* (June 1986), p. 286; *Muslim India* (June 1989), p. 271; *Muslim India* (April 1990),p. 153; *Radiance* (4-10 April 1993), p. 11; and *The Milli Gazette* (1-15 June 2002), p.18.

64 Dilip Awasthi, "Manufacturing Melody: The City is Home to the Country's Biggest Wind Instrument Industry," *India Today* (11 May 1993): 13.

65 Mark Schneider, Breaking the Wave: Explaining the Emergence of Ethnic Peace in a City of Historical Ethnic Violence, Master's Thesis, Political Science Department, University of Michigan, 2004, p.45.

66 Shymlal Yadav, "On the Edge of Oblivion," *India Today* (09 May 2005), p. 8.

67 Meenu Tewari, *When the Marginal Becomes Mainstream: Lesson from Half-Century of Small-Firm Growth in Ludhiana, Punjab*, PhD thesis, MIT, 1996.

68 Salman Khurshid, *At Home in India* (New Delhi: Vikas, 1986), p.37.

69 Munawwar Ali Khan Lodi, "Development of Muslim Industrial Entrepreneurship in India, 1947-1981," *Journal of Institute of Muslim Minority Affairs* 6, 1 (January 1985):7-87. Conversations with A.R. Shervani, Mustafa Rashid's nephew. New Delhi, 24 December 2004. He and his wife Nusrat are exemplary educators.

70 Theodore P. Wright, Jr., The New Muslim Businessmen of India, pp.42-43.

71 *Directory PHD Chamber of Commerce,* 1994.

72 Stefan Mouland, *First We Are People: The Koris of Kanpur Between Caste and Class* (Stockholm: Department of Anthropology, University of Stockholm, 1988).

73 K.M. Mahapatra and Kavita Srivastava, "Leather Goods Industry in Kanpur: Casteism, Religion and Business Inter Linkings," *Economic and Political Weekly* (28 September 2002): 4029-4035.

74 Shelley Vishwajeet, "Its Best Foot Forward," *Business India* (March 29-April 11, 2004): 97-98. Irshad Mirza, the CEO of the Mirza Tanneries served as the Chairman of the U.P. Minorities Commission in 2000-2001.

75 Ibid.

76 Sudeep Chakravarti, "Money Talks," *India Today* (31 January 1993), p. 40.

77 Tahir Beg, " Promotion of Muslim Entrepreneurship under State Support," pp. 223-236, in *Aspects of Islamic Economics and the Economy of Indian Muslims,* edited by F.R.Faridi (New Delhi: Institute of Objective Studies, 1993).

78 "UP Minorities Finance & Development Corporation," *Muslim India* (January 1985), pp 34, 41.

79 *Eighth Annual Report of the Minorities Commission for the Period from 1-4-1985 to 31-3-1986* (New Delhi: Ministry of Welfare, 1989), p. 121.

80 Ibid.

81 *Fourteenth Annual Report of National Commission for Minorities for the period from 1-4-1991 to 31-3-1992* (New Delhi: Controller of Publications, 1995),p. 106.

82 *National Commission for Minorities Annual Report for 2000-2001* (New Delhi: NC, 2001), p. 45-47.

83 As demonstrated by Javed Ahmad Khan and Shariq Nisar in their study, "Collateral (al-Rahn) as Practiced by Muslim Funds of North India," *Islamic Economics Journal of King Abdulaziz University* 17, 1 (2004): 17-33.

84 M.G.I. Bagsiraj, *Islamic Financial Institutions of India: Progress, Problems and Prospects* (Jeddah: Scientific Publishing House, King Abdulaziz University, 1998), pp.19, 25, 29.

85 "Partitioned Spaces," *Indian Express* 26 November 2001, Internet edition. "Less Than Equal," *Radiance* (9-15 December 2001), p.2.

86 Thomas R. Metcalf, *The Aftermath of Revolt (Princeton,* NJ: Princeton University Press, 1965), p. 303.

87 Francis Robinson, *Separatism Among Indian Muslims,* p. 23.

88 B.B. Misra, *The Indian Middle Classes* (London: Oxford University Press, 1961) p. 329, and p. 388.

89 The British, the Kayasthas and Muslims, all three group showed a preference for Urdu as late as 1870s, as archival records in Lucknow show, see Nandalal Chatterji, "The Problem of Court Language in British India," *Journal of Indian History* 31, 2 (August 1953):213-16.

90 Aitchison Commission Report, p. 27 as cited in Zafarul Islam and Raymond L. Jensen, "Indian Muslims and the Public Service, 1871-1915", *Asiatic Society of Pakistan Journal* 9 (June 1964): 85-149, citation on p. 104.

91 Sarojini Ganju, "The Muslims of Lucknow, 1919-1939," pp. 279-298, in *The City in South Asia: Pre-Modern and Modern,* edited by Kenneth Ballhatchet and John Harrison (London: Curzon Press, 1980), citation on p. 282.

92 Ibid.

93 Francis Robinson, op. cit. p. 38.

94 Francis Robinson, op.cit., pp. 42-43

95 Ibid., pp. 45-46.

96 Table adapted from Ibid., p. 46.

97 Aparna Basu, "Growth of Education and Muslim Separatism, 1919-1939," pp. 223-243, in *Essays in Modern Indian History*, edited by B.R. Nanda (Delhi: Oxford University Press, 1980), citation on p. 228. The source of Basu's figures is *Progress of Education in India*, 1927-32, II, Table 99 (B).

98 Aparna Basu, ibid., p. 227.

99 "Position of Muslims in U.P. Services Before Partition," *Muslim India* (September 1994), p. 413.

100 Vallabbhai Patel to G.B. Pant, 15 May 1947, pp. 489-90, in *Selected Works of Govind Ballabh Pant*, XI, edited by B.R. Nanda (New Delhi: Oxford University Press, 1998).

101 G.B. Pant to Sardar Vallabbhai Patel, p. 152, in ibid.

[102] G.B. Pant to Sardar Vallabbhai Patel dated 22 May 1947, in *Selected Letters*, op.cit., p. 147.

[103] G.B. Pant to Tej Narain, Vice President UP Hindu Mahasabha, in *Selected Letters*, op.cit.p 157, and Mukul Kesavan, "Invoking a Majority: The Congress and the Muslims of United Provinces, 1945-47," pp. 91-111, in *Self-Images and Nationality*, edited by P.C. Chatterjee (New Delhi: Allied Publishers, 1989), citation on p. 106, citing archival papers.

[104] Ibid, p. 106.

[105] Ibid, p. 106.

[106] *Selected Works of Govind Ballabh Pant*, op.cit., p. 158.

[107] Ibid, p. 107.

[108] Chaudhri Khaliquzzaman, *Pathway to Pakistan* (Lahore: Longmans, 1961), p. 410.

[109] Mukul Kesavan, op. cit. p. 105.

[110] Review of the present writer's *Khaki and the Ethnic Violence in India: Army, Police and the Paramilitary Forces During Communal Violence* (New Delhi: Three Essays Collective, 2003), in *Strategic Analysis* (January-March 2004) by Keki Daruwala, p. 208.

[111] U.P. State Archives, General Administration Department File 49H/1958, "Inquiry made by the Government of India about the employment of the members of the minority communities," as cited in Steven I. Wilkinson, *The Electoral Incentive for Ethnic Violence: Hindu-Muslim Riots in India*, unpublished PhD dissertation, Department of Political Science, Massachusetts Institute of Technology, 1998, p. 136.

[112] Badruddin Tyabji, *More Memoirs of an Egoist* (New Delhi: Har Anand, 1988), pp. 146-147.

[113] Tavleen Singh, "Ghosts of Perception," *India Today* (6 November 2000), p. 24.

[114] All India Civil List, Issued Half-Yearly (Bombay: Printed & Published under the Authority of the Govt. of India, January 1959), pp. 270-281.

[115] "Representation of Muslims in government and administration in Uttar Pradesh, 1 July 1964" in Paul Brass, *Language, Religion and Politics in North India* (Cambridge: Cambridge University Press, 1974), p. 231.

[116] Interview with Dr. A.J. Faridi, *Shabistan Urdu Digest* (October 1970), p. 9.

[117] N.S. Saksena, "Representation of Muslims in the Police Before Partition", in his *Communal Riots in India* (New Delhi: Trishul Publications, 1990), pp. 128-31.

[118] Shahid Masood, " Muslim Representation in U.P. Services Since Independence," *Radiance* (6 April 1969), pp. 5-6.

[119] N.C. Saxena, "Public Employment and Educational Backwardness Among the Muslims in India, op.cit., p. 171.

[120] "Representation of Muslims in Judicial Service in 1981," *Muslim India* (December 1983), p. 552. This included Judges Mushtaq Ahmad in the 1950s, Nasrullah Baig in the 1960s; Ahmad S. Saghir and Haidar Abbas Raza in the 1980s, all at Allahabad High Court.

[121] Report on Minorities (New Delhi: Ministry of Home Affairs, 14 June 1983), as cited in Mushirul Hasan, *Legacy of a Divided Nation* (Boulder, CO: Westview Press, 1997), p. 291.

[122] S.P. Jain and J.M. Shah, "Socio-Cultural Background and Educational Aspiration," *Behavioral Sciences and Community Development* 7, 1 (March 1973): 44-52.

[123] In U.P. Combined State Service exams, out of the total who entered the exam, 8.46 were Muslims, of which 1.21 were selected, see *Muslim India* (December 1983), p. 553; and in 1980-82, 54, 593 candidates appeared in the exam, of which 1037 were Muslim, out of which 660 were called for interview; out of this number 244 were selected, including 6 Muslims, see *Muslim India* (December 1983), p. 553.

[124] "Police Force: Skewed," *India Today* (31 January 1993), p. 36.

[125] "In BJP-Ruled U.P. Discrimination Against Muslim I.A.S., I.P.S. Officers…" *Radiance* (23-29 February 1992), p.2.

[126] *Eighth Annual Report of the Minorities Commission for the Period from 1-4-1985 to 31-3-1986* (New Delhi: Ministry of Welfare, 1989), pp. 109-110.

[127] *Tenth Annual Report of the Minorities Commission for the Period from 1-4-1987 to 31-3-1988* (New Delhi: Controller of Publications, 1990), pp. 97-99.

[128] Theodore P. Wright, Jr., "The Failure of the Indian Minorities Commission, 1977-1981," *Indian Journal of Politics* 20, 1-2 (February-March 1986), pp. 1-8, cautions the Muslim leadership about the political price and the consequences that may entail the grant of educational and job reservations, advising instead to concentrate on literacy, technical education, and the like. The reservation demand was reiterated in the "Muslim Agenda Uttar Pradesh, 2002," *Muslim India* (February 2002), p. 61.

[129] Jeelani Khan, "Dalit Muslims' Plea for SC Status," *The Milli Gazette* (16-31 December 2002), 5.

[130] Anis Ansari, "Educational Backwardness of Muslims," *Economic and Political Weekly* (17 October 1992): 2289-2291, provides examples from Rampur, Moradabad collected by A.R. Shervani.

[131] *Educational Survey Report on Muslim Managed Schools and Colleges in India with Special Emphasis on Science Education,* compiled by Shamim Shah (New Delhi: Hamdard Education Society, 1985).

[132] Aijazuddin Ahmad, *Muslims in India*, vols. 1-4 (New Delhi: Inter-India, 1993-96).

[133] Brij Raj Chanuhan, "Rural-Urban Interactions of Muslims in Meerut Region," *ICSSR Newsletter* (April-June 1992), p. 54.

[134] Nasim Aijaz, *Spatial Pattern of Female Participation in Economic Activity...with Special Reference to Muslim Women,* unpublished PhD thesis, Agra University, 1990.

[135] N.C. Saxena, "Public Employment and Educational Backwardness Among the Muslims in India, op.cit., pp. 160-162, 166.

[136] Nusrat and Ahmad Rashid Shervani, "Progress of Muslim Girls Education Over 24 Years," *The Milli Gazette* 16-31 May 2001, p.7.

[137] Nita Kumar, "The "Truth" About Muslims in Banaras: An Exploration in School Curricula and Popular Lore," *Social Analysis* 28 (July 1990):82-96.

[138] "Rampant Illiteracy Among Aligarh Muslim Villagers," *Islamic Voice* May 1992, p. 1 & 7.

[139] Zoya Hasan and Ritu Menon, *Educating Muslim Girls: A Comparison of Five Cities* (New Delhi: Women Unlimited, 2005).

[140] Patricia and Roger .J. Jeffrey, "What's the Benefit of Being Educated," pp. 150-183, in *Girls' Schooling ...in South Asia*, edited by Roger Jeffrey and A.M. Basu (New Delhi: Sage, 1996).

[141] Naseem A. Zaidi, *Academic Excellence Among Muslim Students at School Level: A Case Study of Aligarh* (Aligarh: Department of Economics, Aligarh Muslim University, 1996).

[142] *Hindustan Times* 6 October 1873, as cited in M.R.A. Baig, *The Muslim Dilemma* (New Delhi: Vikas, 1974), p. 115.

[143] "Made in Madrasa: An IAS, A Doctor..." *The Times of India* 03 August 2005, Internet edition, reports about Madrasa alumni in various modern professions and services.

[144] Qamaruddin, Status of Madrasa Education in India," Radiance (10-18 August 1997), pp. 33-36; Mohammad Qamar Ishaq, *"Directory of Muslim Educational, Religious and Welfare Organizations in India"* (New Delhi: Institute o f Objective Studies, 1995), pp. 119-212, updated in *Directory of Muslim Educational Institutions in India,* edited by Rahat Abrar and M. Qamar Ishaque (New Delhi: Institute of Objective Studies, 2002), pp. 306-459. Earlier version in *Directory of Muslims Institutions and Organizations in Uttar Pradesh*, compiled by Rahat Abrar (Aligarh: U.P. Rabita Committee, 1993).

[145] Patricia Jeffery, Roger Jeffrey and Craig Jeffrey, "Islamization, Gentrification and Domestication: 'A Girl's Islamic Course' and Rural Muslims in Western Uttar Pradesh," *Modern Asian Studies* 38, 1 (February 2004): 1-53.

[146] "Muslim-Managed Degree Colleges," *Muslim India* (July 1996), p . 319.

147 Mujeeb Ashraf, "Rise and Fall of Etawah College," *Radiance* (23-29 August 1992), p. 12; Nonica Dutta, "Fleeting Impressions: [Karamat Husain] Girls College in Lucknow," *Economic and Political Weekly* (27 January 2001): 279-281.

148 "Largest Muslim Educational Institution After A.M.U." *The Milli Gazette* (11 November 2002), Internet edition; Salman Sultan, "Shibli National College," *The Milli Gazette* (16-31 December 2004), p. 31.

149 "Educational Atmosphere Normal in Azamgarh", *The Milli Gazette* (16-31 October 2004), p. 19.

150 "Muslim Education in Allahabad," *Islamic Voice* (May 1995), p.3;. On this phenomenon see Syed Shahabuddin, "Strangling the Goose that Lay Golden Eggs for Muslim Entrepreneurs," *Radiance* 27 June-3 July 2004), p. 24.

151 Badruddin Tyabji, *More Memoirs of an Egoist* (New Delhi: Har Anand, 1994), p. 145.

152 Theodore P. Wright, Jr. "Muslim Education in India at the Crossroad: The Case of Aligarh," *Pacific Affairs* 39, 1-2 (Spring-Summer 1966): 50-63, citation on p. 53-54. It is not clear what is the source of Wright's figure of 75 percent internal reservation.

153 Violette Graff, "Aligarh's Long Quest for 'Minority' Status: AMU (Amendment) Act, 1981," *Economic and Political Weekly* (11 August 1990): 1771-1781., citation on p. 1772.

154 Badruddin Tyabji, "The Role of the Aligarh Muslim University in Contemporary India," *Indian Journal of Political Science* 4, 1-2 (1970): 27-36, citation on p. 35.

155 Wright, op. cit, p. 60.

156 Graff, op.cit.

157 Conversations with Registrar AMU Nazim Ali, 21 December 2004.

158 *Tenth Annual Report of the Minorities Commission for the Period from 1-4-1987 to 31-3-1988* (New Delhi: Ministry of Welfare, Government of India, 1990), p. 262.

159 Conversation with Registrar Nazim Ali, Aligarh 21 December 2004.

160 Iqbal Ansari, "AMU's Dilemma: Reconciling Merit and Minority Interest," *The Milli Gazette* (16-31 July 2004), p. 3.

161 "Fifty Percent Seats for AMU Students," *The Milli Gazette* (1-15 April 2005), p. 20.

162 Diptosh Majumdar, "Govt. Clears 50% Muslim Quota for PG Courses in AMU", *The Indian Express* (20 May 2005) Internet edition.

163 Saiyid Hamid," Muslims Caught in a Vice," *The Milli Gazette* (1-15 June 2005), p. 2.

164 Muhammad Iqbal, "Muslim Quota in Education," *The Milli Gazette* (16 August-15 September 2005), p. 2.

[165] Dominic Emmanuel, "AMU Quota: Much Ado About Nothing," *The Financial Express* (25 May 2005) Internet edition.

[166] Shymlal Yadav, "AMU: Seat of Contention," *India Today* (06 June 2005), pp. 23-24; Yoginder Sikand interview with Irfan Habib, sent by email on 03 June 2005.

[167] Annie Zaidi, "Quota Trouble," *Frontline* 22, 12 (June 04-17, 2005) Internet edition.

[168] "HC Quashes the Minority Status of AMU," *The Times of India* (05 October 2005), Internet edition.

[169] Naseem A. Zaidi, *Academic Excellence Among Muslim Students at School Level: A Case Study of Aligarh* (Aligarh: Department of Economics, AMU, 1996?), p. 8, idem, "Muslims in Public Services: Case of AMU Alumni," *Economic and Political Weekly* (22 September 2001), pp. 3592-3595; Mahmood Alam Riaz, "Muslims in Public Service: A Comment," *Economic and Political Weekly* (9 March 2002), p. 983, records his disagreement with Zaidi on methodological grounds.

[170] Ibid, p. 261.

[171] http://www.amu.ac.in/history1.htm

[172] Conversation with the University's Media Coordinator Afaq Mahmood, New Delhi 2 January 2005. The University has been recognized as a minority institution in the State Gazette on 27 February 2004.

[173] The Aligarh Muslim University Duty Society's medical college project in Lucknow initiated in the early 1990s came in for pointed criticism by Maqbool Ahmad Siraj in a series of articles he wrote, see "Fanciful Priorities," *Islamic Voice* (September 1992): 1-2; "Guest Editorial: A Look at Indian Medical Colleges," *Saudi Gazette* (31 March 1993), p.6; it is amazing that it took good three months before a rejoinder was written by the project sponsors in "AMU Duty Society Project," *Saudi Gazette* (9 July 1993), p. 6.

[174] Irfan Habib, Suvira Jaiswal and Aditya Mukherjee, *History in the New NCERT Textbooks: A Report and an Index of Errors* (Kolkata: Indian History Congress, 2003).

[175] Omar Khalidi, "Politics of Second Official Language Status for Urdu in India," *Journal of South Asian and Middle Eastern Studies* 27, 3 (Spring 2004): 53-77.

[176] The UP Legislative Assembly approved the bill on 18 March 2005, according to *Radiance* (3-9 April 2005), p. 30.

[177] Ateeque Khan, "Waqfs in U.P.: A Socio-Historic Perspective," *Islamic Culture* 64 (January 1990): 39-67; idem, "Wakf Administration in UP: A Legislative Retrospect," *Islam and the Modern Age* 7, 1 (1990): 53-75.

[178] Hasanuddin Ahmad and Ahmedullah Khan, *Strategies to Develop Waqf Administration in India* (Jeddah: Islamic Research & Training Institute, Islamic Development Bank, Research Paper no. 50, 1998), p. 134.

[179] A majority of the papers in *Wakf Administration: Status and Issues,* edited by S.K. Singh (Rohtak: Spellbound Publications1998) dealt with UP; see also M.A. Qureshi, *Waqfs in India: A Study of Administration and Legislative Control* (New Delhi: Gian Publishing House, 1990).

[180] *Eleventh Annual Report of the Minorities Commission for the Period from 1-4-1988 to 31-3-1989 (*New Delhi: Ministry of Welfare, 1989), p. 81. The Sanskritization policy of the UP administration has not spared even the Muslim endowments given the Sanskrit name of the corporation.

[181] Oddly Anwar Ali, "Wakfs in Uttar Pradesh—Are They to Exist or Extinct for Ever," *Radiance* (29 December 1991-04 January 1992), pp. 6-7, makes no reference to the Waqf Development Corporation.

[182] Obaid Nasir, "Movement to Save UP Auqaf," *The Milli Gazette* (1-15 August 2002), p. 3.

BIHAR

Bihar is today home to 13,722,043 Muslims according to the 2001 Census. The state is endowed with an enviable natural resources base. It is one of the largest producers of fruit and the second largest producer of vegetables in the country. However, this rich state in terms of natural and human resources in the country has been slow to harness its natural and human resources for the development of the state and its people.

In the 13th century, armies of Muslim rulers conquered what is most of Bihar region today. In the wake of the conquering armies came Sufis, who preached Islam by exemplary lives, thereby bringing substantial numbers of people into its fold. From the 13th century to 1764, the region remained under the rule of various Muslim dynasties. During this long era, a number of soldiers, administrators, and merchants belonging to various Muslim groups settled in Bihar. However, in 1764, the East India Company defeated the Nawab of Bengal, who controlled the region. After the Company's conquest, Bihar became part of the huge Bengal Presidency. In 1912, it was separated from Bengal, but Orissa remained with it until 1936. More than half a century later, Bihar went through yet another territorial reorganization, when Jharkhand, the mainly tribal region, was created as a new state in November 2000. The growth of Muslim population can be seen in the Table noted below.

Table I
Muslim Population in Bihar, 1951-2001

Year	Muslim Popn.	Muslim %	Rural Muslim%	Urban Muslim%	Muslim Lit.%	Urdu %
1951	4,373,360	11.28				
1961	5,785,631	12.45	88	12		
1971	7,594,173	13.48				
1981	9,874.993	14.13				
1991	12,787,985	14.8	84.03	15.57		9.89
2001	13,722,048	16.5			42.0	

Source: *Census of India*

Agriculture and Land Ownership

Like neighboring U.P., Bihar had a small number of *zamindars* or landholders among Muslims. Though changes took place since the East India Company's take over in 1764,"in the early 19th century, the old Muslim aristocracy had not withered away. Its members, though deprived of the enormous economic, political and administrative powers enjoyed under the Nawabs of Bengal, were still in possession of vast landed property. The new colonial situation did not destroy the traditional elites."[1] An account written by a *zamindar* at the turn of the twentieth century shows the declining fortunes of the landed classes among Muslims due to opposition to modernization.[2]

At partition, Muslims left a small quantity—1111 *bighas* of land—when migrating to Pakistan, reflecting perhaps both tinier holdings and the small numbers of land holders who left.[3] Post-independence land redistribution measures further cut the income of this group, though some did branch out into large-scale commercial farming.

Bihar is now the third most populous state in the nation. In 2001, its Muslim population was 16.5 percent of the total. It is mostly concentrated in the northern *terai,* wet irrigation belt neighboring Nepal, suggesting a strong preference for an area fit for agricultural production.[4]

The Muslim population in Bihar is predominantly rural, contrary to popular perceptions.[5] However, it is also true that comparatively Muslims are more urbanized than Hindus and others. Given a predominantly rural concentration, it is not surprising that most Muslims are engaged in agriculture and related occupations. According to the Bihar State Minorities Commission, "only 35.9 percent of Muslim households in rural Bihar possess any cultivable land, [whereas], for the general population...the percentage of landowning households is much higher at 58.0 percent.[6] Of those owning the land, only 28.8 percent cultivate it. The rest simply lease the land to the larger cultivators as their own holdings are too small.[7] According to the 1990-91 Agricultural Census of Bihar, the average size of landholding was 2.32 acres, whereas for Muslims it was a mere 1.91 acres.[8] The landholders have a limited stock of agricultural technology, do not own ploughs, water pumps, tractors, or have access to modern methods of irrigation, quality seed and fertilizers.[9] Many are thus forced to hire tractors. Integrated sociological pictures of Muslim villages drawn by academics show rural communities in utter poverty and illiteracy in a state known for its backwardness as a whole.[10]

Traditional livestock rearing, common all over the country, is a valuable source of supplementary income for poor households. For nearly 50 percent of the rural Muslim households, livestock represents an important source of cash income.[11]

Within the agricultural communities are the *Momin/Julaha/Bunker* or weavers, also known as Ansari in Bihar as well as elsewhere. In Bhagalpur alone, there were 10, 000 *bunker* according to a 1989 estimate.[12] During the large-scale massacres of that year, the National Commission for Minorities was informed that an estimated 10, 000 power looms were destroyed. These mainly belonged to the "Muslims who are dependent on silk weaving trade and industry. Bhagalpur has been one of the biggest centers of silk produced in the country."[13] A survey found no rural Muslim households active in manufacturing, and only a few in urban areas.[14]

Like other states, Bihar also has a number of occupational groups among Muslims, such as those related to food preparation: *Mirshikaris* (hunters), *Qasab/ Qasai* (butchers), *Teli* (oil pressers), *Rayin/Kunjra* (green grocers), *Bhat/Bhatiyara* (cooks and inn keepers), *Nanbai* (bakers), *Gaddi* (grazers), *Bihishti/Saqqa* (water-carriers), *Halwai* (sweetmeat makers cooks), *Kalal/Araqi* (distillers); those pertaining to unskilled labor such as *Lalbegi/bhangi/Mehtar* (night soil removers), *Dhobi* (washer men), *Nai* (barbers), *Gaddi* (grazers), *Mali* (gardeners), *Churihar/Shishagar* (bangle makers), *Saiqalgar* (metal polishers), and the like.[15] These groups are generally categorized as backward classes.

The Muslim backward classes in Bihar have been quite articulate since the colonial times, seeking economic justice, like other marginalized groups.[16] When organized along the lines of industry and class—as opposed to mere religious affiliation—the Momins certainly succeeded in gaining some dividends from the state. The Momins' success is best seen in the offices relating to handloom and cottage industries held by one of the most famous Bihari leaders of his time, Abdulqayyum Ansari.[17] In addition to the weavers, *Dhunya* (cotton carders), *darzi* (tailors), *Rangrez* (dyers), are also predominantly Muslim,[18] along with Shershahabadis, whose ancestors may have been soldiers in the army of Sher Shah Suri, the Afghan emperor of India but now simply agricultural workers.[19]

Outside the agriculturalists, weavers and textile related workers, there are a large number of Muslims who are skilled or semi-skilled laborers, such as the *Kullaiyah* (mat weavers), *Atishbaz* (firecracker makers).

Labor, Commerce and Industry

As the seat of the governors appointed by the Mughal emperors and then by the Nawabs of Bengal, Patna attracted a number of merchants to cater to the aristocracy. In the eighteenth and nineteenth centuries, "Khwaja Abdul Ghani, his adopted son Meer Afzal and Afzal's son Khwaja Ashraf were provincial merchants whose sphere of activities included the districts around Patna and were centered in the city of Patna itself...[they] had connections with opium business. Khwaja Ashraf was a considerable dealer in cotton textiles, and the whole family was deeply involved in the saltpeter trade during the 1740s and 1750s...Meer Ishkowla was reputed to possess a big fleet of boats which he used to transport his goods to Calcutta."[20] Among those hanged after the failed Mutiny of 1857 were two rich bankers, "Shaikh Ghasita" and Amir Khan of Patna.[21] Donors of Patna College included another banker, Nawab Syed Wilayat Ali Khan, indicating that banking was not uncommon among Muslims.[22] Needless to say, stray cases of individuals involved in banking do not comprise a class as such. Late in the twentieth century, the Muslim elite of Patna established a cooperative bank in 1987, called the Bihar Awami Cooperative Bank (BACB). In 1988, its share capital was a mere Rs. 6.6 lakhs, earning a minor profit. But it gradually progressed. During 2003, the deposits rose to Rs. 12.27 crores, and the aggregate loan and advances jumped to Rs. 6.19 crores. The bank claims a credit deposit ratio at 49.64 percent compared to 25 percent in nationalized banks, certainly a sign of a success story. The BACB is not legally speaking a Muslim institution, but it in fact is due to the fact that its officers, board of directors, depositors and clients are virtually all Muslim. Since many Muslims feel that the nationalized banks deny credit to them, the BACB serves a crying need for the community.[23]

Education and the Tertiary Sector

Like other parts of India, Bihari Muslims took to modern scientific education imparted through English later than Hindus.[24] But, according to historian Surendra Gopal, "In spite of the Wahabi dislike and opposition to the British, the Muslims, by and large, remained associated with colonial administrative apparatus well into the 19th century. This largely determined their attitude to the learning of English language and the new education, which were sought to be popularized by the English after 1930. Instead of rejecting English language and education, the Muslims of Patna from the very beginning tried to imbibe them. They were conscious that under the existing alien rule only mastery of the English language would give them access to administrative jobs and throw open to them a variety of professions. The Commissioner of Patna requested Shah Ulfat Husain Faryad to give his opinion on the proposal of Lord Macaulay to impart English education to Indians. Faryad supported Macaulay's proposal and was the *first* (emphasis original) Indian to do so. Hence it is not surprising that even when the Wahabi movement with its religious conservatism and hatred for the English attained popularity among a section of Patna Muslims in the second half of the nineteenth century, it could not persuade them to reject English and the new education. Khan Bahadur Mir Abu Saeed set up an educational society in 1865 to which the Commissioner of Patna was an invitee."[25] Gopal's research based on contemporary sources shows Muslim aristocracy supporting educational efforts with money to the institutions and scholarship funds to the students. After 1880, many Bihar students began enrolling at Aligarh, and subsequently many members of the upper middle class traveled to England for higher education.[26] Digging through the archives, Satyanarain Prasad cites many examples of Muslims taking to modern education, concluding that "technical schools of Bihar were filled with Muslims. So the oft-repeated theory that the Muslims kept aloof from western education and consequently did not have a fair share in higher government jobs stands discredited at least in the case of Bihar."[27] Modern education had evidently not reached the poor segments of the Muslim society, according to a contemporary source, a useful reminder lest it is mistakenly assumed that education was widespread.[28] Muslim response to education had a direct bearing on employment. "For several centuries the Muslims formed the ruling elite. Only after the battle of Plassey in 1757 the process of their displacement by the English started. Even then they could not be totally eliminated for the next eighty years [1830s] because Persian remained the language of administration. The upper crust of the Muslim population traditionally studied this language and hence, they continued to provide members to man the administrative structure being fashioned by the English. Further, in the initial phases of their rule, the colonial masters had no option but to depend on the traditional elites because of their knowledge of local conditions for running the administration. The Muslims though no longer members of the ruling race, nevertheless did not lose their position in the new administrative hierarchy and hence continued to enjoy considerable political and administrative influence."[29] In 1881, Hindi was introduced as the language of the judiciary.[30] The Bihar administration also prohibited the use of Persian script in legal transaction. Police officers and other administrative personnel were warned that if they could not read and write Devanagari script, they would be replaced. These measures affected Muslims, who made a high proportion of the scribes and lawyers."[31] Evidently Muslims were quite well represented in the provincial judiciary, despite these measures, unlike neighboring Bengal.[32] Outside British India, Bihari Muslim educated classes had the option of seeking employment in distant Hyderabad, the southern stronghold of Islamic culture, which many did.[33]

Despite the lack of education among the poor Muslims, within the community those who did go to schools made a good 13 percent of the total pupils in the years 1927-32, whereas the Bihar Muslim population at that time was 10.9 percent.[34] It shows that ready acceptance of modern education in the nineteenth century was sustained well into the twentieth century. The Government of India's reservation of 25 percent state employment for Muslims may also have played a part in robust Muslim presence in that sector. But the Congress Party's assumption of power in Bihar in 1937 led to accusation by Muslim League that the minority was not getting its fair share in employment. The League appointed a Commission under Muhammad Shareef to investigate Muslim grievances in the province under the Congress raj, 1937-39. "As regards the percentages of Muslims appointed to various government departments we have to point out that the Muslims form 12.87 percent of the population of Bihar according to the last census [1931]. It has however been an accepted principle that in appointments to the various services in Bihar under the government, the Muslims should have an allotment of 25 percent of all posts. ...it is not possible for a non-official Committee such as this to ascertain the percentages of the Muslim appointments in all the various services, and that this is only possible at considerable expense and labor... The Committee, however, has been able to obtain some statistics relating to some departments from non-official sources...the late Bihar government with its immense staff and huge establishments in its numerous departments could easily have given complete, full and comprehensive figures. From the figures available to us, it will clearly appear that the appointments given to Muslims are very much below 25% and in some cases very much below even that their small population percentage would justify."[35] This was of course the Muslim League position, and not shared by all political opinion in the country.

On its part the Congress government informed the Bihar Legislature in 1937 of Muslim share in the employment as follows: in "the Bihar Police Service (Deputy Superintendent of Police) 33.3 % were Muslims; in Bihar Civil Service (Executive Branch), Muslims represented 22.5%, in Bihar Civil Service (Judicial Branch) as Subordinate Judges and Munsifs, Muslims were 21%; and in Subordinate Civil Service (Sub Deputy Collectors) they had a 29.5% share.[36] Other than the police department, they held a slightly shorter percentage than the guaranteed statutory 25 percent. Nonetheless, the Muslim percentage in the total employed by the provincial government was quite good when compared with the post-independence era.

Since Independence

Drastic changes took place in the politics and society of Bihar at partition. As a province bordering Bengal, many Muslims migrated to the eastern portion of Pakistan. Large-scale migration to Pakistan—which continued up to late 1971— reduced the Muslim percentage in state employment. The Bihar Civil List for 1960— where figures are available for all government departments, the position of Muslims has been similar to that in Uttar Pradesh. Muslim representation ranged from zero in the political and welfare departments to 12 percent in the Bihar Public Service Commission[37] and in the Excise department. The Muslim share of all gazetted posts in Bihar in 1960 was 541 out of 9,773 or 5.53 percent.[38] Of the total 300,000 non-gazetted posts, Muslims held only about one percent.[39] An examination of a less comprehensive list of gazetted officers in Bihar for 1968 revealed 117 Muslim names in a list of 1, 961 officers or 6.92 percent, as against the community's 12 percent in the total population.[40] Eight years later, the Muslim percentage in the civil service had come down further to 5.13 percent.[41] In the judicial service, in 1981, Muslims represented 8.74 percent.[42] In a competitive exam for judicial service, out of a total of 332, only 16 were Muslims. Improvement is noticeable in 1978-80 Bihar Combined State Services examinations.[43] In 1983, the authorities in Patna informed National Minorities Commission that Muslims represented a mere 2 percent in the state jobs, except the Education Department, where they represented 7 percent,[44] which may be due to the larger number of Urdu teachers in government schools. An official report on state personnel reported 1756 holding Bihar Administrative Service posts, of which Muslims numbered 178 or 10.13 percent of the total.[45]

A major reason for the absence of Muslims is their poor educational achievement. Whereas, the general literacy in the rural areas is 44.4 percent, those for Muslims lags behind at 38.0 percent; in urban areas the disparity is even higher at 72.7 for general population and Muslims at a mere 48.8 percent in 2001.[46] Aijazuddin Ahmad, who did a detailed study of Kishanganj in the early 1990s, found the district to be particularly backward in what is universally recognized as an educationally poor state.[47] Another, much smaller, educational survey of the same district by Naim Qasimi confirms Aijazuddin Ahmad's comprehensive work.[48]

One scholar finds a direct correlation between higher illiteracy and areas with a concentration of Muslim population.[49] When primary through higher secondary education is poor, it is inevitable that Muslim-managed degree colleges also have fewer Muslim students. Education of girls and women often takes a back seat in Bihar as it does elsewhere in the country.[50] Bihar boasts of 6 degree colleges managed by Muslims and one medical college founded in Katihar.[51] There are over 1100 government-aided *madrasas* on the rolls of Bihar State Madrasa Education Board, presumably outside the pool of candidates appearing in competitive exams for government employment.[52] Another 900 Muslim educational institutions of varying quality are spread over the state.[53]

At a meeting of the Bihar elite convened in October 1992, the organizers issued a statement describing the community as "educationally and economically backward. Their share in the primary, secondary and tertiary economic activities... commerce and services is very low compared to their population. Their unemployment is high, their educational level is poor. Their enrollment is lower, much lower among the females than among the males. The representation in the professional class, even among the teachers, is very low though their representation among the self-employed workers like Beedi workers and rickshaw pullers is comparatively high."[54] This general statement found confirmation in an empirical survey sponsored by the Bihar State Minorities Commission and prepared by the Asian Development Research Institute, which found that Bihar Muslims are poorer than others in the state. Nearly half (49.5 percent) of the Muslim rural households and 44.8 percent of the urban Muslim households live below the poverty line. This contrasts with the National Sample Survey Organization's findings of the general Bihar population's condition. The NSSO's survey showed that 44.3 percent and 32.9 percent urban and rural population respectively lived below the poverty line.[55]

From time to time sympathetic politicians have asked for reservations for Muslims in educational institutions and employment, but it has not been conceded, except for some groups like the Momins. This brings us to the whole question of reservations, whether it should be for just some backward communities among Muslims or all Muslims as a whole. According to Papiya Ghosh, "Though the backward classes' movement had been active in Bihar since the 1940s, it was during the late 1970s chief ministership of the Janata leader Karpoori Thakur that "Backward Raj" was inaugurated. Following his decision on reservations, the number of Most Backward Class (MBC) Muslim communities rose from six to seven in 1955 and from 14 to 20 in 1978. By 1992 only four out of nine Muslim *biradaris* remained in the Other Backward Classes (OBC) category,[56] i.e. the very basic unit of educationally and economically poor segment of the population. Each "backward" category wants to be declared "most backward" in order to obtain maximum advantage in educational and economic reservations. Thus the Momins moved into the Most Backward Class category in 1984 when the government accepted their demand.[57] A similar demand by the Jamiat al-Rayin (community organization of *Rayin*) for the *Rayin* did not succeed in persuading the state to do so in 1993. In 1994 the *Mehtars, Lalbegis* and *Halal khwors* (night soil removers) who had been categorized as MBCs agitated to be shifted to the Scheduled Caste category, which is obviously blocked as no Muslim can be designated so under the Indian Constitution, paragraph 3, Order 1950. Since the mid 1990s, the demands have also emerged for the entire Muslim community—not just some of its *biradaris*—to be declared backward, although some organizations representing occupational categories want the reservation to be restricted to just their groups, and exclude other Muslims. A reservation demand applicable to all Muslims is thus opposed by sections of Muslims themselves who are more backward—the Momins for example—than the rest of the Muslims.[58] Syed Shahabuddin, representing one opinion has argued that "mere inclusion of Muslim OBCs in the Central and State Lists of OBCs will not do as the more forward castes among the Hindu OBCs will take the cake and leave nothing for the relatively backward Hindu OBCs or for Muslim OBCs."[59] The remedy, according to him, is either having a separate quota for all Muslims or Muslim OBCs alone.

Parallel with the pleas for inclusion in the various backward class categories, have also been demands on state agencies such as the Bihar State Minority Welfare Department. Under its control is the Bihar State

Minorities Financial Corporation established in 1984. The loans it provided have been meager to begin with and when divided between various minority groups the amount is too small to make much difference.[60] In 2001, the Corporation was in deficit due to loan default. Since then it is working as the enforcement agency for the Maulana Azad Minorities Finance Development Corporation based in New Delhi. During 2002-2003, it was involved in creating an infrastructure—the Minorities Bhavan, construction of hostels for students, protective walls for Muslim cemeteries, organization of cultural festivals, and loan schemes and technical training. The Bihar State Minorities Commission (BSMC) established since 1971 is another agency involved in minorities' development. In August 1991 the Lalu Prasad Yadav administration introduced a resolution in the Bihar Legislature giving statutory status to the BSMC two decades after its creation.[61] There is also the Bihar Legislative Council's Minorities Welfare Committee.[62] Set up in 1995, this Committee is charged to look after the well being of the minorities, but it invariably faces problems from the state bureaucracy, which is either unable or unwilling to supply data about the economic condition of the minority communities in the state.

Waqf Board

As in most other states, the Bihar Waqf Board, divided into Sunni and Shia units, is not an efficient organization. In fact it is financially in a deplorable condition, with most of the properties in illegal possession. Like, other Waqf boards, the biggest impediment for *waqf* development is the community leadership's lack of interest in the *waqf* and its inability or unwillingness to expose the involvement of Muslims themselves in robbing *waqf* properties. The problem is compounded by state apathy. Without executive powers, a competent staff and state support, the Waqf Board is unlikely to fulfill its purpose.[63]

Notes

1 Surendra Gopal, *Patna in the Nineteenth Century* (Calcutta: Naya Prokash, 1982),p. 22.

2 Imtiaz Ahmad, "Patna (Azimabad) at the Turn of the Present Century: Based on Some Urdu Writings," pp. 168-113, in *Patna Through the Ages,* edited by Qeyamuddin Ahmad (New Delhi: Commonwealth, 1988).

3 Constituent Assembly of India, *Legislative Debates,* December 1949, p. 16.

4 Aijazuddin Ahmad, *Muslims in India,* Bihar, p. 49.

5 Ibid., p. 58.

6 *Socio-Economic Status of Muslims in Bihar:* A Study Sponsored by Bihar State Minorities Commission (Patna: Asian Development Research Institute, 2004), p. 46.

7 Ibid., p. 46.

8 Ibid.

9 Ibid.

10 Sarfarazuddin Ahmad, *Rural Muslims in Transition* (New Delhi: Commonwealth Publishers, 1991), and Peter Gottschalk, *Beyond Hindu and Turk: Multiple Identity in Narratives from Village India* (Oxford: Oxford University Press, 2000).

11 Ibid., pp. 51-52.

12 "The Bunkers," pp. 22-23, in *Bhagalpur Riots* (New Delhi: People's Union for Democratic Rights, 1990).

13 *Twelfth Annual Report of the Minorities Commission for the Period from 1-4-1989 to 31-3-1990* (New Delhi: Controller of Publications, Government of India, 1992), p. 237.

14 *Socio-Economic Status of Muslims in Bihar,* pp. 53-54; Zeyauddin Ahmad, "Caste Elements Among the Muslims of Bihar," pp. 337-350, in *The New Wind: Changing Identities in South Asia,* edited by K. David (The Hague: Mouton, 1977).

15 Ibid., p. 41.

16 Hasan Nishat Ansari, "Socio-Economic Status and Conditions of the Momins under British Rule," *Journal of Bihar Research Society* 47-48, Parts 1-IV (): 486-520; and the same author's "The Momins: Population and Nationalism," pp. 555-563, *K.P. Jayswal Commemoration Volume,* edited by J.S. Jha (Patna: K.P. Jayswal Research Institute, 1981).

17 "Abdulqayyum Ansari, 1906-1973," *Muslim India* (September 1987): 389.

18 Zeyauddin Ahmad, "Caste Elements Among the Muslims of Bihar," pp. 337-350, in *The New Wind: Changing Identities in South Asia,* edited by K. David (The Hague: Mouton, 1977).

19 Jabir Husain, *Bihar ki Pasmanda Muslim Abadiyan* (Patna: Bihar Foundation, 1994). Rayin are not to be confused with the Arayin, a Punjabi caste.

[20] Kumkum Chattterjee, *Merchant Politics and Society in Early Modern India, Bihar 1733-1820* (Leiden: Brill, 1996), pp. 73-75.

[21] Surendra Gopal, *Patna in the 19th Century* (Calcutta: Naya Prokash, 1982), p. 8. For Amir Khan, see Charles Edward Buckland, *Dictionary of Indian Biography* (London,: Sonnenschein, 1906), p. 12.

[22] J.C. Jha, "Aspects of the History of the Patna College, 1863-1983" pp. 97-113, in *Patna Through the Ages,* edited by Qeyamuddin Ahmad (New Delhi: Commonwealth, 1988), citation on p. 97.

[23] *Socio-Economic Status of Muslims in Bihar*, pp. 141-42.

[24] Satyanarain Prasad, "Muslim Education in Bihar (1854-1882)," *Journal of Indian History* 48, 1 (April 1970): 136-140.

[25] Surendra Gopal, op.cit. 24.

[26] Ibid., p. 24-25

[27] Satyanarain Prasad, op. cit., 136-40.

[28] Imtiaz Ahmad, "Patna; Azimabad at the Turn of the Present Century," op. cit., p. 173, where a contemporary diary speaks of educational poverty among the "Muslims of lower classes."

[29] Surendra Gopal, ibid., pp. 21-22.

[30] Jyotirindra Das Gupta, *Language Conflict and National Development* (Berkeley: University of California Press, 1970),pp. 102-103.

[31] Ibid.

[32] B.B. Mishra, *The Indian Middle Class,* p. 192.

[33] The obvious examples are Mawlawi Khuda Bakhsh Khan, who became the chief justice of the Nizam's High Court in the nineteenth century, and Sayyid Taqiuddin (Home Secretary); Sayyid Abdul Aziz, a minister for education in the twentieth century. More examples in Surendra Gopal, op.cit. pp. 24-25. Sayyid Ali Imam even became the first president of the Nizam's Executive Council, when inaugurated in 1919.

[34] *Progress of Education in India, 1927-32,* II, Table 99 (B) as cited in Ratna Naidu, *The Communal Edge to Plural Societies.*

[35] *Report of the Publicity Committee of the Bihar Provincial Muslim League on Some Grievances of the Muslims,* 1938-39. Patna, December 1939, as reproduced in *Muslims under Congress Rule, 1937-1939: A Documentary Record,* edited by K.K. Aziz (Islamabad: National Commission on Historical and Cultural Research, 1978), pp. 547-548.

[36] *Bihar Legislative Assembly Debates* Official Report, 15th March 1938 (Patna: Superintendent of Government Printing, 1937-39), pp.220-22; I am grateful to Steve Wilkinson for sharing this data with me.

[37] The positive or negative impact of the presence or absence of Muslim members in the Public Service Commissions is often the subject of debate within the community, with opinion often divided. For the record, Justice Sayyid Bahauddin (1911-88) and Professor Sayyid Iqbal Husain (1905-91) have been members of the BSPSC.

[38] Akram Shamsi, "Muslims in Services: Poor Representation in Bihar," *Radiance* 14 February 1965): 5-6.

[39] Akram Shamsi, op.cit.

[40] Compiled from Government of India, Ministry of Home Affairs, *All-India Civil List* (Delhi: Manager of Publications, 1970), pp. 389-410, as cited in Paul Brass, *Language, Religion and Politics in North India*, p. 232. *All India Civil List, Issued Half Yearly* (Bombay: Printed & Published under the Authority of the Govt. of India, 1959, "As Corrected up to 1st July 1958, shows just 30 Muslims, see pp. 199-206 of this civil list.

[41] *Afkar-i Milli* (July 2000) is devoted to the educational and economic condition of Bihar Muslims, and the sources for information are not clearly identified, but I suspect the figure of Muslim employment is from Gopal Singh Panel, see p. 77.

[42] "Representation of Muslims in Judicial Service in 1981," *Muslim India* (September 1983), p. 552; see also "High Courts; Muslim Judges, 1.1.92" *Muslim India* (July 1992), p. 318; and "List of Muslim Supreme/ High Court Judges...Retired Between 1947 and 1979," *Muslim India* (March 1983), p. 146. The Judges included are S. Ali Ahmad, S. Anwar Ahmad in the 1970s, S.H.S. Abidi, Shamim Ahsan, Aftab Alam, and Shamimul Hoda in the 1980s and early 1990s.

[43] "Muslim Performance in Competitive Examinations Held During 1978-80," *Muslim India* (December 1983), p. 553.

[44] *Fifth Annual Report of the Minorities Commission for the Period 1-4-1982 to 31-3-1983* (New Delhi: Controller of Publications, Government of India, 1985), p. 00. Muslims achieved only slight improvement in Public Service Commission exam around this time in Bihar, see Report on Minorities (Delhi: Government of India, 14 June 1983), pp. 34-35, as cited in Mushirul Hasan, *Legacy of a Divided Nation: India's Muslims Since Independence*, p. 290-91.

[45] *Socio-Economic Status of Muslims in Bihar*, p. 63.

[46] *Ibid.*, p. 97.

[47] Aijazuddin Ahmad, Muslims in India, I, Bihar.

[48] "Kishanganj Town: A Study of Muslim Educational Backwardness," *Muslim India* (July 1998), p. 320; and the same author's "Kishanganj ki Taalimi Surat-i Hal," *Afkar-i Milli* (May 1998), p.37.

[49] Arif Hassan, "Educational Backwardness of Muslims in India," *Journal of Objective Studies* 5, 1 (January 1993): 142-54.

[50] "Educational Backwardness of Girls: A Moment of Thought," *The Milli Gazette* (1-15 July 2005), p. 5.

[51] "Muslim Managed Degree Colleges," *Muslim India* (July 1996), p. 319.

[52] *Socio-Economic Status of Muslims in Bihar*, pp. 138-139.

[53] Mohammad Qamar Ishaq, *Directory of Muslim Educational , Religious & Welfare Organizations in India (*New Delhi: Institute of Objective Studies, 1995), pp. 11-46; updated information in Rahat Abrar and M. Qamar Ishaque, *Directory of Muslim Educational Institutions in India* (New Delhi: Institute of Objective Studies, 2002), pp. 37-120.

[54] "Muslim Education, Employment and Economic Status," Text of Syed Shahabuddin's speech at the convention held in Patna, *Radiance* (25-31 October 1992), p.11.

[55] Pranava K. Choudhary, " Muslims Remain Deprived of Government Schemes," *The Times of India* 23 January 2005, Internet edition; "Rabri Government Withholds Minority Report," *NDTV.com* 24 January 2004, Internet edition. NDTV.

[56] Papiya Ghosh, "Partition's Biharis," *Comparative Studies of South Asia, Africa and the Middle East* 17, 2 (1997), p. 28.

[57] Papiya Ghosh, ibid., p. 29.

[58] Ijaz Ali, who heads the movement for "Dalit" Muslims, wants to move his groups from OBC status to SC group and the Muslims in the tribal areas to the category of the STs!, see "On Muslim Reservation", *Muslim India* (October 1999), p. 472.

[59] Shahabuddin's Letter to Asghar Ali Engineer, 8 September 1999, reproduced in *Muslim India* (October 1999), p. 472.

[60] Abuzar Kamaluddin, "Musalmanan-I Bihar ki Maashi Halat," *Afkar-i Milli* (July 2000), p. 78. This issue of *Afkar-I Milli* has a number of articles on Bihar Muslims' educational and economic conditions.

[61] Evidently the Commission was created on 26 April 1971 by a Government order number 5742, but nearly comatose, presenting only three reports to the government in 20 years according to Jabir Husain, "Bihar Aqliyati Commission ko Qanuni Daraja," *Afkar-i Milli* (November 1991): 28-29. The reports are not publicly available.

[62] M.S. Asthanwi, "Third Report of Bihar Legislative Council's Minorities Welfare Committee," *The Milli Gazette* v. 2 dated 01/08/2001, Internet edition.

[63] Hasanuddin Ahmad and Ahmedullah Khan, *Strategies to Develop Waqf Administration in India* (Jeddah: Islamic Research and Training Institute, Islamic Development Bank, Research Paper no. 50, 1998), see chapter "Waqf Administration in Bihar State," pp. 97-110.

DECCAN AND ANDHRA PRADESH

The modern states of Andhra Pradesh, Karnataka and Maharashtra represent the Deccan region, distinct from both northern India and the deep southern India. Like the Urdu-speaking Muslims of north India, the Deccani Muslims comprise a group distinct both from their South Indian counterparts, such as the Malabar Mapillas and the Tamil-speaking Muslims as well as from the Bohras, Khojas, and the Memons of the coastal western India. Hyderabad in Andhra Pradesh has the largest single concentration of Muslims in India in any city.

The Deccan came under the Bahmani sultanate during 1347-1518. Other than the horse dealers[1] and other merchants on the coast, the bulk of the fledging Muslim groups during this period formed a military aristocracy thinly spread over the main population centers. The Muslim aristocracy was too busy soldiering and governing to undertake commercial activities. In the Deccan, migration from Persia,[2] Hadramawt, coastal southern Yemen, the horn of Africa, Afghanistan, and modern North West Frontier Province continued even till the 1940s. Many of these migrants became rich landowners, bankers, or found employment in the Nizam's army.[3]

In the Deccani sultanates, *inams*, rent-free tenures of land, sometimes entire villages were gifted to Muslim divines as well as Brahmans as reward for public service or for the maintenance of charitable institutions, but the British revoked this system in the middle of the nineteenth century when parts of the Deccan came under colonial control.[4] A few of the Muslim religious divines found no contradiction between earning a livelihood, *kasb*, and a devotional life. Many in fact welcomed the royalty to the *dargahs*, and *khanqahs*, accepted cash and lands grants making many *dargahs* the foci of greed, power and ultimately of endless litigation among the Sufi descendants and shrine custodians.

Muslim peasants and cultivators, like their counterparts in other religions, remained economically active in agricultural production, fishing, herding and other manual work. Independent professionals among Muslims were few, except the traditional medical doctors or *hakims*.[5] The Bahmani sultans of the Deccan, and their successors the Adil Shahis and the Qutb Shahis (1500s-1680s) liberally recruited Hindu upper castes of martial reputation like the Nayaks and Marathas as soldiers. Many Brahmans became accountants in the revenue department and record keepers in the bureaucracy.[6] The land ownership remained a firm Hindu monopoly, as described by S.V. Desika Char from various sources.[7] Given the Hindu monopoly over land ownership, it is not surprising that the *zamindar* class was predominantly non-Muslim.[8] The political changes of 1686-87 when the Deccani sultanates were absorbed in the Mughal Empire, and the gradual separation of the Deccan from the declining Mughal Empire by Asaf Jah in the 1720s made little difference to the means of livelihood of various segments of the society.

Agriculture and Land Ownership

Roughly under the same strategic compulsion as the Bahmanis, Qutb Shahis, Adil Shahis and the Mughal *subahdars* before him, Asaf Jah entrusted military positions mainly to Muslims, leaving administrative work and the cultivation of land to the Hindus. Once he became independent of the nominal Mughal emperor of Delhi, he created his own court and nobles by rewarding those who served him well, regardless of community. J.D.B. Gribble's description of this process has stood the test of time: "Asaf Jah had brought with him from Malwa a number of followers, Mahomedans and Hindus, who were attached to his person and fortunes... To the Mahomedan nobles he granted jagirs or estates on military tenure and employed them as his generals...The Hindus...he employed principally in administrative work in the departments of revenue and finance. To them he also granted jagirs as a remuneration for their services, and all these jagirs, whether granted for civil or military purposes, came to be considered as hereditary in the different families... scattered over the country was a large number of indigenous rajahs and chiefs...who were confirmed in their possessions on payment of tribute. The whole... country was divided into three distinct [revenue] portions, consisting first of these feudal *jagirs*, some like the Paigah estates as large as some of the princely states; secondly of scattered portions of territory reserved for the Nizam's privy purse, known as *Sarf-i khas* lands; and thirdly of the Diwani or government lands, the revenues of which were devoted to the expenses of administration."[9] Unlike the Mughal practice of transferring *jagirs* regularly, the Nizams made the *jagirs* hereditary, in order to weave a network of loyalty around their persons as well as to proclaim independence from Delhi. Yet, "unlike the zamindars and taluqdars of other parts of India, the jagirdars of Hyderabad had no proprietary rights over their jagirs."[10] On the eve of jagirdari abolition in September 1949, besides the Sarf-i Khas, "there were 1500 jagirdars, not to mention the numerous *hissedars* (shareholders) and *guzarayabs* (other dependents)."[11] The Nizam and the nobility—a landed gentry which included some Hindus—together held forty percent of the total area of the state.[12] Approximately 57 percent of the earners and working dependents were engaged in the 'exploitation of animals and vegetation,' pointing to the predominance of agriculture and agrarian classes in the economy in 1931, in which Muslims were a minority.[13] In 1944, it was estimated that Muslims constituted 24.3 percent of the ordinary cultivators; they did not as a rule own land.[14] Only a small number of landowners, who cultivated the land or hired the labor to do so, included Muslims.[15]

Labor, Commerce and Industry

In the early eighteenth century Deccan, the Muslim minority continued to monopolize the highest positions, but Hindus played an important role not only in administrative functions but also in banking and money-lending.[16] Like their coreligionists in many other parts of India, the Deccani Muslims shunned trade and industry.[17] At best Muslims were petty shopkeepers and retailers of perfume, groceries, foodstuffs, and cloth, not big businesses owners or industrialists.[18] In 1929, the Nizam's Government established an Industrial Trust Fund (ITF) with an initial capital of one crore, which grew to over five crores in 1948 according to one source.[19] The purpose of the ITF was to help the progress of industry in general.[20] Given the access to political power, some Muslims took advantage to promote themselves or their relatives through this scheme. The Socialist Party, a political group hostile to the capitalists in general, claimed that the ITF "has been deliberately utilized for helping Muslim industrialists in order to conserve the economic power of the Muslim ruling class. Eighty to ninety percent of the investments of the ITF are in concerns owned or managed by Muslim capitalists who are invariably the relations of high officials."[21]

Contrary to the Socialist Party's assertion, dispassionate academic research has established that such was not the case, as many upper caste Hindu industrialists also took advantage of the ITF.[22] Some Muslim beneficiaries of the ITF included Mir Laiq Ali (1905-71), a civil engineer, who became a successful entrepreneur earning the sobriquet of the Rockefeller of Hyderabad![23] Mir Laiq Ali owned, operated or managed Sirpur Paper Mills, Hyderabad Roller Flour Mills, Nizam Sugar Factory, Singareni Collieries, Deccan Airways, and Hyderabad Construction Company, besides being the managing director of many other companies. He became the President of the Nizam's Executive Council in November

1947, also presiding over the ill-thought attempt at Hyderabad's independence from India in 1948. Laiq Ali's business partner was Abdulkarim Babu Khan who was a contractor for public works, and some retail trade.[24] Camar [Qamar] Tyabji, the son in law of Sir Akbar Hydari, the Nizam's Prime Minister, was the managing director of three major companies, controlling a capital of 2 crores and 75 lakhs in 1948, according to a contemporary source.[25] The Alladin family of Secunderabad owned and operated the Allwyn Metal Works, producing 14,000 refrigerators in the late 1960s. The state government took over the company in 1969. The Alladins also owned Hyderabad Asbestos and Cement Products, Bakelite Hylam and an aerated water factory. The family patriarch Ahmad Nawaz Jang (1882-1954) was perhaps the only industrialist to get a title from the Nizam—that of Nawab Ahmad Nawaz Jang Bahadur. His son, Dost Muhammad Alladin (1909-73), inherited and ran the family financial network, becoming the youngest President of the Hyderabad Chamber of Commerce. In addition to these industrial families of old Hyderabad, a number of others also made their mark on the industrial scene among Muslims. One such was Muhammad Vazir, who established the famous tobacco factory Vazir Sultan in 1930 known for its signature product, the Charminar cigarettes. Beating the stereotype of Deccani Muslims as slothful, decadent lotus eaters, Muhammad Hanif moved out of his native place to set up a successful furniture business in late 1940s in Calcutta's famed Elliot Road.[26] Finally, no account of Hyderabad Muslim businessmen in old Hyderabad can be complete without reference to Khan Bahadur Abdulkarim Babu Khan, d. 1968. He held shares in various companies including managerial directorships of Sirpur Paper Mills, Sirsilk Mills, Hyderabad Construction Company, Nizam Sugar Factory, Hyderabad Roller Flour Mills, and Hyderabad Vegetable Products.[27]

Modern Education and the Tertiary Sector

The ownership of revenues of large tracts of lands by some 1500 *jagirdar* families created the false picture of Deccani Muslims as rich landlords, while the facts were otherwise. First of all they did not *own* the lands; they owned only the land revenues. Second, "on the average…the mode of the living of the *jagirdar* class left a great deal to be desired. Steeped in the habits of a bygone feudal age, receiving *nazars*, gifts in cash and kind and other parasitical incomes without simultaneous exertion, many a *jagirdar* had become negligent of the affairs on his *jagir* and indulged in a good deal of extravagance, pomp and ceremony. Indebtedness, in spite of large incomes had soared in many cases. The *jagirdars* and their dependents as a class could not be said to be reasonably educated despite the means at their disposal."[28] "The condition of the Muslim *jagirdars*," Zahid Ali Kamil, contended, "is pitiable. They have to depend for their income on the generosity of their Hindu *naibs* or *mukhtars*, [agents] who take jolly good care to see that the *jagirdars* always remain in their clutches, partly through heavy interest bearing debts…and partly because they can successfully make the *jagirdar* believe that without them he will not be able to collect a pie from the *ryots*. Very often they advise the *jagirdar* never to step into his *jagir*…When Muslim women are holders of *jagir*, the situation is considerably worse."[29] Turning to the rural administration, we find that "out of 99,184 village officers, only 2514 are Muslims, while 96670 are Hindus. The *Pattedars*, *Inamdars* and *Rusumdars* are likewise predominantly Hindus. For instance, against 10 lakh and odd Hindu *Pattedars*, the number of Muslim *Pattedars* is barely 60,000. Similarly, among *Inamdars* 70,000 are Hindus and 10,000 are Muslims. Among *Rusumdars*, 3500 are Hindus and 200 Muslims.[30] Land ownership was small, most Muslims in the rural areas being tenant cultivators. The entrepreneurial class, as we have just noted, was miniscule. Similar was the case with modern independent professionals consisting of small number of engineers and allied professionals, medical doctors and health care personnel, lawyers and the like.

Therefore a large number of Muslims depended on state employment, rooted in the nature of the government introduced by the Nizams in the eighteenth century, by which the major army, police and executive positions were given to Muslims and the rest to the Hindus. The system continued with little change for more than a century. In the 1860s, public education became a state responsibility when Salar Jang I allocated a budget for its pursuance and promotion, resulting in the expansion of government employment. "From 1884 onwards, the government published a "Civil List" at least once a year which besides providing the total number of officials gave a breakdown by community, "according to Bustan-i Asafiya, as noted below.

Table I
Gazetted Officials of the Hyderabad State, 1884-1951

Year	*Hindus*	*Muslims*	*Parsis*	*Europeans & Xians*	*TOTAL*	*Source/Remarks*
1884	99	459	40	90	688	
1885	67	327	22	35	451	
1886	61	282	38	60	441	
1887	61	326	37	74	498	
1891	72	411	39	64	586	
1893	65	383	41	86	575	
1894	63	400	40	83	586	
1895	67	443	49	82	641	
1896	65	365	39	88	557	
1897	62	358	37	80	537	
1898	89	544	50	92	775	
1899	74	607	44	87	812	
1900	78	614	46	88	826	
1901	71	369	43	83	566	
1902	70	430	45	83	628	
1903	76	423	46	82	627	
1904	80	418	41	75	614	
1905	63	380	28	78	549	
1906	79	417	41	79	616	
1907	74	419	46	82	621	
1908	85	486	41	86	698	
1909	96	488	47	93	724	
1910	89	463	43	70	665	

1911	85	461	41	91	678	
1912	85	552	46	104	787	
1913	90	534	46	106	776	
1914	92	518	44	111	765	
1915	117	522	50	95	784	
1916	123	534	41	94	792	
1917	115	511	38	96	760	
1918	131	562	36	85	814	
1919	136	572	33	76	817	
1920	143	604	29	72	848	
1921	161	659	26	62	908	
1922	156	716	35	69	976	
1923	166	759	38	72	1035	
1924	167	756	41	64	1028	
1925	170	756	41	64	1031	
1926	197	792	29	76	1094	
1927	198	817	33	76	1124	
1928	198	817	33	76	1124	
1929	214	806	35	70	1125	
1930	227	840	37	71	1175	
1931	252	893	33	72	1250	
1941	421	1268			1765	121 other than Hindus and Muslims
1949	1355	1626	31	110	3122	*The Quarterly List**

Source up to 1931, Manikrao Vitthalrao, *Bustan-i Asafiya*, VI (Hyderabad, 1932), pp. 42-46; for 1941, see Mohan Guruswamy, "Hyderabad 1948 Revisited," posted on http://www.indiadefence.com/hyderabad.htm . *Hyderabad Reborn: First Six Months of Freedom* (September 18, 1948-March 7, 1949, compiled by Binod U. Rao, Director of Information (Hyderabad: Government of Hyderabad, 1949), p. 15. *The Quarterly Civil List of the Hydeabad Government,* corrected up to January 1, 1949 compiled in the Office of the Controller-General of Accounts and Audit, Hyderabad: Government Central Press, 1949.

While the percentage of Hindus increased over the forty-five year period from 1884-1941, the percentage of Muslims stayed about the same seventy percent. The percentage of Parsis, Christians and Europeans fell. The category 'gazetted official' constituted only one level of those employed by the government. It did not include the much lower-paid treasury guards, office peons, clerks etc."[31] By 1948, the percentage of Hindus had drastically increased showing the Nizam's sensitivity toward making the bureaucracy more representative of the society. The Muslim percentage was still 48 percent of the total. However the Operation Polo of 1948 heralded drastic changes. The Europeans left completely by the end of that year, and Muslims in the top positions drastically decreased by 1951. The exact figures showing a community-wise break up of the bureaucracy of Hyderabad State in 1951 can be found only when figures for that year are available. The 1958 All India Civil List clearly shows a precipitous Muslim decline; there appear to be just 59 Muslim gazetted officers at the time.[32]

Reflecting the poor performance of Muslims in modern technical education, the Nizam's State Railway established in 1872 had few Muslims. For instance, according to the Manager, out of a work force of 15, 452 only 2,211 were Muslims, in 1936, far fewer than was the case with civil service. Hindus predominantly staffed the NSR, with a sprinkling of Anglo-Indians, Indian Christians and others.[33]

The Hyderabad State Force on 15 August 1947, according to an official source, numbered about 17,000[34] to 22, 393 men.[35] The Nazm-i Jamiat or Afwaj-i Biqaida, or the Mughal, pre-modern army units dating from Asaf Jah's own times in early 1720s were not modernized in the nineteenth century. They remained untrained in modern warfare and displayed antiquated weapons fit for a museum even in the later 1940s and numbered 10,000 to 11, 000, according to military historians.[36] Regardless of the exact numbers, the Nazm-i Jamiat was demobilized in 1949, according to the state economic advisor.[37] The police force was predominantly, though not exclusively Muslim.[38] In an official publication in 1949, the Military Government of Hyderabad claimed that the previous government had increased the police force "from 17,000 to 35,000 at a tremendous pace between January and September 1948."[39] The Military Government's publication then coyly informs its readers that "the force is being reduced to its normal strength, while recruitment has started among non-Muslims,"[40] an obvious euphemism for excluding Muslims.

Education and Tertiary Sector

Hyderabad boasted of two major centers of higher education. The Nizam College founded in 1887, taught its students through English, whereas Osmania University did so through Urdu. Osmania University, established in 1918, offered employment to both the traditional Muslim literati as well as the modern educated Hyderabadis of all religious affiliation. In 1948, it employed several hundred personnel on its expanding campus and off-campus colleges.

The conclusion about the Muslims share in the economy of old Hyderabad is fairly clear. They owned the land revenue in large numbers as the *jagirdars* of various levels. Muslims neither owned land on a large scale nor did cultivation on a large scale. There were only a small number among shopkeepers and entrepreneurs. However, Muslims dominated the civil services, army and police, especially the highest offices and the lowest ranks, leaving some room for Hindus and others in the middle level, especially those requiring technical skills or specialized applied sciences. Though no statistics are available, a large number of Muslims found employment as domestic servants within the homes of the *jagirdars* and the richer families of the society. The situation drastically changed in the wake of Partition.

After Independence: Aftermath of Operation Polo

Negotiations between the Nizam and the government of independent India went on for most of the year resulting in a Standstill Agreement on 29 November 1947, a stop gap arrangement before the future relations between the Nizam's Dominion and New Delhi could be worked out.[41] In the meantime, the Rizakar militia or those pretending to be Rizakars harassed, and in some cases perpetrated violence against innocent Hindus resulting in some deaths.[42] The Indian government thereafter sent tanks and armor supported by air power as the Nizam was still not agreeable to being part of India. The Hyderabad State Force surrendered on 18 September, within a week. The Operation Polo had an enormously negative impact on the Deccani Muslims, comparable to the partition-related events in North India and Bengal. No one knows the exact number of deaths before, during and immediately after the surrender of Hyderabad forces, but estimates vary from a high of 200,000 to a low of 20,000.[43] While the defeat of the Nizam's army and inclusion of the state of Hyderabad was welcomed by people, including Muslims, the end of the Nizam's Dominion also entailed the erosion of privileges as well as representation in employment for the Muslims in the various sectors of the economy, namely:

1. Jagirs and related privileges.
2. Employment in the offices of feudal estates like the Sarf-i Khas, Paigahs and other bigger *jagirs.*
3. Employment in the government or quasi-government departments.
4. Domestic service with the Jagirdar families.
5. Hyderabad State Force and the Irregular Force.

The Jagirdari Abolition Act of 1949 ended the feudal system of land revenue collection, affecting not only the immediate family and relations of the *jagirdars* but also a large number of employees, dependants and their hangers-on.[44] The suppliers of goods and services to the *jagirdari* class also felt the impact of their clients' misfortune.[45] The Nizam and his immediate family received a generous privy purse from the new administration.

Figures for Muslim Evacuee lands and properties are available for Delhi, U.P. and Bihar, but complete statistics for Hyderabad are not. The revelation in 2003 that more than 250 acres of Evacuee land in a district changed hands under suspicious circumstances is the barest hint to a full inquiry to come up with a full disclosure.[46] What is known is of course the cases of harassment of innocent Muslims accused of being "Intending evacuees," as seen through the case of Nawab Zulqadr Jang (d. 1951), a doddering old nobleman who suffered the indignities of police interrogation.[47]

The big business groups consisting of Mir Laiq Ali, Camar Tyabji, Alladins, and Babu Khan had a varied fate. The Government took over Mir Laiq Ali's companies and properties as he moved to Pakistan in rather dramatic circumstances in March 1950.[48] Tyabji's fortunes declined due to reasons unknown or undisclosed. The Alladins survived, as they had no visible political connections to the former regime. In the 1960s, their company the Allwyn Metal Works produced 14,000 refrigerators annually, before the government took over in 1969. Babu Khan survived the hostile circumstances, partly by constructing the Congress Party's headquarters, the Gandhi Bhavan without cost, as a gift to the new rulers.[49] Barring a handful of officers, the rank and file in the Hyderabad State Force was disbanded on 1 April 1950, along with the Irregular Force, rendering some 33,000 individuals and their families penniless.[50] Assuming a conservative figure of 05 members per family, this would amount to a staggering 165,000-affected people.[51] The police force also went through some purges, though the exact numbers are unknown.[52] The civil service went through a massive shake-up, especially at the top level. At least three *subahdars*—Mustafa Ali Khan (Aurangabad), Amir Ali Khan, Habib Muhammad (Warangal) — equivalent to the commissioners in the British provinces, were dismissed from service.[53] Three district collectors, Muhammad Hyder (1914-73) of Osmanabad, Mir Moazzam Husain (of Adilabad), Baqir Husain Qureshi (of Karminagar) were also removed from service and jailed.[54] A third district collector, Sayyid Zainulabidin (d. 1976) of Raichur, decided to take voluntary retirement fearing adverse reaction if he persisted in office.[55] No one to date has been able to record the exact numbers of removal from active duty, but the numbers run into thousands according to S.N. Reddy (1898-1978) a former police commissioner.[56] Justice Pingle Jaganmohan Reddy, then a judge in the High Court noted: "Good Hyderabad officers were arrested, removed, demoted and badly treated merely because they were Muslims."[57] Against this evidence, a contemporary government report blandly asserted that "fewer than 100 out of a total of nearly 4000 officers were suspended."[58] Stories of dismissals and harassment are legion, only a few making it to print, such as those of Mawlawi Habiburrahman, then a Secretary in the Department of Commerce.[59] D.R. Pradhan, a bigoted ICS officer, specifically asked Habiburrahman to falsely implicate an innocent employee of his Department for being a Rizakar, failing which he was hinted at adverse consequences. Habiburrahman took early retirement rather than be responsible for an innocent man's victimization.[60] In the environment of post-1948 changes, some bureaucrats in the central government's Income Tax Department Office made Muslim taxpayers a special target. In the words of Iqbal Masud, who worked in Hyderabad in the late 1950s and 1960s "I had to dispose off the Nizam's cases and the cases of rich Muslims. I found that the Income Tax administration had practically declared a war against them...Many absurd mistakes had been committed. I was Deputy Commissioner of Appeals. Normally such humble creatures (officially we were 'administrative judges') did not take important decisions leaving it to the taxpayers to fight it out at the Income Tax Appellate Tribunal or at the High Court or Supreme Court levels. Being an inexperienced bureaucrat, I took my task literally, which was to render justice, even to Muslims. As I began to dictate orders granting relief, my steno-typist who was a South Indian Brahmin, became alarmed. "Sir, this is dangerous. The Department will call you "communal". He was frank, I told him, and 'I know this, Srinivasan. But let's have fun in watching what happens.' Srinivasan looked at me in wonder...The fun 'came' but of a Gothic kind. The Income Tax Department screamed in protest...I was transferred ...from Hyderabad to Bombay."[61] "The Nizam is under continued harassment by revenue collectors," corroborated the *Business Week*, a New York journal.[62]

To the credit of the Military Governor, Maj.Gen. J.N.Chaudhuri, he appointed Lt. Col. M.A.Rahman (1881-1961) as Chairman of the Hyderabad Public Service Commission to instill confidence among his coreligionists, many of who were fleeing to Pakistan for safety and better prospects.

Evidently he could not change the tone of the new administration installed by New Delhi, under the direction of Sardar Patel as the Minister for States. Ironically, Lt. Col. M.A. Rahman migrated to Pakistan in 1950, advising others to do so as well, according to Anwar Soofi, then a young Hyderabad Civil Service (HCS) officer.[63] HCS was the equivalent of ICS in the Nizam's Dominion. Soofi, along with at least 20 other officers migrated to Pakistan, in the same manner as did the Muslim ICS officers around 1947 from other parts of India.[64] Some penned their reasons for migration, and the reasons almost always boiled down to three: actual discrimination, anticipated discrimination, and better prospects in Pakistan.[65] The Manager of the Nizam State Railway, Syed Mahmood Alam (d. 1996), left for Pakistan after repeated harassment due to his kinship ties to Mir Laiq Ali, the Prime Minister.[66] Men and women in lower positions followed the lead given by the top civil servants, exemplified by the case of Pasha Begum Soofi, an educational administrator, who migrated to Pakistan in search of greener pasture.[67] A majority of civil servants, however, still remained in Hyderabad.[68] But distrust of Muslims was obvious. According to Syed Hashim Ali, as late as 1962 the AP Governor S.M. Srinagesh told him it was the state policy not to appoint a Muslim District Collector and a Muslim Joint Collector simultaneously. When he pointed that in the rest of the state districts both the appointments were held by Hindus, the Governor had no answer![69] Muslims, of those who remained, some complained of demotion and promotion blocked. For instance Hasanuddin Ahmad, HCS/IAS was demoted from the post of director to assistant director right after 1948. Upon complaint, his superiors *verbally* informed him that it was the policy of the state to appoint only Hindus as heads of departments![70] Zaheer Ahmad, who held important positions even after the Operation Polo, died complaining of being isolated in the new environment.[71] This is not to say that there were no exceptions; there in fact were, for example, the case of Syed Abid Husain, who started out as an HCS officer, then received the rank of an IAS officer. After several successful assignments in various central government departments, Husain became India's ambassador to the United States in 1990. Taking an entirely opposite view from the one prevailing in the community, he once remarked that "actually in India, it is Hindus who are discriminated against."[72] Similar to Syed Abid Husain, the successful careers of Judge (better known as poet) Sikandar Ali Wajd (1913-83); Mahamid Ali Abbasi (d. 1989), Secretary of Finance and Industry between 1960-67; and Vice Chancellor Syed Hashim Ali (1924-2003) of Osmania and Aligarh universities indicates that at least some who started their career before 1948 escaped discrimination in the new regime. In 2005, there were a mere five Muslim IAS officers in the state.[73]

Unaffected Groups

Two groups of Muslims who were not affected were the rural poor and the independent professionals. The incorporation of Hyderabad into India and the resultant political change had little impact on landless cultivators' condition, except to the extent it did on others when the *jagirdari* was abolished in 1949.The tiny group of engineers and allied professionals, health care personnel and others felt little change. Lawyers trained in the Nizam's legal system began to feel the narrowing of the prospects due to change in the court language from Urdu to English. School teachers and the faculty at Osmania University were also adversely affected due to the change in the language of instruction. The Muslim presence in Osmania steadily declined. In 1990, of the 215 professors, 23 were Muslims; of the 60 chairmen of Board of Studies, a mere 5 were Muslims.[74] In 1997, out of the 332 full professors, there were only 27 Muslims, 12 from the familiar groves of Arabic, Islamic Studies, Persian and Urdu departments.[75] Seven years later in 2004, not much improvement is discernable as out of its 17 college principalships, there is not a single Muslim holding that position, and there are just 55 in the faculty consisting of several hundred professors, readers and lecturers. If the departments of Arabic, Islamic Studies, Persian and Urdu are excluded, the Muslim numbers will be further reduced.[76] The posts of Vice Chancellors have been given to Muslims: Muhammad Sulayman Siddiqi was appointed Vice Chancellor (VC) on 3 February 2005, and Ali Yawar Jang has been the VC during 1948-52, and Syed Hashim Ali during 1982-85.

ANDHRA PRADESH

In November 1956 the Hyderabad state was broken up and divided along linguistic lines. The Madras state's coastal Andhra (Circars) and Rayalaseema merged with Telangana to form the state of Andhra Pradesh. Marathwada, the Marathi speaking western portion of Hyderabad merged with Bombay, renamed Maharashtra, while the Kannada speaking districts merged with Mysore, later renamed as Karnataka.

The Muslim population in Andhra Pradesh since 1961 is presented in the following table.

Table II
Muslim Population in Andhra Pradesh, 1961-2001

Year	*Muslim Popn.*	*Muslim %*	*Rural Muslim%*	*Urban Muslim%*	*Muslim Lit.%*	*Urdu Pop. %*
1961	2,715,021	7.55	55.0	45		
1971	3,520,021	8.09				
1981	4,533,700	8.47				
1991	5,923,954	8.9				8.37
2001	6,986,856	9.2			68.0	

Source: *Census of India*

Landownership and Agriculture

The Andhra Pradesh State Minorities Commission conducted an empirical socio-economic survey of minorities in 1988/89. A key finding is "an interesting departure of occupational structure of the minorities compared to the total population. While in the State population only about 30% of workers is engaged in non-agricultural operations, the corresponding proportions among Christians are 46 % and Muslims, a staggering 82 percent."[77] The Report is consonant with the findings in many other parts of the state. For instance, most of the Muslims in the Rayalaseema are landless laborers, just as is the case with the 55 percent of the rural population in Andhra Pradesh.[78] When not involved in cultivation, many of the rural Muslims are simply unskilled laborers[79] or occupied as cotton cleaners and mattress makers. These Muslims go by various names such as *Dudekula*, *Julaha*, *Naddaf/Laddaf*, *Nurbaf*, and the like, all meaning roughly the same with minor variations: cotton cleaners.[80] Although not as large in number as in Bihar and U.P., the Muslim cotton cleaners and weavers are large enough to be able to organize and get themselves enlisted as an OBC group entitled to reservations in jobs and educational institutions.[81] Scattered all over Andhra Pradesh are villages, populated sometimes with Muslim-majority to the surprise of many—including academics, who remain blissfully ignorant of rural Muslims.[82] This was brought forth dramatically when a Muslim woman Fatima Bi, was elected the *sarpanch*, elected head of the village Kalva Bugga in Kurnool. In an astonishing feat, this determined woman, spurred by a United Nations Development Program's poverty eradication project, transformed her impoverished village into a self-sufficient economy.[83] But for the most part, Muslim women in rural Andhra Pradesh have not been able to benefit from the government's self-help schemes, according to press reports.[84]

While little is known about the Muslim peasantry, no doubt due to the fact they are practically indistinguishable from their Hindu counterparts, relatively more is known about Muslim labor engaged in a number of industries. The woolen carpet industry in Andhra Pradesh dates back to the medieval times when Persian carpet weavers arrived in the Golconda sultanate attracted by the highly Persianized court of the Qutb Shahis in the fifteenth and sixteenth centuries. Today the two major centers are in Eluru and Warangal.[85] More than 4 million workers roll *bidis*, tobacco rolls, in various parts of India at the turn of the twenty first century, Andhra Pradesh being no exception.[86] Muslims, particularly, children are found in numbers disproportionate to their total national population in this industry, according to one study.[87] The informed journalist Maqbool Ahmad Siraj estimated that 80 percent *bidi* workers were Muslim.[88] Though no empirical survey has corroborated Siraj's observation, in a 1989 survey of top *bidi* manufacturers, there was not a single Muslim, leaving one to infer that few Muslims have graduated from being workers to owners.[89] Still lower in economic status than the *bidi* workers are Muslim *Mehtar*, scavengers, whose numbers are not known but are large enough to be enumerated as a Backward Class. It is interesting that the Backward Classes Commission, 1982, headed by N.K. Muralidhara Rao, recommended moving the *Mehtars* from the Backward Class category to the Scheduled Caste list. If done so, it will entitle the group to preference in reservation on par with Hindu Scheduled Castes.[90] The one occupational group that has experienced upward economic mobility is those of the *Qassab/Qasai* called Qurayshis in the Deccan. Though an estimate of numbers is absent, it probably runs in thousands. Though entitled to reservation in employment and education as a result of inclusion in the category of Backward Classes,[91] few take advantage, according to a leader of the Jamiat al-Quraysh, the organization representing the butchers. Instead many have become successful businessmen, some even exporting meat abroad. Some have even branched out into businesses other than the ancestral occupation, exemplified by the success story of Muhammad Salim, who entered the hotel industry in 1996 and now owns three hotels in Hyderabad.[92]

Urban Workers

But the vast majority of Muslim laborers in the cities and towns of Andhra Pradesh are semi-skilled and unskilled workers. Semi-skilled workers include large number of children making lacquer bangles, quilts and embroidery work, employing about 3,500 workers in the shadow of Mecca Masjid alone.[93] Virtually unknown to the Muslim leadership, several thousand Muslims have become *dhobi*, washer men.[94] Muslim occupational groups include *Attar* (perfumers), *faqir*, also known as *Gosangi* (religious mendicants), *Garardi* or *Garodi* (folk entertainers), and *Hajjam* (barbers), all desperately poor.[95] Muslim families of Chilakaturipeta,

Guntur, construct temples, carve Hindu idols, and install deities in the sanctum sanctorum as laid down by *shilpa shastra*.[96] A few have gone into reviving old weaving techniques to weave silk textiles, catering to the expanding market of heritage-conscious expatriate Indians.[97] Conventional wisdom simply assumes that Muslim women are confined to home due to *purdah*, female seclusion. This is far from being the case in Andhra Pradesh and elsewhere.[98] Unlike these employed men and women, socio-economic surveys since 1950s and 1960s identify a dismal picture. Muslims represented a majority of the street beggars,[99] a large chunk of slum-dwellers,[100] and a majority of the rickshaw-pullers.[101]

At the death of Nizam Osman Ali Khan in 1967, the Sarf-i Khas employees, mainly peons, caretakers, watchmen, drivers, cooks and the like were dismissed or "retrenched", to use the idiomatic expression then current in India.[102] Many of the "retrenched" employees took to rickshaw pulling.[103] The practices of some industrial giants, like the Birlas, has resulted in the gradual removal of Muslims from industries taken over from Mir Laiq Ali, exemplified by the case of Sirpur Paper Mills, where Muslim workforce has come down from 80 percent in 1948 to less than 12 percent in 1995 according to a member of the Legislative Assembly.[104]

The old walled city of Hyderabad, where the majority population consists of Muslims, was deemed weak in three measures of urbanization, proportion of working population, existence of manufacturing industries and commercial activities according to a 1962 survey.[105] In 1979, the government established a Society for Employment and Training in Twin Cities (SETWIN) to promote self-employment. It conducted a survey,[106] about the same time, so did *Siyasat* daily newspaper. Together, they came up with a catalog of poverty, poor schools, lack of infrastructure, and the like.[107] Still another survey by Mutual Assistance and Voluntary Institutions in India (MUAVIN) in 1991 shows no improvement.[108] A similar conclusion derives from a number of academic studies focusing on economy, housing and health.[109] A major study by Ratna Naidu concluded that 50 percent of the working population in the old city was in the informal sector, Muslims,

SCs and the STs are regularly in debt, more Muslims are unemployed than Hindus. Given the poverty, it is unsurprising that more old city Muslims live in *kuccha* houses than in *pucca* ones.[110]

Modern Education and the Tertiary Sector

Echoing the findings of these academics, the Andhra Pradesh Minorities Commission's 1989 Survey summarized the Muslim minority's socio-economic status. It showed acute illiteracy and educational poverty among Muslims in all parts of the state, but particularly in coastal Andhra and Rayalaseema, and even more so among women. When Muslims are educationally poor, it is unsurprising that they do not enter competitive exams leading to jobs.[111] Muslims represented barely three percent of the successful candidates in the AP State Public Service Commission examination held in the 1980s at all levels of jobs.[112] A census of nearly 30,000 employees in Kurnool, a minority-concentration district, showed that Muslims made up a mere 12.6 percent of the government employees. In 1971-72, there were 100 vacancies for Munsifs in the state. In the written test, out of the 30 Muslims who appeared, only five were called for interview, of which only two were selected.[113] A decade later, Muslims represented 9.48 percent of the judicial service.[114] In 1984, the government informed Sultan Salahuddin Owaisi, then an MLA, that "at present there are 4 District Judges, 4 Judges and 18 Munsifs in the state", probably a handful of the total.[115] At the High Court, during 1956-2006, there have been only 10 Muslim judges out of a total of 141, according to Justice B.S.A. Swamy.[116] The Police Department, a huge employer of Muslims before Andhra Pradesh was formed in 1956, has now fewer Muslims.[117] In 2000, 10,803 SCs, 4,250 STs, 10,074 Muslims, and the rest 33,853, presumably Hindus and Christians, represented the AP Police.[118] Documentation of discriminatory practices in hiring Muslims is not available, which is difficult in any case. There have been many Muslim members of the AP Public Service Commission (e.g. Baqir Ali Mirza); even chairmen such as Ghulam Hyder (1960-66) and Abdul Karim Khan in 2002. Both deny discrimination against their coreligionists. However, it must be understood that discrimination is rarely open, manifest and obvious. It is often subtle, wrapped in innocuous terms, but always fathomable to those who can read between the lines. For example, the AP Government Oriental Manuscripts Library and Research Institute (OMLRI) holds some of the choicest and largest number of Arabic, Persian and Urdu manuscripts. But despite the quality and quantity of the manuscripts that need senior staff, the Government framed rules requiring a PhD in Sanskrit or Telugu as prequalification for the post of the Director or Commissioner of OMLRI, thus precluding anyone with Arabic, Persian and Urdu qualifications to aspire to the Institute's highest posts.[119]

Since Muslims are not in stable jobs, government employment entitling them to housing loan, home ownership in the community is lacking. The share of Muslims in small-scale industries was found to be a negligible 03 percent. The Muslim participation in various schemes of the government for people with small means, industrial units formed with bank loans, participation in the training programs organized by the Small Industry Services Institute, all seem to leave much to be desired. Indebtedness is the natural outcome of poverty. About 55 percent of the Muslims and 40 percent of the Christian households were found to be in debt, as against the state average of about 32 percent. Part of the blame for this state of affairs is due to the absence of Muslims in the democratic institutions of the state from the highest level of state legislature and cabinet to the lowest level of *panchayat*, and the semi government cooperative marketing societies. For instance, no Muslim in the AP state cabinet ever became a finance minister or minister for education, or held any other cabinet portfolio with revenue, to be able to channel government policy in a fair manner, even if not unduly favoring one group over the other.[120]

Oddly, the 2001 Census report for Andhra Pradesh shows more Muslim literates in A.P. than Hindus. It may be because the definition of "literate" is perhaps anyone who can read Urdu letters—which many Muslims can, having read the Qur'an, but it is questionable to categorize such persons as literate. Despite such high "literacy" level, Muslims represent a lower percentage than any community as workers.[121] Does this point to discrimination?[122] A full investigation conducted by the Government with unrestricted access to the information can bring out the true picture.[123]

The demand for reservation for Muslims along the lines of other backward classes has been there since 1994, when Chief Minister Vijaya Bhaskara Reddy, actually conceded the demand, but it never materialized from a mere promise to legislative or executive action. The reservation demand was raised during the Chandrababu Naidu administration during 1995-2004.[124] On 12 July 2004, the Chief Minister C.Rajasekhara Reddy announced five percent job quota for Muslims through a Government Order Ms. 33, issued by the Backward Classes Welfare Department.[125] The Government Order was challenged by Hindu chauvinist groups, the only ones to oppose the move in the AP High Court. The Court struck down the Order, but significantly declared that the Muslims as a group were entitled to affirmative social reservation in education and employment, if identified as a socially and educationally backward group by the Backward Classes Commission.[126] Soon after the Court order, the Government and the AP Backward Classes Commission appointed in November 2004, chaired by D. Subrahmaniam examined the Muslim reservation question. It recommended reservation for Muslims in education and employment as a group.[127] Armed with the required procedural tool of a Commission's recommendation, the state government introduced legislation on October 4, 2005 seeking reservation for Muslims. The following day the Legislative Assembly passed the Bill, nearly unanimously, with the sole opposition of two BJP votes.[128] Unlike the reservation question in Bihar and U.P., the Muslim opinion in AP was not divided, as the caste question is non existent in the Deccan region as whole. Under the legislation, children of parents earning more than 2,50,00 rupees per annum will be excluded from the reservation.

Closely tied to the question of reservation is the state of Muslim education, which is poor at the primary through higher-secondary level.[129] Despite enthusiasm, a staggering 84 percent of Muslim women are illiterate according to a survey, which clearly contradicts the Census's bright picture of Muslim education.[130] Nearly 300 madrasas are found in the state, producing graduates who are incapable of entering the professional job market.[131] Some improvement in professional education is noticeable judging by the growth of engineering, medical, and pharmacy colleges. Muslim educational societies have established as many as 10 engineering colleges and two medical schools.[132] There are ten Muslim-managed degree colleges; unlike the professional schools, they have been established much earlier.[133] Given the high capitation fee charged to the students, only the rich can afford the professional colleges.[134]

Reservations are not the major avenue for improving the condition of the minorities. There is the State Minorities Commission formed as far back as 1979 whose annual reports are not consistently available to judge its performance over a quarter century. The statements of 1987 and 1997 placed by the chief ministers in the State Assembly give an impressive list of achievements for the minorities' welfare.[135] The AP Department of Minorities' Welfare (established in 1993) budget figures shows that not much is available to it, as compared to, for example, for the welfare of Scheduled Castes, Tribes, and Backward Classes. The annual budgets for the AP Dept of Minorities Welfare are given below:

Table III
Annual Budget of the AP Dept of Minorities Welfare, 1993-2005

Year	*Budget Amount in Crores*
1993-94	Not available
1995-96	4.81
1996-97	Not available
1997-98	25.00
1998-99	28.37
2000-01	27.24
2001-02	34.40
2002-03	36.61
2003-04	Lumped w/SC, ST, BC Welfare budget

2004-05	39.03
2005-06	49.00

Source: Government of AP Budget Figures posted on http://ap.gov.in/budget/

In the absence of an independent assessment, it is difficult to say how much of the budget is actually spent and how much is mere public relations material. On the allocation of 49 crore rupees in the 2005/06 budget, Majlis leader Akbaruddin Owaisi declared it inadequate, amounting to a meager 55 rupees for the minorities in the entire state.[136] The National Minorities Commission (NCM)'s Vice-Chairman M.S. Usmani certainly conveyed his clear dissatisfaction with the Department's performance in August 2004.[137] The state finance minister's budget speeches since 1995 list government-sponsored welfare measures pertaining to housing, economic development schemes, Waqfs, appointment of Urdu teachers, establishment of IITs, Polytechnics, Urdu residential schools, loan schemes, construction of wedding halls, to name only the most important. Roughly the same heads are covered in a Strategy Paper on Welfare of Minorities issued by the Chandrababu Naidu administration in 2001.[138] The activities of the Department of Minorities Welfare Center for Educational Development in advancing the educational level through providing free books, coaching, counseling and guidance for career development are perhaps the most successful effort. The AP State Minorities Finance Corporation (APSMFC) was established in 1984, and began functioning the following year. The state government and Maulana Azad National Minorities Finance Development Corporation jointly finance it. During 1985-2004, it provided loans to 1.90 lakh beneficiaries totaling Rs. 122.56 crores. In addition it provided grants to 1.72 lakh beneficiaries totaling an amount of Rs. 19.22 crores.[139] However the APSMFC seems to have invited more adverse comment than appreciation. For instance, a scandal involving misuse of funds worth several crores was discovered in September 2003, leading to an outcry.[140] Two years later APSMFC was again in news regarding the controversy over the transfer order of the Managing Director and its reversal, leaving the purpose and mission of the Corporation in disarray.[141]

Overseas Remittances and Small Businesses

The one silver lining in the otherwise dismal picture of employment is the remittances sent by migrant workers in the oil-rich Persian Gulf states and elsewhere in the Middle East. There are only estimates—several thousand Muslim young men have been overseas residents since the early 1970s. The impact on the economy is visible through a number of tangible signs; for instance, banks have opened in the old city locations where there were none earlier, especially those transacting foreign currencies; and there is increase in land prices, construction and housing repair, opening of deluxe taxi services and the like from the old city to the airport. While Indians of all religious and regional groups migrate to the Middle East, it is the general impression that Muslims have migrated in proportions larger than others.[142] The "Gulf Boom" impression is so widespread that even as sober a journalist as Maqbool Ahmad Siraj joyfully exaggerated the phenomenon as "Hyderabad Muslim Economy from Penury to Opulence."[143] More cautious analysis is needed to judge the outcome of the Gulf boom, especially considering the short term of job visas, lack of protection against unscrupulous employers in distant lands, and above all, the fact that most Gulf workers are unskilled laborers rather than skilled professionals.[144] Finally only a few actually know how to invest the "petro-dollars".

A slight improvement is also seen in private businesses that Muslims have gone into. In the 1960s in the Vishakhapatnam coastal industrial belt, an economist discovered Muslims to be proportionate to their population numbers in entrepreneurial activities.[145] By contrast Gujaratis, Marwaris, and Punjabis own most medium and major industries in Hyderabad, with only one in Muslim ownership during 1950-1980, according to G. Ram Reddy.[146] But improvement is clearly visible since Ram Reddy's findings. They now represent 11.97 and 15.48 percent of the small firms in 1983 and 1994 respectively, a clear improvement.[147] The

Hadramawti Arabs, long known as small-scale fruit-growers, became exporters to the Middle East.[148] Prosperity has come to a number of butchers, as meat consumption has expanded due to the gradual disappearance of vegetarianism among the upper caste Hindus, although the spread of meat consumption has not prevented anti-Muslim groups from attacking animal transportation during Eid, or against meat plants, as was demonstrated during the agitation against Al-Kabeer Meat Plant in Medak.[149] The publication of a business directory in Urdu at the turn of the twenty first century is both an index of growth of Muslim owned businesses and the resilience of Urdu in Andhra Pradesh. Though not all the businesses advertising in the directory are Muslim owned, they certainly predominate.[150] Similarly, a Muslim, Darwish Ghiyasuddin, heads the AP Tea Merchants Association and claimed that a majority of distributors are Muslim. The feudal and service classes of the Deccani Muslims long lampooned money as *hath ka mail,* or dirt to be washed off as soon as acquired. However, a new generation of men has begun to take advantage of market forces and have entered the banking sector. For instance, Sayyid Abid Hasan Rizwi (d. 1992) founded the Charminar Cooperative Urban Bank (CCUB) in 1985. The CCUB had a spectacular rise and fall. Starting with a small amount of deposits, it increased its deposits from a mere 17 crores in 1996 to a staggering 8,000 crores in 2002, before irregularities began. Matters came to a head when its chairman committed suicide on 26 February 2002 due to involvement in questionable practices.[151] Two smaller, less spectacular, examples are those of the Toor Baitulmal[152] and Darussalam Cooperative Bank in operation from the 1960s and 1980s respectively.[153]

Waqfs

Like other states, the endowed properties in Andhra Pradesh are quite rich. In fact they may be richer than some of the other states. As per the Waqf Survey Commissioner's report in 2001, there are 35, 703 *waqf* institutions in the state comprising 3632 mosques, 1600 *dargahs* (sufi shrines) 11, 373 *ashurkhanas* (Shiite shrines), 7380 *chillas*, 8371 graveyards, 1122 *idgahs*, 359 *panjas*, and 1776 miscellaneous properties worth 1385 crore rupees.[154] But more than half the properties are under illegal occupation,[155] including by Government itself! According to Muhammad Fariduddin, Minister for Minorities Welfare, in late 2004 "there are 1.45 lakh acres of *waqf* properties in which 60.000 acres of land are encroached."[156] Notable examples of *waqf* properties under the government's illegal occupation are Ishaq Madani Dargah in Vishakhapatnam comprising prime 5000 acres of land and nearly 250 acres of land in Guntur.[157] The Forest Department illegally acquired 488 acres of land belonging to the Dargah of Hazrat Mir Mahmud Awliya in 1995 in Kishan Bagh in Hyderabad.[158] It is not the Government alone that is the illegal occupier of *waqf* lands and properties. Politicians, sometime even those who are vociferous against the government encroachment, are equally involved as exposed through press reports throughout the 1990s and early 2000s.[159] The Waqf Board office is in complete disarray, a familiar situation in almost every state, but perhaps worse in AP where a financial scam led to the murder of an official in 1993.[160] On 21 September 1997, the present writer witnessed chief minister Chandrababu Naidu's unannounced visit to the Board office. The air quality in the office was so bad that Naidu could not stay there for long. Badly sneezing, the Chief Minister asked the surprised officials whether they have become immune to dust. The office itself was in a total mess with documents stacked ceiling high in no particular order. The chief minister was informed that there were 12000 files pending of which a mere 750 had been disposed off. Suggested improvements in the Waqf Board have come from many quarters,[161] but no improvement is visible.[162] The impotence of the Board is exemplified by the occupation of land adjoining its own office in the Haj House on the Public Garden Road in the capital.[163] Year after year, the Waqf Board provided *biryani* without charge on various religious functions, incurring huge waste of money totaling seven lakhs per annum. The appointment of an IPS officer S.A. Huda in December

2004, it is hoped will improve the *waqf* performance. He is clearly moving with drastic action by introducing economy measures.[164]

Notes

1 Horse dealers kept arriving in the Deccan, as late as the nineteenth century, exemplified by the cases of Abdullah of Risala-yi Abdullah and the family of Sir Mirza Ismail, see M.R.A. Baig, *In Different Saddles* (Bombay: Asia Publishing House, 1967) for Abdullah, and Mirza Ismail, *My Public Life* (London: Allen & Unwin, 1954); further information in Omar Khalidi, "Memoirs of Gen El-Edroos of Hyderabad," *Quarterly Journal of the Pakistan Historical Society* 42, part II (April 1994): 182-213.

2 Sanjay Subrahmanyam, "Iranians Abroad: Intra-Asian Elite Migration and Early Modern State Formation," *Journal of Asian Studies* 51, 2 (May 1992): 340-363.

3 For these groups see Omar Khalidi, "The Hadhrami Role in the Politics and Society of Colonial India, 1750s-1950s," pp. 67-81, in *Hadhrami Traders, Scholars and Statesmen in the Indian Ocean, 1750s-1960s*, edited by Ulrike Freitag & William G. Clarence-Smith (Leiden: E.J. Brill, 1997); "Sayyids of Hadhramaut in Early Modern India," *Asian Journal of Social Sciences* 32, 2 (2004): 329-352. "The Pathans in the Deccan: An Introduction," *Islam and the Modern Age* 22, no. 3 (August 1991): 214-29; "The Shi'ites of the Deccan: An Introduction," *Rivista degli Studi Orientali* 64, no. 1-2 (1990): 5-16; "African Diaspora in India: The Case of the Habashis of the Dakan," *Hamdard Islamicus* 4 (Winter 1988): 3-22.

4 However, the system remained unchanged in Hyderabad State until 1949 Jagirdari Abolition Act. To this day, many Brahmins's surname is Inamdar.

5 Most skills of a majority of these hakims were outdated compared to Europe, even as far back as 17th century, as indicated by the arrival of Dr. Peter de Laan, a Dutch surgeon based in the settlement at Masulipatnam to treat a Qutb Shahi princess in Golconda, who charged a staggering sum of 800 pagodas as fee, see Francois Bernier, *Travels in the Mogul Empire, 1656-58*, I, edited by A. Constable (London: Constable, 1891), p. 301.

6 Athar Ali, *The Apparatus of Empire: Awards of Ranks, Titles, Offices to the Mughal Nobility, 1574-1658* (Oxford: Oxford University Press, 1985); Satish Chandra, *Parties and Politics at the Mughal Court, 1707-1740* (Oxford: Oxford University Press, 2002); B.B. Misra, *The Indian Middle Classes* (London: Oxford University Press, 1961), claims that Hindus almost exclusively manned Mughal revenue department, see p. 187. Names such as *Munshi* (letter, report writer), *Majumdar* (the Bengalized form of *majmuadar*, revenue official), *Talukdar* (*taluqadar*, or landlord) and *Chitnis* (*chitthi nawis*, letter, report writer) are obvious examples of the Mughal legacy.

7 S.V. Desika Char, *Hinduism and Islam in India: Caste, Religion, and Society from Antiquity to Early Modern Times* (Princeton, N.J.: Markus Wiener, 1997), p. 89.

[8] Irfan Habib, "The Social Distribution of Landed Property in Pre-British India," *Enquiry,* New Series II, 3 (Winter 1965): 62-64.

[9] J.D.B. Gribble, *History of the Deccan*, II (London: Luzac, 1896), pp.5-6.

[10] A.M. Khusro, *Economic and Social Effects of Jagirdari Abolition and Land Reforms in Hyderabad* (Hyderabad: Department of Publications & Osmania University Press, 1958), p. 3.

[11] A.M. Khusro, ibid., p. 4. But 1500 jagirdars did not mean 1500 individual jargirdars, as the annual revenues were divided into various family members.

[12] Ibid..p. 1.

[13] Lucien Benichou, p. 15.

[14] Ibid., p. 14.

[15] S.C. Dube, *Indian Village* (Ithaca: Cornell University Press, 1956). The Indian village is Shahamirpet, not far from Hyderabad.

[16] Omar Khalidi, "Business Rajas: The Gujaratis, Gosains, and Marwaris of Hyderabad," *Deccan Studies* 4,1 (January-June 2006). pp. 49-79.

[17] Claude Markowits, "Les homes d'affaires musulmanes dans la premiere moitie du xxe siecle," pp. 111-126, in *Islam et Societe en Asie du Sud*, edited by Marc Gaborieau, Paris: Editions de l'Ecole des Hautes Etudes en Sciences Sociales/Collection *Purusartha* 9, 1986).

[18] Abuzafar Muiduddin Hasan, "Tazkirah-yi Muasharat-i Hyderabad," pp. 15-67, in *Suqut-i Hyderabad,* edited by Omar Khalidi (Hyderabad: Dar al-Ishaat Kul Hind Majlis-i Taamir-i Millat, 1998).

[19] *The Hyderabad Problem: The Next Step*, foreword by Jayaprakash Narayan, (Bombay: Hyderabad Struggle Committee, Socialist Party, 1948), p. 29.

[20] Meheroo Jussawala, *Industrial Finance in Former Hyderabad State, 1941-1956,"* unpublished PhD thesis, Department of Economics, Osmania University, 1961.

[21] *The Hyderabad Problem: The Next Step*, p. 29.

[22] C.V. Subbarao, "Role of the State in Industrialization: The Case of Hyderabad," pp. 208-242, in *The South Indian Economy: Agrarian Change, Industrial Structure and State Policy, 1914-1947,* edited by Sabyasachi Bhattacharya et al (New Delhi: Oxford University Press, 1991).

[23] Conversations with Begum Mir Laiq Ali and her sons, Karachi 1998.

24 The Birlas took over most of the Laiq Ali's businesses when he fled to Pakistan, see *State Government and Politics: Andhra Pradesh*, edited by G. Ram Reddy & B.A.V. Sharma (New Delhi: Sterling, 1979), p. 515.

25 *The Hyderabad Problem: The Next Step*, p. 30; Appendix II.

26 Muhammad Hanif, "Meri Aap Beti," *Rahbar-i Sanaat wa Tijarat* (January-February 1998): 63-68, and letter to the author from Kolkata dated 29 September 1998. Hanif has the distinction to publish perhaps the only Urdu journal dedicated to the promotion of business and industry.

27 Conversations with Bashiruddin Babu Khan, Hyderabad, 30 December 2004.

28 A.M.Khusro, op. cit. p. 12.

29 Mir Zahid Ali Kamil, *Communal Problem in Hyderabad* (Secunderabad: Hyderabad Printing Works, 1936), p. 248.

30 Ibid., p. 47-48.

31 John Roosa, *The Quandary of the Qaum: Indian Nationalism in a Muslim State, Hyderabad 1850-1948,* unpublished PhD thesis, University of Wisconsin-Madison, 1998), p. 97-98.

32 *All India Civil List*, issued Half Yearly (Bombay: Printed & Published under the Authority of the Govt. of India, January 1959), pp. 177-183.

33 V. Sarasvati Rao, "Development of the Nizam State Railways," pp. 9-21, in *Memoirs of Cyril Jones,* edited by Omar Khalidi (New Delhi: Manohar, 1991), citation on p. 21.

34 Syed Ahmad El-Edroos, "Memoirs of Maj. Gen. Syed Ahmed El-Edroos," edited by Omar Khalidi, *Journal of Pakistan Historical Society* 42 (April 1994): 184-313, figure on p. 205.

35 Constitutional Affairs Secretariat, H.E.H. The Nizam's Government, File number 35/57F, preserved in the State Archives, as cited in *Operation Polo Against Hyderabad 1948*, S.N. Prasad, ed. (New Delhi: Historical Section, Ministry of Defense, Government of India, 1972), p. 122. The government's official publication gives a figure of 17, 870, see *Hyderabad Reborn: First Six Months of Freedom,* September 18, 1948-March 7, 1949, compiled by Binod U. Rao, Director of Information (Hyderabad: Government of Hyderabad, 1949), p. 15.

36 Muhammad Ashraf, "The Hyderabad Army," *Military Historical Society Bulletin* 9, 34 (November 1958),p. 36 gives the lower figure, whereas Syed Ahmad El-Edroos, "Memoirs of Maj. Gen. Syed Ahmed El-Edroos," edited by Omar Khalidi, *Journal of Pakistan Historical Society* 42, I (April 1994),p. 205 gives a higher number.

37 *A Review of Hyderabad Finance*, issued by the Economic Advisor, Finance Department (Hyderabad: Government of Hyderabad, 1951),p. 193. It gives a figure of 10,000 men.

[38] Omar Khalidi, *Khaki and the Ethnic Violence in India* (New Delhi: Three Essays Collective, 2003), pp. 58, 81.

[39] *Hyderabad Reborn: First Six Months of Freedom*, p. 19.

[40] Ibid.

[41] For the political and military developments of 1947-48 in Hyderabad, see *Hyderabad: After the Fall*, edited by Omar Khalidi (Hyderabad: Hyderabad Historical Society, 1988).

[42] Omar Khalidi, "Rise and Fall of a Muslim Militia: The Rizakars of Hyderabad, 1940-1950," *Journal of Henry Martyn Institute* (January-June 2002): 3-26.

[43] See *Hyderabad: After the Fall*, and A.G. Noorani, "Of A Massacre Untold," *Frontline* (March 03-16, 2001), internet edition.

[44] A.K. Imadi, *The Nobles of Hyderabad: A Study in Social Change*, PhD thesis, Department of Sociology, Osmania University, 1978.

[45] A.M. Khusro, op. cit.

[46] V. Krishna Ananth, "A Controversy in Hyderabad," *Frontline* 20, 8 (2003) Internet edition.

[47] S. Sri Kishen, *45 Years a Rebel* (Hyderabad, 1952), p. 43-45.

[48] Mir Laik Ali, *Tragedy of Hyderabad* (Karachi: Pakistan Cooperative Book Society, 1962). He does not talk about his businesses or even his dramatic escape from house arrest in Hyderabad.

[49] Abdulkarim Babu Khan, d. 1968, spent two months in jail when Mir Laiq Ali fled to Pakistan in March 1950. The Government alleged that he was involved in Laiq Ali's escape.

[50] For the process of disbandment , see Syed Ahmed El-Edroos, p.205 and Muhammad Ashraf, "The Hyderabad Army", *Military Historical Society Bulletin* 9, 36 (May 1959), p.84. For the enlistment of a handful of officers of HSF, see Omar Khalidi, *Khaki and the Ethnic Violence*, op.cit., p.9.

[51] I have combined the HSF and the Irregular Force number, about 22,000 and 11,000 respectively to make a total of 33,000.

[52] Omar Khalidi, *Khaki and the Ethnic Violence*, pp.80-81.

[53] Interview with Shahid Jawid, grandson of Mustafa Ali Khan (d. 1980) in San Francisco, January 16, 2005; with Justice Sardar Ali Khan, son of Amir Ali Khan in Hyderabad, 29 December 2004, and Salih Habib, son of Habib Muhammad, in Chicago February 03, 2005. Habib Muhammad was imprisoned from 1948-1953 on unproven charges.

[54] William Dalrymple, *At the Court of the Fish-Eyed Goddess* (London: Harper Collins, 1998), see the chapter "Under the Charminar," pp. 219-240; and conversations with

Syed Ahsan, nephew of Baqir Husain Qureshi, San Jose, California, 21 May 2005; with Masood Hyder, Muhammad Hyder's son in Boston, August 1996.

55 Conversation with his son Sayyid Abdulmutakabbir, Hyderabad, June 1976.

56 C. Sri Kishen, *45 Years a Rebel* (Hyderabad, 1952), p. 205. Muneer Ahmad Khan, *Muslim Leadership in Hyderabad,* PhD dissertation, Osmania University, 1980,cites similar figures from contemporary newspapers, see p. 141.

57 P. Jaganmohan Reddy, *Down Memory Lane: The Revolutions I Lived Through* (Hyderabad: Booklinks Corporation, 2002), p. 327.

58 *Hyderabad Reborn: First Six Months of Freedom*, p. 15.

59 Mawlawi Habiburahman, *Chand Yaddashtain* (Hyderabad: Bahadur Yar Jang Academy, 1986).

60 Srinivas Lahoti, *Yeh Log* (New Delhi: Anjuman-i Tarrqi-yi Urdu, 1989), pp. 23-25.

61 Iqbal Masud, *Dream Merchants, Politicians, and Partition: Memoirs of an Indian Muslim* (New Delhi: Harper Collins, 1997),pp.58-59.

62 "India's No. 1 Tax Target," Business Week (20 September 1958), p. 151.

63 M.A. Rahman's son, M. Atiqur Rahman, ICS did not follow his father to Pakistan. He was India's ambassador to Iran and Germany besides other diplomatic posts. I am thankful to Salman Haider, former Foreign Secretary, Ministry of External Affairs for this information. Like his father, Atiqur Rahman wrote his name as M.A. Rahman.

64 Conversation with Anwar Soofi, Miami, Florida, July 29, 2004, the officers include Muhammad Abduljabbar, Mustafa Ahsan, Mustafa Akbar, Abul Arif, M.M. Ahmad, Hamiduddin Ahmad, Basit Baig, Farooq Baig, Khwaja Nizamuddin Hasan, Jamil Husain, Liyaqat Jang, Mir Nawaz Jang, Moin Nawaz Jang, Abbas Ali Khan, Mushtaq Ahmad Khan, Nasim Ahmad Khan, Bashir Husain Siddiqi, Mahdi Ali Siddiqi, Muhammad Tahir Siddiqi, Anwar Soofi, S.B. Sufi, Sayyid Taqiuddin. Mahdi Ali Siddiqi.

65 Mahdi Ali Siddiqi, *Bila Kam wa Kast: Khudniwisht Sawanih Umri* (Karachi: Shuaba-yi Tasnif wa Taalif, Jamia Karachi, 2002).

66 Syed Mahmood Alam, *Islam, Christianity and World Peace* (Manila: The Author, 1987). Written while resident in the Philippines, the introductory portion of the book is about the author's life in Hyderabad.

67 Pasha Begum Soofi, *Hamari Zindagi* (Karachi: Iwan-i Urdu, 1973).

68 Sabir Kamal, *Chand Namwar Civiliyan* (Hyderabad, 1998), lists only the HCS officers.

69 Syed Hashim Ali, "Baten jo yad rah gayin," *Sabras* (August-September 2000), p. 33.

70 Hasanuddin Ahmad, HCS, IAS officer, chairman of the AP State Minorities Commission (1990-91), interview, Hyderabad, January 20, 2004. He did write about this matter in *Munsif* ,daily newspaper, October 18, 2004, Internet edition in a piece on Sayyid Khalilullah Husayni, founder of Majlis-i Taamir-i Millat.

71 Akbar S.Ahmad, "Muslim Society in South India: The Case of Hyderabad," pp. 173-87, in *Hyderabad: After the Fall*, edited by Omar Khalidi (Hyderabad: Hyderabad Historical Society, 1988), citation on 185.

72 "Actually in India, It is Hindus, who Are Discriminated Against," Interview to *The Pioneer*, New Delhi, 08 November 1992, as reproduced in *Radiance* (22-28 November 1992), p. 2. It must have been an extraordinary statement to make in the bitterly anti-Muslim environment at the height of the Hindutva movement for Baburi Masjid demolition.

73 Muhammad Shafiquzzaman, Ahmad Nadeem, Rajen Habib Khwaja, Syed Ali Murtaza Rizwi, and Muhammad Ali Rafat. "Muslim Officers Shun State," *Deccan Chronicle* (10 October 2005) Electronic edition.

74 Osmania University Diary (Hyderabad, 1990).

75 Figures based on Osmania University Diary, 1997 as cited by Masood Ali Khan, "Education of Muslims in Andhra Pradesh," p. 143, in *Education and Muslims in India Since Independence*, edited by A.W.B. Qadir et al (New Delhi: Institute of Objective Studies, 1998).

76 *Siyasat* 9 September 2004, Internet edition.

77 *Report on Socio-Economic Survey of Minorities in Andhra Pradesh, 1989*. Prepared by Osamania University, Sponsored by The AP Minorities Commission (Hyderabad, 1989). This mimeographed pamphlet of a bare 17 pages is a summary of the survey conducted nearly 15 years ago. Mirza Ansar Baig, the then Chairman of the Commission, who has the voluminous Report claims that since the Report has not been placed in the AP Legislature, it cannot be made public. Personal interview, Hyderabad, 10 August 1990.

78 "55 Percent of Rural Population Landless: Survey," *The Hindu* (09 January 2004), Internet edition.

79 "Muslims Lag Behind in Development: Study," *The Hindu* (16 July 2004), Internet edition. This study was conducted in Anantapur by five NGOs, represented by K. Qasim Peeran and Renuka Devi.

80 S.A.A. Saheb, "Dudekula Muslims of Andhra Pradesh," *Economic and Political Weekly* (15 November 2003): 4908-4912. For an earlier account, see M.S.A. Majid, "Cottage Industries of South India and the Muslims," pp. 16-19, in *Muslim Year Book of India and… Pakistan*, edited by S.M. Jamil (Bombay: Bombay Newspaper Company, 1948).

The most comprehensive work on this subject is in Telugu by I. Daud, *Nurbashyiulu: Charitra-Sanskriti* (Hyderabad: Vishalandhra Book House, 2001).

81 See the biographical piece on "Qasim Ali Abid," a leader of the Muslim weavers and a member of Rajya Sabha, from 1972-78, in *Siyasat* (29 June 1981), p. 4.

82 A handful of anthropologists excepted, for example see the study of a miniscule Muslim group of country doctors in East and West Godavari, Krishna and Guntur, by P. Meera Khan and V.K.R. Manchiraju, "The Baids of Andhra Pradesh," *Man in India* 46, 1 (March 1966): 14-32.

83 Mohammad Siddiq, "Woman Village Head Wins UNDP's Award," *India Abroad* (9 October 1998), p. 8. Rivalries within the village however, put Fatima Bi in difficult circumstances, see "UN Award-Winner in Dumps," *The Hindu* (1 December 2003), internet edition.

84 "DWCRA Fails to Reach Muslim Women," *Deccan Chronicle* (18 November 2001) Internet edition.

85 G. Subramaniam, B. Ramakrishana Rao, and A. Babu Rao, "Woolen Carpet Industry in Andhra Pradesh: A Survey," *SEDME* 9, 1 (March 1982): 45-59. Earlier account in J.D. Rees, *Lord Connermara's Tours in India, 1886-1890 (*London: Kegan Paul, 1892), pp. 274-76.

86 Madhu M. Raghunath, *A Living Wage: Strategies for Implementation of Minimum Wages: The Case of the Indian Beedi Industry*," MCP thesis, Department of Planning, M.I.T., 2001.

87 Mulla Asgherali M.M. Jaffer, "World Federation Frees the Debt-Slaves of India," *Shia World* (March 1987):1-3, This refers to a Muslim community of *bidi* rollers in Avalkonda, Chittoor district.

88 Maqbool Ahmad Siraj, "Decline of the Muslim Artisan," *Radiance* (25-31 October 1987), p.6.

89 "Beedi Barons: Rolling in Money," *India Today* (15 November 1989): 50-52.

90 Scheduled Caste by definition excludes Muslims and Christians, only Hindus, Sikhs and Jains can be SCs according to the Constitution. See *Report of the Backward Classes Commission, 1982,* headed by N.K. Muralidhara Rao (Hyderabad: Government Central Press, 1986). p. 31.

91 Ibid., p. 26.

92 Interview with Muhammad Salim, former Chairman Waqf Board, Hyderabad, 16 December 2004.

93 Jeremy Seabrook, *Notes from Another India* (London: Pluto Press, 1995), see the chapter "The Lacquer Bangle Makers of Hyderabad, pp. 176-182.

94 "Shahr ke Musalman Dhobi," *Munsif* daily newspaper (16 October 1999) Internet edition.

95 *People of India*, vol. 13, *Andhra Pradesh*, 3 vols. edited by K.S.Singh (New Delhi: Affiliated East West Press, 2003), contains anthropological information, albeit often unreliable.

96 "Sculptures Beyond Religious Barriers," *Deccan Chronicle* (August 16, 1999) Electronic edition.

97 Yasmin Mahmood and David H. Wells, "Progress Through Preservation," *Saudi Aramco World* (September-October 2000): 2-9. This is the brainchild of Abid Hasan Safrani, d. 1984, an associate of Netaji Subhash Chandra Bose.

98 Hajira Begum, Satyananda Sahoo, and M. Mohsin, "Work Participation and Labor Supply of Muslim Women: Determinants and Constraints," *Indian Journal of Economics* 298/75 (1995): 363-396.

99 *Report on a Socio-Economic and Health Survey of Street Beggars in Hyderabad—Secunderabad City Area* (Hyderabad: Indian Institute of Economics, 1956).

100 *Report on Socio-Economic and Health Survey of Hut-Dwellers of Hyderabad City,"* (Hyderabad: Indian Institute of Economics, 1959); Ratna Naidu, "A Study of Slums in Hyderabad-Secunderabad," *Indian Journal of Social Work* 39 (1978): 297-312.

101 *A Socio-Economic Survey of Rickshaw Drivers in Hyderabad City Area (*Hyderabad: Indian Institute of Economics, 1962).

102 See the biography of Jahandar Afsar, who formed a union to fight for the rights of these employees, Musa Iqbal, *Jahandar Afsar: Hayat wa Khidamat* (Hyderabad, 2002).

103 Sadiqa Peerbhoy, "A Fading Vignette," *The Statesman* (9 March 1977).

104 "Muslims Neglected in Sirpur Paper Mills," *Radiance* (22-28 October 1995), p.4.

105 *Bulletin of the Hyderabad Metropolitan Project* (Hyderabad, 1966).

106 Waheeduddin Khan, "How Hyderabad Was Studied," *Bulletin of Madras Development Seminar Series*, Supplement , 13, no. 12 (December 1983):175-82.

107 *Qadim Shahr ka Maashi Survey*, conducted by Amjad Baghi (Hyderabad: Siyasat, 1985), in the same volume, pp. 69-76, a summary of SETWIN survey is given.

108 M.A. Siraj, "A Socio-Economic Profile of the Old City," *Islamic Voice* (November 1991), p.5.

109 A. Narendra, "Economic Decline in Hyderabad," *Urban India* 19, 2 (1999): 31-45; Odette & Alain Vaguet, *Du Bidonville a l'epidemie: la crise urbaine indienne a Hyderabad* (Talence Cedex, France: Centre d'Etudes de Geographie Tropicale, CNRS, Domaine Universitaire de Bordeaux, 1993); Fatima Ali Khan, Cliff Moughtin, and Sheila Prasad, "Urban Design and Spontaneous Developments: A Case Study in Hyderabad," *Interchange* 6 (1991): 9-40.

[110] Ranta Naidu, *Old Cities, New Predicaments: A Study of Hyderabad* (New Delhi: Sage, 1990), pp. 98-100.

[111] Mohammad Shafiquzzaman, *Problems of Minorities' Education* (Hyderabad: Booklinks, 2001), written by an IAS who has worked in the Minorities Welfare Department, thus highly informative about the state role in education.

[112] *Report on Minorities* (New Delhi: Ministry of Home Affairs, 14 June 1983), as cited in Mushirul Hasan, *Legacy of a Divided Nation*, p.290.

[113] Jaafar Sharif, "Muslim Representation in Andhra Judiciary," *Radiance* (24 March 1974), p. 10.

[114] "Representation of Muslims in Judicial Service in 1981," *Muslim India* (December 1983), p. 552.

[115] *Muslim India* (April 1984), p. 189. In the 1950s, the judges included A.M. Ansari, Sayyid Taqi Bilgrami, Siyadat Ali Khan, Khaliluzzaman Siddiqi; in the 1960s, Sharafuddin Ahmad, Qamar Husain, K.A. Muktader, and Muhammad Mirza. Sardar Ali Khan was appointed a judge in AP High Court in 1980, serving until 1992; thereafter, Syed Shah Muhammad Qadiri was appointed a judge in 1986, between 1995-97, three Muslims, Muhammad Habib Shams Ansari, Bilal Nazki, and Sayyid Saadatullah Husaini were appointed judges of AP High Court. Qadiri became a judge of the Supreme Court in 2003.

[116] B.S.A. Swamy, *A Caste Captures AP Judiciary* (Hyderabad, 2005), p. 3.

[117] Omar Khalidi, *Khaki and the Ethnic Violence in India*, pp. 80-83.

[118] National Crime Records Bureau, *Crime in India* (New Delhi: Ministry of Home Affairs, 2000).

[119] "Memorandum on Oriental Manuscripts Library in Hyderabad," *Radiance* (23-29 August 1987), p. 4.

[120] Omar Khalidi, "Muslim Ministers in the State Cabinets: The Cases of Karnataka and Andhra Pradesh (1956-2000)", *Radiance* (16-27 October 2001), pp. 16-17.

[121] Aniket Alam, "More Literates among Muslims than Hindus," *The Hindu* (16 September 2004) internet edition.

[122] Abdul Karim, an engineer, went to court when denied promotion and succeeded! See "New Engineer in Chief for Panchayat Raj," *The Hindu* (11 July 2004) Internet edition.

[123] K.S. Shafiq, "Muslim Backwardness," *Radiance* (24 December 1995), p.11, cites several experiences of discrimination against Muslims when he was working as Deputy Commissioner for Labor at Hindustan Shipyard in Vishakhapatnam, at AP State Industrial Undertaking, and at Administrative Staff College in Hyderabad.

124 *Inclusion of Muslims in Backward Classes, Report of an Opinion Poll*, conducted by *Siyasat Daily* (Hyderabad: *Siyasat*, 1995). The poll found overwhelming support among Muslims.

125 "Five Percent Job Quota for Muslims Announced," *The Hindu* 13 July 2004, Internet edition.

126 "HC Strikes Down Muslim Quota GO, Orders BC Panel," *Deccan Chronicle* (21 September 2004), Internet edition.

127 Only excerpts from the Commission's report have appeared in the Urdu press, and neighboring states have sought the report in order to consider reservation. The full text of the report when made available to the public would be revealing.

128 "State Assembly Passes Muslim Reservation Bill," *The Hindu* 6 October 2005, Internet edition.

129 Muhammad Shafiquzzaman, *Problems of Minorities Education.*

130 Zoya Hasan and Ritu Menon , *Educating Muslim Girls: A Comparison of Five Cities.*

131 Rahat Abrar and M. Qamar Ishaque, *Directory of Muslim Educational Institutions in India* (New Delhi: Institute of Objective Studies, 2002), pp. 1-31.

132 Aizza, Anwaruluoom, Madina, Mukhaffam Jah, Nimra, Noor, Owaisi, Shadan, Syed Hashim, and Vazir Sultan engineering colleges; Deccan Medical College, MESCO College of Pharmacy. The principal promoter for Shadan Medical College announced government approval in 2005.

133 "Muslim-Managed Degree Colleges," *Muslim India* (July 1996), p. 319.

134 "Minorities Do Not Benefit from Self Financing Schools," *Islamic Voice* (October 2001) Internet edition, being the statement of Muhammad Fasihuddin, an activist exposing scams in the minority colleges, see "Minority Rights Leader Passes Away," *The Hindu* (03 March 2004) Internet edition.

135 "AP Chief Minister N.T. Rama Rao's Statement on Minorities Welfare," *Muslim India* (December 1988), pp. 569-561; "AP CM Naidu's Report on Minorities Welfare…24 February 1997," *Muslim India* (October 1998), pp. 443-444.

136 Akbaruddin Owaisi's speech in the AP Legislative Assembly as reported in *Siyasat* 2 March 2005, Internet edition.

137 "Mahkama-yi Aqliyati Bahbud ki Karkardagi…" *Siyasat* (27 August 2004) Internet edition.

138 *Strategy Paper on Welfare of Minorities* (Hyderabad: Government of Andhra Pradesh, Minorities Welfare Department, 2 February 2001).

139 *Emergence of APSMFC* (Hyderabad: APSMFC, 2004), document provided by the Managing Director M.A. Azeem in Hyderabad, 26 December 2004.

[140] Probe Sought into Affairs of Minorities Finance Corporation," *The Hindu* (30 September 2003) Internet edition.

[141] "Ex-MD Forces His Way Into Office," *The Hindu* (02 February 2005) Electronic edition.

[142] Syed Majeedul Hasan, "Indian Muslims and Foreign Exchange Remittances: A Sample Survey," *Journal Institute of Muslim Minority Affairs* 1 (1980): 89-97.

[143] Maqbool Ahmad Siraj, "Hyderabad Muslim Economy from Penury to Opulence," *Islamic Voice* (November 1991): 20.

[144] The fate of Hyderabad workers caught in the Gulf War I of 1991 is the subject of Afzal Shariff's *Indian Muslim Labor* (New Delhi: Anmol, 1998).

[145] Wayne E. Nafziger, *Caste, Class and Entrepreneurship: A Study of Indian Industrialists* (Honolulu: University of Hawaii Press, 1978), p. 78.

[146] G. Ram Reddy, "Caste, Class and Dominance in Andhra Pradesh", p. 297 in *Dominance and State Power in India,* I, edited by Francine Frankel and M.S.A. Rao (New Delhi: Oxford University Press, 1989).

[147] *Directory, Federation of Andhra Pradesh Chamber of Commerce & Industry* (Hyderabad, 1983, 1993).

[148] "Figs from Barkas Tickle Palates in Europe," *Deccan Chronicle* (5 September 2004) Internet edition.

[149] Ayalur Balakrishnan, "Hindu Organizations Threaten to Tear Down Al-Kabeer Plant," *Saudi Gazette* (11 September 1994), p. 11; Safi Abdurrahim, "Al-Kabeer: A Giant Name in Meat Industry," *Arab News* (Jeddah) (6 February 1996), p. 6. Al-Kabeer is run by Ghulamuddin Maqbool of Mumbai in partnership with S.C.Subberwal, a Hindu.

[150] *Deccan Business Directory,* compiled by Syed Riazuddin and Amani M. Ameeruddin (Hyderabad: Urdu Market Research & Advertisers, 2001).

[151] "Charminar Chief Banked on His Clout," *Deccan Chronicle* (26 February 2002), Internet editon.

[152] M.G.I. Bagsiraj, *Islamic Financial Institutions of India: Progress, Problems and Prospects* (Jeddah: Scientific Publishing Center, King Abdulaziz University, 2003), p34.

[153] In 1993, a scam was uncovered at Darussalam Cooperative Bank, see the *Deccan Chronicle* report reproduced as "Financial Scandal at Daruussalam Educational Trust, Hyderabad," *The Minaret* (New York 16 January 1994), p. 8.

[154] A.P. State Wakf Board, *Annual Report for years 1997-2000* (Hyderabad: The Board, 2000); and an unpublished document entitled *Hon'ble C.M. Review Meeting on 18-10-2004 at 12:30PM,* given to me by S.A. Huda, Officer on Special Duty, in Hyderabad December 2004; "More than Half Wakf Land is Encroached," *Deccan Chronicle* (23 September

2001). Internet edition. Sultan Omer in his thesis claimed an even higher figure of waqf properties, see Public Policy Towards Muslims: A Case Study of Hyderabad, Master of Philosophy dissertation, Department of Political Science, Osmania University, 1980, p. 154. He lists 42, 341 properties as opposed to 35, 703. Either he counted differently or was supplied a different figure by the Waqf Board of his time (1980) or the properties were sold away illegally between the two decades!

155 Ibid.

156 "State Firm on Quota for Muslims, Says Fariduddin," *The Hindu* (20 November 2004) Internet edition.

157 "Wakf Land Encroached on by State Government," *Deccan Chronicle* (20 April 1999), "Wakf Land in City Under State Threat," *Deccan Chronicle* (02 August 1999); "Wakf Land Either Encroached or in Dispute,": *Deccan Chronicle* (03 November 2001), Internet edition.

158 Interview with Bashiruddin Babu Khan, Hyderabad, 11 January 2004.

159 See R. Balaji, "ACB Probes Massive Graft in Wakf Board," *Deccan Chronicle* (21 July 1992), p.1; Shaik Ahmed Ali, "Wakf Revolving Fund Vanishes into Thin Air," *The Times of India* (26 December 2001), Internet edition; "Ramulu Turns Guns on Virasat [Rasool Khan, MLA]," *Deccan Chronicle* (2 August 2002) Internet edition.

160 M.A. Mannan, "Unholy Mess: Scam Stalks Wakf Board," *India Today* (15 March 1993), p. 17.

161 Hasanuddin Ahmad and Ahmedulla Khan, *Strategies to Develop Waqf Administration in India* (Jeddah: Islamic Research & Training Institute, Islamic Development Bank, Working Paper no. 50, 1998), pp. 79-97. Syed Dastagir Pasha, "Socio-Economic Potential of Awqaf in Andhra Pradesh and their Administration," pp. 149-158, in *Awqaf Experience in South Asia,* edited by Syed Khalid Rashid (New Delhi: Institute of Objective Studies, 2002).

162 "Wakf Board Does it Again," *Deccan Chronicle* (1 January 2005), p. 13. About an illegal sale of 39.16 acres of Waqf land in a village in Vijayawada.

163 "Haj House se Muttasil Imarat," *Munsif* Urdu Daily (02 May 2005), Internet edition.

164 J.S. Iftekhar, "Wakf Board Tightening the Purse Strings," *The Hindu* (12 September 2005) Internet edition.

KARNATAKA

The Kannada-speaking region of the Deccan was variously divided politically and administratively into the princely state of Mysore, Hyderabad Karnatak and Bombay Karnatak from around the 18th century. Muslim presence in the region dates from the thirteenth century, but increased after the military conquest by Muhammad Tughlaq. He conquered the region with the rest of the Deccan in early fourteenth century. From that period on, Karnataka was ruled in succession by the Vijayanagar rulers, the Adil Shahis of Bijapur, Mughals and then by the Wodeyar rajas. Mid-eighteenth century saw the rise of Haydar Ali, a military commander of Mysore, who seized power from the reigning Wodeyar raja in 1763. Tipu Sultan succeeded his father Haydar Ali upon his death in 1782. The reign of Tipu is crowded with a number of wars with neighbors and the foreigners. He ruled barely 17 years, and died fighting the British in 1799. The British restored the Wodeyar dynasty of Mysore that ruled much of the region until independence in 1947, but significant parts of the Kannada areas remained in Hyderabad State and Bombay Province until the 1956 State reorganization. In 1973, the Mysore State was renamed Karnataka. The Muslim population in Karnataka since 1961 may be seen in this table:

Table I
Muslim Population in Karnataka, 1961-2001

Year	*Muslim Pop.*	*Muslim %*	*Rural Muslim %*	*Urban Muslim %*	*Muslim Lit. %*	*Urdu Pop. %*
1961	2,323,376	9.87	56.4	43.6		
1971	3,113,298	10.63				
1981	4,104,000	11.05				
1991	5,234,023	11.06				9.66
2001	6,463,127	12.2			70.1	

Source: *Census of India.*

Land Ownership and Agriculture

According to a socio-economic survey of religious minorities done in 1994, nearly 50 percent of the minorities live in rural areas.[1] Though the category of minorities includes small groups such as Buddhists, Jains, and Sikhs, even so the percentage of Muslims as urban-dwellers is very high. Consequently it makes sense when the survey found that only a miniscule 3.1 percent of Muslims are cultivators.[2] Independent academic research by Mumtaz Ali Khan seems to confirm the survey.[3] In a survey of 245 villages in Tumkur in 1982, 59 percent of the Muslims were found to be engaged in non-agricultural occupations, such as laborers, menials, artisans, professionals and salaried workers.[4] Muslims constitute a disproportionate percentage of non-farm self-employed persons, thus in the informal sector.[5] But wherever there are Muslim-dominated villages, such as Gulwar in Gulbarga, most are engaged in agriculture.[6] The only big landowner in Karnataka may have been the Nawabs of Savanur, a tiny principality in what is now Dharward and Belgaum districts.[7] Communal violence is generally regarded an urban phenomenon, though there are plenty of exceptions; for instance, M.K. Doddi, an obscure, Muslim-dominated village of 40 hardworking families, near Channapatna the toy town, simply "ceased to exist" in 1990, when it was wiped out by a violent Hindu mob, in the words of Sudheendra Kulkarni.[8] Few Muslims own land.[9] In fact, Muslims own fewer acres of land, draft and milch animals than even the Scheduled Castes.[10] As in other parts of the country, Karnataka has its share of Muslims engaged in lowest-income occupations such as snake charmers and bird tamers.[11]

A number of Muslims have been involved in sericulture. Sericulture in Karnataka owes its beginnings to official experimentation in the late eighteenth century. Though the record of Tipu's efforts is fragmentary, he certainly was enthusiastic about sericulture. It is recorded that in 1785, he was searching abroad for silkworms and for people expert in rearing them. He evidently sent representatives to Bengal, and beyond in the Persian Gulf, to obtain worms and experts. Tipu's efforts bore no immediate fruit but the tree clearly survived. The industry is said to have been revived in 1802 by a member of the Mastan family, the great-grandfather of F.M.Abdul Quddus of Channapatna. He prepared in 1932 an account of his family's involvement in the industry since that time.[12] The revival, it is clear, had the support of the great Purnaiya, finance minister under Tipu, and subsequently regent and minister after the Wodeyar restoration. The largely Muslim town of Closepet, now Ramanagaram, founded in 1800, became a noted sericulture center along with Yelandur. More widely, mulberry was cultivated and Muslims took up rearing and reeling, particularly in the Bangalore district.[13] However, in the 1870s, attacked by persistent bacteria, the silkworms perished and even the introduction of fresh stock did not substantially improve the worm-culture. A few seri culturalists, like M.H.P. Ghatalah, survived against great odds, but not many.[14] In early 2004, UNDP enquiries revealed that 90 percent workers and entrepreneurs in this business were Muslims.[15] The silk industry faces stiff competition from synthetic silk manufacturers of China and Japan.

Labor, Commerce and Industry

A number of Muslims are found in semi-skilled labor such as *darzi* (tailors), and *karigar* (workers) in ivory inlay work; makers of Bidri ware were historically located in the town of Bidar.[16] Others in the semi-skilled category of workers include the *Baghban* (gardeners), *Bihishti* (water porters), *Chhapparband* (roofers), *Dhobi* (washer men), *Faqir* (mendicants), *Hajjam* (barbers), *Qasai/Qureshi* (mutton and beef butchers) respectively, *Mochi* (cobblers), *Naalband* (horseshoe makers), *Pendar* (horsemen), *Sikkaligar* (blacksmiths), and the like.[17] But larger number of Muslims, particularly children, is employed as *bidi*-rollers, *agarbatti* (incense stick-makers), *Laddaf, Momin, Naddaf* (cotton cleaners) and the like. [18] Such working class groups, needless to say, live below the poverty line as documented by G. Thimmaiah,[19] and the income level of Muslims is lower than those of the Hindus.[20]

Some times "...the fact that Muslims seem to have remained on the fringes of society has made them more versatile. Their greater enterprise cannot be explained by a lack of interest in the land, for they, like the Wangla peasant, are small landowners. Many of my peasant informers regarded a shop as a gold mine. When I enquired why they themselves did not open shops, they insisted emphatically that it would never do for a peasant to squat on the floor of his shop and offer goods to passers-by, who might be of lower castes or even untouchables. 'A Muslim can do this, but not a peasant. They also claimed that if a peasant opened a shop (and there in fact are two caste shops in the village), he could never make money like a Muslim shopkeeper, because a peasant was expected to be charitable and therefore obliged to sell goods on credit, a Muslim need not do this."[21] But overall, only a small number of Muslims have been in businesses both historically as well as at present in the twenty first century. Only 0.3 percent of the minorities were reported to be engaged in wholesale business and 1.5 percent of the Muslim population was engaged in retail businesses, and only 0.3 percent in street vending.[22] Like handicrafts elsewhere, the Bidri ware has flourished due to an expanding market.[23] Channapatna, the town known for silk rearing, is equally famous for handcrafted toys, employing mostly Muslims.[24] Many have prospered by responding to the demands of changing tastes of the market.[25]

Cooperative banks have a long history in the country, often established by caste-based organizations; Muslims are new comers to this field. Karnataka Muslims have pioneered Muslim entry into these cooperative banks[26] and achieved spectacular success, exemplified by the rise of Amanat Cooperative Bank established in 1977, according to its website.[27] Its membership was reportedly close to 40,000 in early 2000. However, certain fraudulent practices involving a staggering 61 crore rupees in 2001-2002, resulted in a huge loss of community confidence in the bank and its authorities.[28] A systematic survey of Muslim business people of the state may reveal a number of success stories. In his pioneering study of the new Muslim businessmen in India, Theodore Wright found only a few Karnataka businessmen, but deeper probes are likely to unearth many more.[29] For instance, there are success stories associated with the major construction firm India Builders Corporation of Ziaullah Sharif who have been in the business for three generations since the maharajas' time in Bangalore;[30] other famous companies include Syed Muhammad Beary Group,[31] HMS Granites, H.M. Group of Construction Companies, and the like. Waheeda Rahman (b. 1938) a well known film star of the 1960s and 1970s started a new career by launching a company Good Earth Foods along with a friend Ashrafa Sattar.[32] As the hi-tech capital of India, Bangalore now has a number of Muslim entrepreneurs, such as S.M.M. Azeez of Toyama Electric Private Limited,[33] and Muhammad Majeed of Sami Labs, a leading producer and exporter of nutraceuticals,[34] to name only a few in a growing list.[35] A small town in Karnataka, Bhatkal is home to an ancient Muslim community with reputation as traders.[36] Many among the Nawait community of Bhatkal[37] are in businesses, small and medium, with deep connections to the Persian Gulf states.[38] One of the community members, Syed Muhammad Arshad Muhtashim, a Mangalore-based builder, was reported to start a commercial airline.[39] However, the relative prosperity of the Bhatkal Muslims has attracted the envy of competitors who, in collusion with the Hindutva brigade, created riots aimed at the destruction of businesses, as has been the case since the 1980s culminating in 1993's major anti-Muslim violence.[40] In Kolar, previously famous for its now extinct gold mines, Muslim shopkeepers and owners of silk industry, suffered enormous losses in the violence that took place in 1990, ruining many in the process. Channarayapatna, a sleepy little town less than a hundred miles from Bangalore was the scene of anti-Muslim violence in which businesses worth $100,000 were destroyed in January 1983, according to journalists.[41]

On its part, the state government has begun to play a role in the advancement of the community. It provided one crore rupees to establish a Karnataka Minorities Development Corporation Limited (KMDC) in 1985.[42] According to the KMDCL figures, it has given 3922.97 lakh rupees as Margin Money or business loans during the financial year 2004 to 74249 beneficiaries.[43] From the beginning critics complained of inadequate funds at the disposal of the KMDCL, certainly not matching the needs.[44] The Corporation has a number of loan categories, including those for students pursuing professional education, for women entrepreneurs, for vocational training, for digging bore wells, for animal husbandry and the like.[45] The Corporation faces problems common to all government schemes, in particular loan default, as well as dishonest executives.[46]

Education and the Tertiary Sector

A detailed description and analysis of the state of education among Muslims is absent. An 1870 British report on the subject, based on statistics from 8 towns in princely Mysore, shows Muslims to be a lower percentage of the student population when compared to other communities.[47] A little more than a century later, a survey of Bangalore schools done by Mohammed Peer finds the educational condition not greatly different from that prevailing in the nineteenth century.[48] Most of the Urdu medium schools in Karnataka—and there are many more than realized—are producing mere matriculates who do not plan to pursue higher studies.[49] A survey of Muslim-managed high schools in mid 2004 came to the following conclusions: "Most Urdu medium schools are doing miserably; privately-managed but government-aided Urdu-medium schools in Bidar and Gulbarga seem promising; the best results are those by privately-managed English-medium schools in south Karnataka districts; the results of Muslim pupils in schools run by other communities are better than those run by Muslims themselves, such as Anjuman-i Islam Schools in Hubli, Anjuman-i Hami-yi Muslimin in Bhatkal and al-Mahmood in Shimoga.[50] As regards the question of Urdu-medium schools, it is clear that the Muslim community prefers English medium schools given the unequal competition Urdu schools face with English and Kannada-medium schools. An alternative approach may be to teach Urdu as a mandatory subject to those desiring to learn it while the rest of the education is imparted through English.[51] Evidently, such is the trend, according to Maqbool Ahmad Siraj.[52] Despite the trend, there are at least a hundred, if not more madrasas in the state.[53] The goal of full literacy is far from achieved in Karnataka, particularly among the women and the rural areas, as "Muslims have the lowest level of education after the 7th standard."[54] When the base of education—primary through higher secondary education is week, it is understandable why Muslim students do not successfully compete in examinations leading to admissions into professional colleges. Little wonder that Muslims are not proportionate to their numbers in engineering, medical and dental colleges in the state as a 1984 survey concluded.[55] To boost the number of Muslims in professional colleges, organizations such as the Al-Ameen Educational Society established a medical college in 1984 in Bijapur, and engineering, dental and pharmacy colleges in other parts of the state.[56] A similar set of colleges have been established in Gulbarga by Khwaja Bandah Nawaz Educational Society in Gulbarga, capped by the opening of the medical college in 2000.[57] There is an engineering college in Bhatkal established by Anjuman-i Hami-yi Muslimin[58] and a dental college run by Farooqiya Educational Society in Mysore. Besides the professional colleges, educational societies have been running numerous schools and colleges in arts and commerce.[59] Independent assessment of these professional and technical colleges suggests that these institutions benefit Muslim students willing or capable of paying huge capitation fee.[60] Poor but meritorious students are often denied admission.[61] The capitation fee system benefits less qualified children of affluent parents such as those working overseas. Since financially able Muslim students are not always available, professional college seats are sold to non-Muslims, a bonanza for college authorities.[62] Sometimes, institutions have been established without assessing the needs, resulting in white elephants.[63]

Some documentation on the ethnic and religious composition of the Mysore rulers Haydar Ali and Tipu Sultan's army is known, but we do not have similar information about the administrative personnel during their rule.[64] We know for instance that his administration included Purnaiya, who had served his father as well, and a large number of Hindus were in his employment.[65] Although Tipu abolished jagirs, except for his sons and senior commanders, he did not create a class of *jagirdars,* unlike his counterparts in Hyderabad.[66] Thus Mysore did not have a large *jagirdari* or land owner class when Tipu was defeated and killed in 1799. The British exiled the sultan's sons to Vellore in the Madras Presidency, then to Calcutta in 1806, where the great-grandsons even became sheriffs in 1891 and 1913. The rest of the Sultan's court dispersed, some taking refuge in Hyderabad.[67] A new administration took over after the Sultan's defeat and death. Even after the British conquest of Mysore, the legal and administrative system did not change overnight. When judicial courts were established in 1805, the language of legal proceedings was still Persian, to the advantage of Muslims. Only in late 1830s was Persian replaced by English.[68] The line of enlightened maharajas who ruled Mysore for nearly a century and a half, 1800s to 1947 seem to have treated their Muslim subjects fairly, including the appointment of Mirza Ismail, as the diwan from 1926-1941.[69] Evidently Muslims were recruited to the "extent of 50 percent in Mysore Infantry, Lancers etc."[70] Furthermore, "they enjoyed 10 percent of intake in all technical and professional institutions. In appointments at the probationers' level, one person out of every seven persons was a Muslim. This practice was invariably followed in all departments of the Government."[71] Given these liberal measures, it is not surprising that in 1950, Mysore Muslims were recruited to 10.6 percent of the open government positions even though they accounted for only 6.3 percent of the population.[72] According to another source, Muslims held "13 percent of class I, II, and III posts in government service" in the 1950s and 1960s. [73] Muslims represented in 1981, 7.7 percent of the state judiciary.[74] In 1984, the Muslims represented 9.45 percent of the government services, lower than was the case earlier.[75] The Minorities Commission reported in 1989-90 that "the representation of Muslims in 16 [Government] departments is less than 5 % and in other departments it is between 5 and 10 %. In the Department of Food and Civil Supplies Muslims are just 3 %. Karnataka Government Secretariat has 4.52 Muslim employees."[76] Ten years later in 1994, the government-sponsored a survey of 88 percent of the Muslim population of the state. It found that the percentage of Muslims and Swethambar Jains in public services was less than the overall average for all minority communities.[77]

The State Minorities Commission came to the same conclusion, with the additional comment that there is inverse relationship between higher posts and Muslims![78] The most recent (1999) report on the subject makes similar reading.[79] Muslims are not proportionate to their population numbers in the state police service, as in many other departments.[80] In 1984, minorities as a whole represented 8.7 percent of the total police force, as against the total minority population percentage of 9 percent.[81] About a decade later in 1995, out of a total force of 53,000, Muslims numbered 3336, according to the government.[82] Figures available in 2000 show that Muslims represented 3951 of the police force as against 8500 SCs, 2185 STs, and 36296 all others.[83] In other words, in five years, Muslims improved their position only slightly. Following the pattern in other departments, it is safe to assume that even these belong to the lower ranks of the police. Syed Sadaqat Peeran, a member of the State Public Service Commission in the mid 1990s, attributes poor performance of his coreligionists to poor education and preparation rather than any other factor.[84] When basic education is poor, few make it to colleges. Even when in colleges, many do not have high occupational aspirations.[85] Independent professionals like doctors and engineers in the Muslim community were also disproportionate to the total population.[86] Considering the backward condition of the Muslims, Karnataka government declared Muslims to be an "Other Backward Class" (OBC) through a Government Order issued on 13 October 1986 when Ramakrishna Hegde was the chief minister.[87] This measure was followed by another G.O. issued on 17 September 1994 during the tenure of Chief Minister Veerappa Moily placing Muslims under II B category of reservation of 4 percent exclusively for Muslims.[88] Along with Kerala, Karnataka is the second state to declare the entire Muslim community economically and educationally backward, and eligible for reservation in educational institutions and employment. In fact Karnataka has taken the lead in establishing an unprecedented ministry for minority welfare on 28 June 2002, heralding a new era in modern Indian history.[89] It is too soon to judge the ministry's performance, but the precedent thus set augurs well for the minorities. Unlike other states, the Karnataka cabinets have had Muslims holding critical portfolios such as finance, thus making it possible to move the levers of power for ameliorative measures for a poor community.[90]

Muslim Waqf Board

According to a report of the Karnataka Waqf Board, there are a total of 18, 680 *waqfs* in the state.[91] But as elsewhere, Minorities Commission officials reported that "there are innumerable cases of illegal encroachments and occupation of these properties by the Government as well as the powerful sections of the community. The Commission is flooded with complaints of every sort regarding the illegal use and mismanagement of these properties. "During our tours, the members of the Commission were taken around and shown the places where such encroachments or illegal use or occupations has taken place. The Commission felt unable to remedy these matters."[92] Given the comments of the Minorities Commission, it is obvious that the situation in Karnataka is hardly unique.[93] As usual, some of the problems lie within the Waqf Board, as some of its chairmen have been removed due to illegal activities, often an inside job.[94] One of the major *waqfs* in Bangalore, The Agha Ali Askar Estate, occupied by Windsor Manor, the prime city hotel, had been leased out to it for a ridiculously low rent by unscrupulous or negligent officials. Thanks to the efforts of the Waqf Board, the Supreme Court directed the Windsor Manor, belonging to the Welcome group of hotels, to either vacate the premises or pay rent at the prevailing rates.[95] Such intervention is exceptional rather than the rule.

Notes

1 *Report of the High Power Committee on Socio-Economic and Educational Profile 1994 of Religious Minorities in Karnataka,* chairman K. Rahman Khan (Bangalore: Karnataka State Minorities Commission, 1995), p. 2.

2 Ibid., p. 30. The survey included 88 percent of all Karnataka Muslims, a high percentage, making the survey highly reliable.

3 Mumtaz Ali Khan, *Muslims in the Process of Rural Development: A Study of Karnataka* (New Delhi: Uppal, 1994); and the same author's "Planning Processes and Muslim Responses in Rural Karanatak, *ICSSR Newsletter* (1991): 75-79.

4 V.M. Rao, *Barriers in Rural Development* (Bangalore: Institute of Social and Economic Change, Working Paper, 1982).

5 Maitreyi Bordia Das, *Employment and Social Inequality in India: How Much Does Caste and Religion Matter?* Unpublished PhD dissertation, University of Maryland-College Park, 2002, p. 110.

6 C.G. Hussain Khan, *Marriage and Kinship among Muslims in South India* (Jaipur: Rawat, 1994).

7 K.N. Chitnis, *The Nawabs of Savanur* (New Delhi: Atlantic Publishers, 2000).

8 Sudheendra Kulkarni, "A Muslim-Dominated Village That Ceased to Exist," *The Sunday Observer* (14-20 October 1990) as reproduced in *Radiance* (4-10 November 1990), p. 6.

9 Ratna Naidu, "The Muslim Community in Bidar Since 1948," pp. 158-172, in *Hyderabad: After the Fall,* edited by Omar Khalidi (Hyderabad: Hyderabad Historical Society, 1988).

10 Abusaleh Shariff and Mehtabul Azam, *Economic Empowerment of Muslims in India* (New Delhi: Institute of Objective Studies, 2004), p. 47.

11 "Resettling Snake Charmers," *Islamic Voice* (August 2000) Internet edition.

[12] S.R. Charsley, *Culture and Sericulture: Social Anthropology and Development in a South Indian Livestock Industry* (London: Academic Press, 1982), pp. 74-75.

[13] Aruna Chandaraju, "Mysore Silk: Extending its Repertoire," *Swagat* (December 2005): 130-134, provides an excellent non-technical summary of the silk manufacture.

[14] *Mr. M.H.P. Ghatalah, His Life and Work* (Madras: Indian Patriot Press, 1916).

[15] http://hdrc.undp.org.in/childrenandpoverty/REFERENC/CASESTUD/SILKROUT/04siib.htm. "Blood on Silk," *Frontline* (06-19 January 2001) Internet edition, showing large number of children in this labor.

[16] Maqbool Ahmad Siraj, "The Silver Cloud that Hangs Over Bidar," *Arabia: The Islamic World Review* (April 1983):77-78.

[17] Anthropological profiles of these groups are in *People of India: Karnataka*, 3 vols., edited by K.S. Singh et al (New Delhi: Affiliated East-West Press, 2003).

[18] There is an incomplete list of such occupational groups—strangely called castes in "Karnataka Socio-Economic-cum-Educational Survey: Socio-Economic & Educational Profile of Muslim Community, 1984" *Muslim India* (September 1987): 414.

[19] G. Thimmaiah, *Inequality and Poverty: A Case Study* (Bombay: Himalaya Publishing House, 1983), regarding a 1974/75 study in Bangalore.

[20] Abusaleh Shariff and Mehtabul Azam, *Economic Empowerment of Muslims in India*, p. 18.

[21] Trude S. Epstein, *Economic Development and Social Change in South India* (Manchester: Manchester University Press, 1961), p. 62.

[22] *Report of High Power Committee on Socio-Economic and Educational Survey, 1994 of Religious Minorities in Karnataka*, p. 5.

[23] Ratna Naidu, "The Muslim Community in Bidar Since 1948," pp. 158-172, in *Hyderabad: After the Fall.*

[24] Maqbool Ahmad Siraj, "A Visit to Toy Town," *Arabia: The Islamic World Review* (December 1983),p. 80.

[25] Azmatullah Sharif, "Toy Town Transforms with the Trend," *Deccan Herald* (29 March 2005), Internet edition..

[26] M.G.I. Bagsiraj, *Islamic Financial Institutions of India: Progress, Problems and Prospects* (Jeddah: Scientific Publishing Center, King Abdulaziz University, 2003).

[27] http://www.bankersindia.net/bankexpo/bankexpo.htm?banks/amanath/display.htm.

[28] "Ceasefire in Amanath Bank," *Islamic Voice* (August 2003) Internet edition; "Amanath Bank Episode: Reckless Nepotism undid the Good Work," *Islamic Voice* (September

2003) Internet edition; and "Rahman Khan's Rejoinder," *Islamic Voice* (October 2003) Internet edition.

29 Theodore P. Wright, Jr., "The New Muslim Businessmen of India," pp. 37-46, in *Changing South Asia: Development and Welfare*, edited by Kenneth Ballhatchet and David Taylor (London: School of Oriental & African Studies, 1984). Wright's study is based on advertisements of Muslim businesses in *Radiance*, a similar study based on advertisements in *Islamic Voice* of Bangalore and *The Milli Gazette* of New Delhi has a great potential.

30 Conversation with Ziaullah Sharif in Bangalore, January 2004.

31 Outside Karnataka few have heard of Beary Muslims, mostly farm labor, mainly concentrated in Mangalore area, see AbdulWahhab Doddamane, *Muslims in Dakshina Kannada: A Historical Study* (Mangalore: Green Words, 1993); Azmatullah Sharif, "Sunrise in the West Coast," *Islamic Voice* (January 2005) Internet edition.

32 Vasanti Sundaram, "Life on Her Own Terms," *The Hindu* (1 February 2004), p.5.

33 A.S. Paneerselvan, " Hi-Tech Entrepreneurs of Bangalore," *Business India* (31 January-13 February 1994)123-127

34 "Businessmen in the News," *Business India* (10-23 November 2003), p. 27.

35 Yasmin Mahmood, "India's Silicon City," *Saudi Aramco World* (November-December 1997): 37-42.

36 Victor S. D'Souza, *The Navayats of Kanara* (Dharwad: Kannada Research Institute, 1955).

37 Victor S. D'Souza, *Navayat of Kanara: A Study in Culture Contact* (Dharwad: Karnataka Research Institute, 1955).

38 http://groups.msn.com/nawayat/_homepage.msnw?pgmarket=en-us.

39 "Bhatkal Tycoon to Start Airline," *The Milli Gazette* (1-15 October 2004), p.1.

40 Muhammad Abdurrahim Qurayshi, "Bhatkal main Firqwarana Kashidagi," *Milli Ittihad* (16-31 July 1993), p.5; Arshad Siddiqui, "Administration, BJP Nexus in Bhatkal Riots," *Radiance* (11-17 July 1993), p. 8; "Bhatkal Muslims' Economy at Stake," *Radiance* (10-16 October 1993), p.2; Mohd. Zeyaul Haque, "Bhatkal: A Divided Town," *The Nation and the World*, reprinted in *Muslim India* (September 1996), p. 411.

41 Maqbool Ahmad Siraj, "Muslim Businesses are a Target in South India," *Arabia: The Islamic World Review* (20 April 1983), pp. 37-38.

42 "Karnataka: Report on the Welfare Program for Minorities," *Muslim India* (December 1985), p. 551.

[43] *The Karnataka Minorities Development Corporation Limited, 17th Annual Report and Accounts, 2002-2003* (Bangalore: KMDCL, 2003), p. 5 and the Balance Sheet, 1986-2004 to the author through Maqbool Ahmad Siraj.

[44] Mohamed Fakhruddin, "The Karnataka Minorities Development Corporation Needs More Funds than Patronization," *Radiance* (6-12 October 1991), p.8.

[45] *Karnataka Minorities Development Corporation ke Programon aur Kamiyabion ka Ek Mukhtasar Khaka* (Bangalore: KMDCL, 2004), a pamphlet in Urdu enumerates various schemes and achievements.

[46] "Minorities Development Corporation Chief [Mohammed Obeidullah Sharief] Held," *The Hindu* (23 March 2005) Internet edition.

[47] Cited in Hafeez Malik, *Sir Sayyid Ahmad Khan and Muslim Modernization in India and Pakistan* (New York: Columbia University Press, 1980), p. 151.

[48] Mohammed Peer, *Muslim Education in India: Problems and Prospects* (Mangalore: Karnataka Muslim Pragathi Parishat, 1991).

[49] Usha Ramkumar, "Women's Education in Western Ghats Region of Karnataka," *Economic and Political Weekly* (23 May 2002): 3076-2080. Maqbool Ahmad Siraj, "A Threshold Test," *Islamic Voice* (July 2004), p. 6.

[50] Maqbool Ahmad Siraj, "A Threshold Test," *Islamic Voice* (July 2004), p. 6.

[51] "Kannada Medium Must in Primary Schools," *The Hindu* (10 August 2003). Internet edition. The government policy is in clear violation of the constitutional clauses guaranteeing education through mother tongue.

[52] "Overview of Muslim Education in Karnataka," *Radiance* (24-30 October 2004): 12-14.

[53] Mohammed Qamar Ishaq, *Directory of Muslim Educational, Religious & Welfare Organizations in India* (New Delhi: Institute of Objective Studies, 1995), pp. 65-70; updated information in Rahat Abrar and Mohammed Qamar Ishaque, *Directory of Muslim Educational Institutions in India* (New Delhi: Institute of Objective Studies, 2002).

[54] *Report of High Power Committee on Socio-Economic and Educational Survey, 1994 of Religious Minorities in Karnataka*, p. 2.

[55] "Karnataka Socio-Economic-cum-Educational Survey: Socio-Economic & Educational Profile of Muslim Community, 1984" *Muslim India* (April 1987): 172; *Muslim India* (May 1987): 222; *Muslim India* (June 1987): 268; *Muslim India* (July 1987): 317-318; *Muslim India* (August 1987): 366; *Muslim India* (September 1987): 414; *Muslim India* (October 1987); 459.

[56] *Al-Ameen Movement: A Glance* (Bangalore: Al-Ameen Educational Society, n.d.)

57 Conversations with Syed Khusro Husaini, son of the *sajjada nashin* of the Dargah Hazrat Khwaja Bandah Nawaz, Hyderabad, October 2000; Nishat Arif Husaini, "Padma Shri for Husaini," *The Milli Gazette* (16-31 July 2004),p . 16.

58 *Anjuman Platinum Jubilee* (Bhatkal: The Anjuman, 2001).

59 "Muslim Managed Degree Colleges," *Muslim India* (July 1996), p. 319, lists 7 such colleges in Karnataka, but the numbers must have gone up since that date.

60 Raj Chengappa, "Capitulation on Fee," *India Today* (15 June 1984), p. 57; Rekha Kaul, *Caste, Class and Education: Politics of Capitation Fee Phenomenon in Karnataka* (New Delhi: Sage, 1993).

61 Fouzia Zaheer, "Don't Let Dreams of Intelligent Muslims Die," *The Milli Gazette* (1-15 October 2002), p. 13. is probably the only one to go public when denied admission despite qualifications.

62 Syed Shahabuddin, "Strangling the Goose that Lay Golden Eggs for Muslim Entrepreneurs," *Radiance* (27 June-03 July 2004), p. 24.

63 "Ghousia Polytechnic for Women: Excellent Facility, Few Users", *Islamic Voice* (October 1988) Internet edition.

64 Tipu's army included Muslims of various ethnic backgrounds including Mahdawis, some of whom were exiled in 1797 to Channapatna, the famous "toy town." See Mohibbul Hasan Khan, *History of Tipu Sultan* (Calcutta: The Bibliophile, 1951), pp.276-77; 325, 348.

65 Kate Brittlebank, *Tipu Sultan's Search for Legitimacy* (Delhi: Oxford University Press, 1997), p. 34.

66 Kate Brittlebank, ibid. pp. 90-91.

67 Every so often news reports appear in the press about the pitiable condition of Tipu's descendants living in West Bengal.

68 Ikram Kawish, *Askar I Maysur* (Madras, 1992),p. 15.

69 Mirza Ismail, *My Public Life* (London: Allen & Unwin, 1954). His great-grand daughter Sabah Khaleeli was reported to be a franchise owner of orange juice products.

70 "Memorandum Presented by the Muslims of Mysore District to the Karnataka II Backward Classes Commission in December 1983," *Muslim India* (September 1984) p. 434.

71 Ibid.

72 *Mysore Legislative Assembly Debates*, 7 August 1953, as cited in Steven Wilkinson, *Votes and Violence* (Cambridge: Cambridge University Press, 2004), p. 114.

[73] Donald E. Smith, *India as Secular State* (Princeton: Princeton University Press, 1962), p. 418. Oddly, the *All India Civil List*, corrected up to 1st July 1958, issued Half Yearly (Bombay: Printed & published under the Authority of the Government of India, January 1959), lists a mere 9 Muslim names in the Mysore State civil service.

[74] Representation of Muslims in Judicial Service in 1981," *Muslim India* (September 1983), p. 552; see also "High Courts; Muslim Judges, 1.1.92" *Muslim India* (July 1992), p. 318; and "List of Muslim Supreme/ High Court Judges…Retired Between 1947 and 1979," *Muslim India* (March 1983), p. 146. These included Judges S.A. Hakeem in the 1980s, Ahmad Ali Khan in the 1970s; M.M. Ali Mirdhe in the 1990s.

[75] "Karnataka Socio-Economic-cum-Educational Survey: Socio-Economic & Educational Profile of Muslim Community, 1984" *Muslim India* (October 1987): 459.

[76] *Report of the State Minorities Commission-II* (Bangalore: Government of Karnataka, nd.), p. 41. The report was submitted without date to Veerendra Patil, Chief Minister between 1989-90.

[77] *Report of High Power Committee on Socio-Economic and Educational Survey, 1994 of Religious Minorities in Karnataka*, p. 4.

[78] *Second Report of the State Minorities Commission*, submitted by R.H. Goodwala, then chairman (Bangalore: Government of Karnataka, n.d.) It is a sad commentary on the Commission that it does not even date its published report. The report in question was submitted to Ramakrishna Hegde, Chief Minister between 1983-88.

[79] "Karnataka Administrative Service 1999 Results: An Analysis," *Muslim India (*August 2002),p. 380.

[80] Omar Khalidi, *Khaki and the Ethnic Violence in India*, pp. 83-84.

[81] Seventh Annual Report of the Minorities Commission for the period 1-4-1984 to 31-3-1985 (New Delhi: Controller of Publications, 1987), p. 376.

[82] *National Commission for Minorities Second Annual Report (Financial Year 1994-95) (*New Delhi: Controller of Publications, 1997), p. 43.

[83] National Crime Records Bureau, *Crime in India 2000* (New Delhi: Ministry of Home Affairs, 2000).

[84] Conversations with Syed Sadaqat Peeran, Bangalore, January 20, 2004.

[85] Ambarao T. Uplaonkar, *Social Background and Occupational Aspirations of College Students: A Case Study of Karnataka State* (Delhi: Ajanta Publications, 1988). The study is focused on Gulbarga students.

[86] *Report of High Power Committee on Socio-Economic and Educational Survey, 1994 of Religious Minorities in Karnataka*, p. 25.

[87] Ramakrishna Hegde's letter to Syed Shahabuddin dated 25 July 1986 reproduced as "Reservation for Muslims in Karnataka," *Muslim India* (September 1986), p. 402.Text of the G.O. in *Muslim India* (December 1986); 559-560.

[88] Information on the G.O. number SWD 150 BCA dated 17 September 1994 supplied from official record in Bangalore by Maqbool Ahmad Siraj to the present writer.

[89] A. Jayaram, "Minster for Minority Welfare, A First for the State," *The Hindu* (29 June 2002) Internet edition.

[90] Omar Khalidi, """Muslim Ministers in the State Cabinets: The Cases of Karnataka and Andhra Pradesh (1956-2000)" *Radiance* 16-27 October 2001): 16-17.

[91] Report on the Karnataka Board of Wakfs," *Muslim India* (February 1989), p. 67.

[92] *Second Report of the State Minorities Commission* (Bangalore: Government of Karnataka, n.d.),p 55.

[93] Hasanuddin Ahmad and Ahmedulla Khan, *Strategies to Develop Waqf Administration in India* (Jeddah: Islamic Research & Training Institute, Islamic Development Bank, Research Paper, no. 50, 1998), see "The Waqf Administration in the State of Karnataka," pp. 117-123.

[94] "Waqf Board Chairman [Khalid Ahmad] Removed," *Islamic Voice* (July 2003), Internet edition.

[95] Maqbool Ahmad Siraj, "A Landmark Win for Waqf Board," *Radiance* (30 January 2005), p. 13.

MAHARASHTRA

The Muslim presence in the coastal western India dates from the 7th century, when various groups of Arabs arrived on the Konkan coast.[1] The military conquest of the Deccan by Alauddin Khilji in 1294 heralded the beginning of the Muslim presence in the Deccani hinterland, augmented by the shift of the capital to Dawlatabad by Muhammad Tughlaq in 1327. The Marathi-speaking region of the Deccan was variously divided politically and administratively into the Bahmani Sultanates and its off shoots, the Nizam Shahis of Ahmadnagar, the Adil Shahis, the Mughals and Shivaji's domain in the medieval era Thereafter the region went under the control of various Maratha dynasties. In the early nineteenth century, it came under British control as the Bombay Presidency and Province. But a large chunk of the Marathi speaking areas such as the Berars remained under Hyderabad until 1853, as did Marathwada until 1956. In that year, states reorganization on linguistic principle took place through the break up of Hyderabad State, resulting in the merger of Marathwada with Maharashtra. The Muslim population in Maharashtra since 1961 is as follows:

Table I
Muslim Population in Maharashtra, 1961-2001

Year	*Muslim Popn.*	*% of Total Popn.*	*Rural Muslim%*	*Urban Muslim%*	*Muslim Lit.%*	*Urdu Popn.%*
1961	3,027, 639	7.67	44.9	55.1		
1971	4,233, 023	8.40				
1981	5,805, 785	9.25				
1991	7,628,755	9.7				7.27
2001	10,270,485	10.6			78.1	

Source: *Census of India*

Agriculture and Landownership

As in the case of other states, only a few studies regarding the economic conditions of Muslims are available, and thus what is known is presented here until better data becomes available.[2] From the general pattern of Muslim participation in the rural economy of the Deccan, it safe to infer that Muslims as direct cultivators—as opposed to simply non-agricultural labor—are fewer, though perhaps differing by regions within Maharashtra. Some Konkani Muslims are certainly involved in mango and coconut growing, a seasonal activity. In the 1880s in Marathwada, historically, Muslims represented only around 25 percent of those engaged in agriculture as against nearly 80 percent of the rest of the population.[3] A survey in rural areas of Ahmadnagar revealed Muslims to be mainly landless laborers.[4] The only significant landlords in the Bombay Province may have been Muhammad Ali Nakhuda Roghay, the Konkani magnate in the nineteenth century[5] and the Nawabs of Janjira,[6] a tiny principality of the Abyssinians on the coast, less than 90 miles south of Bombay before the princely states' abolition in 1947. A small number of Konkanis are also involved in agriculture.[7] At least 1111 bighas of agricultural land were left behind by Muslims departing for Pakistan from the Central Provinces (of which Berar was a part), according to official figures.[8] Since not all Muslims migrated to Pakistan, it is possible that some landowners stayed put. An attempt to change existing laws pertaining to inheritance of lands in Maharashtra is perhaps an indication that there is enough land-owning Muslim population to merit the submission of a memorandum to the authorities.[9] Nearly one hundred sugar factories in Maharashtra are owned and operated by peasants. Large in scale and efficient in operation, these factories are organized as cooperatives, with half a million cane-growers as their members.[10] In Sangli district one such cooperative even elected a Muslim as its chairperson, perhaps a hint that some Muslims may be involved in sugar cane cultivation.[11] *Baghban*, or *mali* (gardeners) and fruit sellers are found in large numbers in Maharashtra, particularly in Kolhapur area, where they have a near monopoly on banana retail trade and distribution as well as over the famed Nagpur oranges, according to Nasim Siddiqi, Chairman of the State Minorities Commission.[12] Some of the *Baghban* have become wealthy as evidenced by the lavish celebration of Milad al-Nabi under the sponsorship of the Baghban Association. But otherwise, most rural Muslims in Maharashtra appear to be agricultural or non-agricultural workers without land.[13]

Labor, Commerce and Industry

Historically, most Muslims in the region appear to be in various traditionally skilled, semi-skilled, and unskilled occupations. Those who are in skilled professions include *Attar* (perfumers) and *Kaghazi* (papermakers). Then there are several groups of men with traditional skills, sometimes interrelated, such as *Barudgar* (fireworks makers), *Dharad* (ironsmiths), *Tambadkari* (metal workers), *Misgara* (copper, brass smiths), *Naalband* (horse-shoe makers), *Qalaigar* (tinsmiths), *Richihara* (needle fitters), and *Saiqalgar* (metal arms-makers), now grinders of scissors and knives. Those professions relating to textiles and foot wear include *Patwegars*, silk tassel twisters, weavers of fine clothes such as Himroo and Shimroo, Kimkhwab and Paithani saris, *Rafugar* (cloth repairers), *Rangrez* (dyers), and *Darzi* (tailors); *Maniyar* or *Manihar* (bracelet makers), *Kafshgar* (embroidered shoemakers). Among those offering goods and services in food are:

Bhadbhunja (grain parchers), *Bhatyara* and *Kanjar* (sellers of chicken and eggs), *Bojgara* (beer makers) of Kolhapur, *Goniwala* (grain sellers). *Teli*[14] (oil-pressers), *Tamboli* (betel nut and tobacco-sellers), *Bhoi*, *Daldi* (fishermen), *Multani* (sellers of dried fish), butchers (of goat and cows, buffaloes), is a major category of occupations, both historically and now.[15] Some of the butchers have progressed from self-employed shop-owners to employers. A miscellaneous category of skilled workers includes *Saltankar* (tanners), *Takara* (stone carvers), *Gaundi* (brick layers), *Hajjam* (barbers), *Phaniband* (comb makers). Semi-skilled category encompasses *Dhobi* (washer men). Unskilled categories include those *Halalkhwors* (scavengers), *Garori* and *Madari* (village magicians), *Mahawat* (elephant drivers), *Sarban* (camel drivers), *Pakhal* (bearers), *Lakarhara* (hewers of wood), *Bihishti* (drawers of water), Pathan *chowkidar* (security guards),[16] and *Naikwari* (messengers). In other words, if they are not directly cultivators, most Muslims have been in the informal sector, as seen through a rare autobiography of Husain Jamadar, a social activist of subaltern origin from Kolhapur.[17] Daily wage earners, like textile mill workers are normally a highly insecure group dependent on the management's hire or fire at will in a labor-surplus economy. It has also happened that if you belonged to the wrong religion, you were a security risk. "They are laying off Muslims," said a Labor Welfare Officer in Bombay to journalist Taya Zinkin, "this is quite deliberate policy...Mill owners have to think of their factory first and if there are ugly riots as in Jamshedpur and they have large numbers of Muslims, who knows if the mills will not have to be shut down either because there are riots, or because half of the labor force is afraid of going to work in case there are going to be riots. Of course I protest against this policy but I can see the employers' point of view. The sad thing is that these days employing Muslims is security risk."[18] To this startling information, the journalist protested, "But how can they lay off Muslims? I thought that under Indian law employers cannot dismiss people at will?"[19] The Labor Welfare Officer responded, "The practice in the textile industry is not to have many permanent workers but to hire at the gate from day to day. Usually, of course it is the same people, more or less, who get the job, but now the policy is not to hire Muslims at the gate."[20] The journalist's conversation in 1964 was repeated with greater resonance in 1992-93 during the Bombay pogrom when Muslims were laid off wholesale by many in the private sector.

Unlike Uttar Pradesh and Bihar, in Maharashtra, there are far fewer Muslim artisans. The *Momin* of Maharashtra, called as elsewhere by various names of *Ansari*, *Julaha* and *Bunkar*, are traditionally associated with handloom weaving. *Momin* were dispersed over a fairly large range of professions from the nineteenth century. Involvement with agriculture was common, though they were reluctant to work as mere laborers. Many Muslim weavers took great pride in their skills and saw abandonment as a last resort. In some instances, *Momin* weavers preferred moving to other areas to become handloom weavers or mill-workers as an alternative to becoming farm hands or industrial labor. In the late nineteenth century, a large number of Muslim weavers from the Gangetic plains began moving to western India. The foremost historian of the community, Mumin Muhiuddin attributes the cause of migration to catastrophic events in the 1850s, namely the riots in Hanumangarhi (contemporary Fayzabad-Ayodhya) in 1856, and the Revolt/Mutiny of 1857. According to Muhiuddin's account, Muslim weavers decided to leave under conditions of distress, even political persecution.[21] However, economic historians argue that the decline of the Mughals and the successor states in northern India resulting in the decline of patronage was perhaps the more compelling reason for migration. The economic historians' reasons appear more logical since the migration had begun before the 1850s and continued down to the late nineteenth century.[22] Once arrived, many of them concentrated in small towns in northern Maharashtra, along the Agra-Bombay highway, including Dhule, Malegaon, Bhiwandi and Bombay itself.[23] There was also a significant settlement in Yeola and Sangamner, Kamptee and Nagpur area.[24] Initially they came by foot or cart, but later, train became the most common mode of migration. Those who settled in Bombay often became skilled workers in the textile mills, but those who came to inhabit the smaller towns frequently tried to maintain the profession of handloom weaving. Generally, they produced here very different kinds of cloth, suited to the taste of Maharashtrian customers, from those they had made in their home regions. One study found the condition of *Momin* weavers to be worse than their Hindu counterparts.[25] In early 1990s, it is estimated that there are a million and a half *Momins* in Maharashtra. They have been clamoring for inclusion as an Other Backward Class category entitling them to benefits in educational institutions and employment, regardless of name variation: *Julaha*, *Momin* or *Ansari*.[26] Evidently the state government recognized only *Julaha* as the category for inclusion among the OBCs, but eventually the central government agreed to include two: *Julaha Ansari* and *Momin Ansari* in Maharashtra on the recommendation of National Commission for Backward Classes.[27]

In contemporary Maharashtra, the economic condition of the *Momins*—both handloom-weaver and power loom owners— fluctuates with developments in the market and politics, such as the violence in November 2001.[28] In early 2003, the power looms industry in Bhiwandi was reported to be in poor shape leading to widespread unemployment.[29]According to Homi J.H. Taleyarkhan, "Out of the total power looms in the country, the share of Maharashtra is [a staggering] 55 percent with the weavers mainly concentrated in the districts of Thane, Nasik and Kolhapur."[30] Unlike the coarse cloth associated with the handloom and power loom industry, the Muslim weavers of Aurangabad area have been weaving the Paithani saris and Himroo shawls making the city synonymous with the fabrics.[31] The Aurangabad fabrics go back several centuries, but a revival took place under the patronage of the Nizams of Hyderabad in the nineteenth century. In particular, the Qureshi family preserved the art associated with the Paithani. Today the Master Craftsman, Ijaz Ahmad Qureshi, 13th in the generation of the Qureshis, runs the Aurangabad Himroo Industry and Paithani Weaving and Training Center, a success story, with government support.[32]

Mumbai probably has the largest number of Muslim laborers in the country as the nation's commercial capital. Within Mumbai lies Dharavi, Asia's largest slum. Made up of ramshackle corrugated tin sheds, it is home to more than 600,000 people with a high proportion of Muslims.[33] But it is a unique shantytown. Local workshops with cheap labor churn out leather goods, pottery and jewelry worth nearly one billion dollars a year. There are numerous success stories among its many Muslim residents, such as Malik Yusuf the leather merchant,[34]Sharifuddin Waziruddin, a successful *zardozi* merchant,[35] Abul Baqaa, who developed a surgical thread unit with exports of over Rs. 1.75 crore at one point.[36] Abul Baqaa and other Muslim businessmen were however ruined when Hindutva mobs burnt, destroyed and looted Muslim businesses in the wake of Bombay pogroms of 1993.[37] A majority of the garment and jewelry workers in Bombay are Muslim; most of these workers lost what little they had besides lives.[38] By definition slums are poor, except for some success stories; even these are prone to destruction during violence, especially targeted against Muslims, as has been the case in Gujarat most recently in 2002. The vast majority of Dharavi dwellers and their children are without infrastructure and schools,[39] many turning to hawking.[40] Foreign competition is a big source of worry for many local manufacturers. China is emerging as a huge competitor in consumer goods in the world markets, driving away many Muslim businesses as others.[41]

In the mid-1960s, Badruddin Tyabji, the then Vice-Chancellor of Aligarh Muslim University, given his excellent connections with the commercial world of Bombay, wrote to some Bombay industrialists seeking employment for his University graduates in their firms. All but one—Dharamsey Khatau of Khatau Group of Industries— apparently responded favorably.[42] Since then things may have changed. One of the disturbing findings of a study by Asghar Ali Engineer and Sunil Dighe is the near absence of Muslims as workers in the private industrial companies such as Hindustan Sugar Mills and J.K. Singhanias, both Marwari-owned.[43] The bias against Muslims is the undertone of a fictional work *Reaching Bombay*

Central by Shama Futehally in which the writer notes how a Muslim was fired when merely suspected of promoting a co-religionist.[44] The anti-Muslim statements given by business tycoons such as V.H. Dalmia and Ramnath Goenka in support of the Hindutva movement explain why they discriminate against Muslims.[45] The big businesses rationalize their reluctance to hire Muslims on grounds of Muslim presence—such as Haji Mastan and ferocious Pathan moneylenders—[46] in the underworld of Mumbai, and the western coast in particular, with links to the Persian Gulf states.[47]

Reservation of jobs in the private sector is an unresolved issue in the nation as yet, but the lead given in Maharashtra through legislation in 2004, made it possible for certain groups to benefit from affirmative action. Muslims are not included in this category.[48]

No account of Muslims in business and industry can be complete without a detailed study of mercantile communities such as the various sects of the Bohras, Khojas, and Memons.[49] Such studies have already been done by Jonah Blank, Hanna Papanek and Sergey Levin,[50] and will not repeated here as our concern in this book is the Urdu-speaking Muslim communities. Displacing Surat, which was Mughal India's chief seaport, Bombay emerged as colonial India's seaport and commercial capital in the late eighteenth century. The great success stories of Bombay are generally associated with Gujaratis, Marwaris and Parsis. However, "similar riches were made by those Konkani Muslim families, such as the Kurs, the Roghays, and the Ghattys, who entered the China trade and also traded in pearls with Madras. Muhammad Ali Roghay, who earned the title Nacoda [nakhuda, "boat-lord"] because of the large number of ships he owned, traded in China in partnership with one of the [Parsi magnate named] Readymoneys. The Konkani Muslim *shetia* [magnates] had a considerable advantage in the trade, because, like the Parsis, their community had long been associated with shipbuilding.[51] Roghay, best known among his community, was of course not the only one, as "Konkani Muslims also had several private docks at Majagaon for building smaller crafts (dhows)."[52]

Under the pro-business environment of colonial Bombay, many Muslim commercial houses flourished throughout the colonial era as evidenced by the establishment of Muslim chamber of commerce in Bombay and beyond. By the 1940s, one could even speak of a substantial Muslim business class as documented in a directory.[53] However, the partition and its consequences greatly weakened Muslim presence in the business world. Younger, resourceful entrepreneurs migrated to Pakistan for better prospects or in dread of poor treatment in a Hindu-dominated India.[54] Their fears were not entirely wrong. For a decade after partition, the unjust laws of the Evacuee Property Act paralyzed business transactions as banks did not consider Muslims credit-worthy, and property transactions were frozen resulting in advantage to competitors. An exception to this case was K.A. Hamied's pharmaceutical business, which actually prospered.[55] Since that time, Bohra, Khoja, and Memons have continued to flourish, though they too have had to face the fury of the Shiva Sena and other Hindutva organizations in the riots and pogroms of 1984 and 1992-93 as Theodore P. Wright demonstrated.[56] Only one Muslim-owned company, the Chemical and Pharmaceuticals Limited is among the large-scale industrial-manufacturing units.[57] Along with other Muslim businesses, the CEO of this Company, Yusuf Hamied, left Mumbai as a victim of Shiva Sena threat to his life.[58] Another Muslim-owned company in pharmaceuticals is Medley Pharmaceuticals, a large exporter. Though not in large-scale businesses, two companies have done well: Rizvi Builders and the Inqilab Group of Publications. Rizvi Builders is one of the biggest construction firms in Mumbai. Started by Akhtar Hasan Rizvi of Jaunpur in 1973, it has now branched out into other businesses such as hotel management. Rizvi Builders have also started a school of architecture.[59] Like Rizvi Builders, Tain Construction Company, established by Tanveer Inamdar, is a leading construction firm in Pune.[60] Examples of other successful ventures are exemplified by the cases noted here: Al-Habib Engineering Private Limited of Mumbai, an exporter to the Middle East since 1980, though they began as a manpower agent earlier.[61] The Pune-based Nexgen Logistix, run by

Faisal Ali is a new infrastructure technology company with several million US dollar business.[62] The *Inqilab* Group of Publications is one of the leading newspaper publishing groups in Mumbai with papers such as *Inqilab* in Urdu and *Mid-Day* in English, Gujarati and Marathi editions, and *Sportsweek*. The company originated when Abdulhamid Ansari began his journalism career in the 1940s.[63] The Hyderabad-born ad czar Mohammed Khan runs Enterprise Nexus, a giant in the business. From humble beginnings, Ghulamuddin Maqbool established in 1981 a successful meat processing plant Al-Kabeer, with operations within India and abroad.[64] The success stories of these new businessmen outside the traditional mercantile communities show that it is possible for some individuals to overcome their family background and tread new paths. However, whether belonging to the mercantile communities or not, all Muslim businesses face the threat of targeted destruction as has in fact happened in Bhiwandi and Mumbai in 1984 and 1992-93. In Bhiwandi, "one factor in the violence may well have been the vying over the standards of living—provoked by the fact that a section of Muslims were becoming fairly prosperous as a result of the power loom boom."[65] During the 1992-93 pogrom in Bombay, according to a careful report in by Merle Almeida and Austin Lobo, "The trades that have been most affected are timber, leather, garments, embroidery, bakeries, gems and jewelry—trades predominantly owned by Muslims or those whose factories or workshops were located in Muslim areas. P.N. Mogre, secretary-general of the Indian Merchants Chamber, estimates the cost of January riots as approximately 750 crores. Around 90 percent of the bakeries in the city are owned by Muslims. More than 350 bakeries were burned down during the riots...were run by small entrepreneurs."[66] The pogrom slowed foreign investment and shook investor confidence in an environment barely recovering from decades of license permit raj.[67] Muslims own around 800 restaurants, another easy target of the mobs during violent events.[68] Sholapur, an industrial town in southern Maharashtra, witnessed planned destruction as Muslim businesses "suffered extensive damage running into crores of rupees in areas like

Begumpet, Mangal Chowk, Jodabawi, Ashok Chowk, and Mangalwarpet."[69] The repeated failure of the state to predict, prevent or immediately quell violence once it breaks out calls into question its impartiality resulting in the destruction of Muslim economy. Under the conditions of peace, professional guidance and access to credit, motivated Muslim entrepreneurs are quite capable of doing as well as others, as has been demonstrated in Kolhapur. A study of engineering enterprises in Kolhapur indicates that in the merit rating for upward change in organizational set-up and in establishment of new firms, Muslims scored the highest merit points in 1979. Similarly, Muslim entrepreneurs showed excellence in other areas such as personnel and production management and creation of new enterprises.[70] In Pune, Muslims in petty production have done well, raising hope for their coreligionists in the state as a whole.[71] The Maharashtra state government established a Maulana Azad Alpasankhyak Vikas Mahamandal (MAAAVM) or minorities' finance development corporation, on 20 August 2002 fulfilling an electoral promise. Out of a paid up capital of Rs. 50 crores, it received 16 crores in 2004 enabling it to help 2500 people for self-employment and entrepreneurship. Some schemes within the MAAAVM have been quite successful, though loan recovery is not always possible due to a large number of defaulters.[72]

Urban and rural cooperative banks have served the useful purpose of meeting the needs of the small borrower, generally shunned by the commercial banks.[73] Muslims have been latecomers to this burgeoning sector,[74] though some examples have come up lately, for example the Charminar Cooperative Bank, Darussalam Cooperative Bank in Hyderabad and a number of others in Mumbai and elsewhere, sometimes called Islamic banks.[75] However, "most of these institutions...are localized. Their scale of operation is very small. They are unregulated and uncontrolled...unless they are reorganized and put under some kind of legal framework, not much progress can be expected."[76] Whether due to internal issues or due to the negative publicity by the media, one such financial institution Baitun Nasr folded up in 2003 after three decades of existence.[77]

Education and the Tertiary Sector

Muslims in the British Presidency of Bombay took little part in modern education in early colonial era. According to Christine Dobbin, "By the mid-nineteenth century, the Muslim community throughout the Presidency was noted for its unwillingness to espouse the new English education. The problem was particularly acute in the cities, where Muslims in general spoke Urdu and so required a separate system of elementary schools before they could go to even the Anglo-Vernacular level."[78] Since they were poor at elementary level, it is unsurprising that "Muslims played a very small part in higher education."[79] Higher education among Muslims was restricted to the richest in the society, particularly to those belonging to the mercantile communities such as the Bohras, Khojas and Memons.[80] However, thanks to the untiring effort of such members of the Bombay Muslim elite as the brothers Qamaruddin and Badruddin Tyabji, Muhammad Ali Roghay Nakhuda, Ghulam Muhammad Munshi, and others, Anjuman-i Islam was founded in March 1876 to advance the backward minority's education.[81] Badruddin Tyabji, coming as he did from the tiny sect of Sulaymani Bohras, was conscious of various classes within the Muslim community. Keeping the class divisions in mind, he urged that Anjuman "schools be opened to meet the wants of various classes, mercantile, technical and agricultural. He stressed the need for girls' schools. He urged that oriental learning should be blended with Western education in literature, the arts and the sciences."[82] The Anjuman was able to improve the educational condition of the community only to a small extent. Badruddin Tyabji told an educational commission "that of the 15, 247 students matriculated in the Presidency from 1859 to 1881, only 48 were Muslims. The Anjuman-i Islam published even more damning figures: out of 175 students at Elphinstone College, there were only 5 Muslims, at St. Xavier's College there was only one Muslim out of 71 students, and at the Free General Assembly's Institution, none at all."[83] The Muslim leadership, though admitting that the community itself was responsible for educational poverty, sought government help.[84] The Presidency's government made its own calculation about Muslim education: "At the end of 1884, it was calculated that though Muslims formed 18 percent of the population of the Presidency, they were only 1.83 percent of all students in government arts colleges, and 3.87 of all high school students.[85] Consequent to the educational poverty, in a memorial to the government by Anjuman-i Islam "it was alleged that so few Muslims were in the government service that they may be said to be practically excluded from all positions of trust, honor, and emolument."[86] The dismal picture of Muslim employment was despite the presence of co-religionists like Khan Bahadur Kazi Shahabuddin (1832-1900) being a member of the Public Service Commission.[87] The Anjuman wanted recruitment qualifications relaxed in order to induct more Muslims into the services.[88] In 1871, not a single Muslim name could be found in the list of high civil and judicial officials.[89] As late as 1882, the proportion of Muslims employed in the public services by the Government was unduly small, according to one report.[90] Against these assertions, however, William Lee-Warner, a government official "pointed out that Muslims comprised eleven percent of all government officials and municipal and local fund employees throughout the Presidency."[91] A scheme was finally agreed upon whereby Muslims were to be guaranteed a number of free studentships in government high schools. Since the Bombay Presidency was a large area, the differences within its various parts were not always understood. For instance, in Khandesh, Ahmadnagar and Dharward areas, Muslims "enrolled in Government schools in proportion roughly to Muslim population."[92] Outside the Bombay Presidency, many districts of the Central Provinces and Berar today form part of Maharashtra. The majority of the people in these districts spoke Marathi while Muslims spoke Urdu. The Berar or the Hyderabad Assigned Districts as it was known in the colonial times or modern Vidarbha, is an agriculturally rich region seized from Hyderabad in 1853 under an unjust Anglo-Nizam treaty. In the nineteenth century, according to a historian, the state of Muslim education in Hyderabad Assigned Districts was better and Muslims were in large number in public employment.[93] In fact, Muslim pupils in schools far exceeded the total Muslim percentage in the provincial population by the 1920s.[94] From the 1920s, primary through secondary education increased in Bombay province as a whole. In 1927, Muslims, excluding Sindh, "comprised 8.6 percent of the provincial population but 13.8 percent of the student force," a clear advance thanks to the favorable environment created by the Government and the private efforts of the community channeled through the Anjuman-i Islam and other organizations.[95] By the late 1940s, Muslims of Bombay, Central Provinces and Berar, comprising the post-1960 Maharashtra had made rapid advances in education. They were certainly not a backward minority in any sense.

The post-1947 was difficult for Muslims everywhere including the territories comprising Maharashtra today. The Congress Party showed little understanding of Muslim interests throughout India. This was particularly so in the Congress right wing represented in Bombay by Sardar Patel, and chief ministers B.G. Kher and Ravi Shankar Shukla of Bombay and Central Provinces respectively. In 1947-48, for instance, Ravi Shankar Shukla, "drew up a scheme of compulsorily retiring Muslim employees, high and low, beginning with the police department. Muslim schools, some for long the Nizam's beneficiaries...were closed down. All prominent Muslims...were put under surveillance."[96] Several thousand took refuge in the Nizam's Dominion, outside their control.[97] Many Muslims from all parts of the two provinces migrated to Pakistan leaving behind the poor and the illiterate segments of Muslim society.[98] An overall assessment of the state of Muslim education at all levels and in every region, rural and urban in Konkan, Khandesh, Marathwada, Vidharbha, and Mumbai is lacking. According to A.H. Kamat, in rural Maharashtra " so far as Muslims are concerned, they are in sizeable numbers only in some of the bigger villages and while they have maintained the same pace of progress as other sections of society in western Maharashtra and Vidarbha, they seem to be lagging behind in Marathwada."[99] One reason, many Muslim organizations want to establish their own schools is to escape from the anti-Muslim bias shown in many textbooks, particularly of history.[100] While the saffronization of textbooks is often associated with Uttar Pradesh and other north Indian states, Maharashtra is no exception since pre-independence days exemplified by the Vidya Mandir scheme.[101] Post independence examples of biased books are plentiful.[102] Another impediment to Muslim education is the legal issues pertaining to recognition, inclusion of the Scheduled Castes and Tribes in the minority institutions and so forth.[103] Undeterred by theses difficulties, a series of reports show burgeoning interest and pursuance of education by Muslims across gender.[104] Most commentators writing about Urdu assume it to be the language only of North India, a vague term. It is an eye opener to many observers—both academic and journalistic—that Maharashtra has more Urdu-medium schools than Uttar Pradesh.[105] In a study of literacy campaigns in Maharashtra, Denzil Saldanha found that "Muslims have been able to attain the NLM (National Literacy Mission) norms in total sample in the Maharashtra districts. Primarily the learners from this community from Ratnagiri and Nanded districts contribute this high success rate. Learners from these districts were studying in their mother tongue Urdu. Some of them had familiarity with deciphering the script as a result of religious instruction. The Muslim women in general and especially in these districts demonstrated a high degree of motivation supported by religious leaders and community elders. In Latur district, in contrast, a lower percentage of evaluated Muslims attained the NLM norms. A major factor was perhaps their studying in the Marathi medium which generally was not their language in domestic sphere."[106] The Anjuman-i Islam itself runs a string of schools, colleges, and other institutions, making it the largest Muslim organization in Maharashtra. Enrollment into Urdu medium schools has gone beyond just poor Muslims to other segments of the society.[107] Of the total number of students, roughly 55 percent are Muslim in 2005, the rest from other communities, according to the President of the Anjuman.[108] The Anjuman also runs the M.H. Saboo Siddik College of Engineering, and other professional schools. There have been allegations that students are forced to give capitation fee in order to be admitted thus depriving deserving but poor pupils from pursuing professional courses.[109] However, the chairman of the Anjuman, Ishaq Jamkhanawala, denies his detractors' accusations.[110] Maharashtra's cultural capital Pune, long known for its upper caste Hindu educational institutions run by the Joshis, the Gadgils, and the Abhyankars is now joined by the Azams and the Inamdars running two highly successful institutions, the Haji Ghulam Muhammad Azam Education Trust and the Maharashtra Cosmopolitan Education Society.[111]

In addition to secular Urdu schools, Maharashtra boasts of nearly 200 madrasas.[112] A directory of social and educational organizations in Maharashtra lists close to 500 institutions in the state, all dedicated to various aspects of educational and economic development.[113] Even excluding those belonging to the mercantile communities of Bohras, Khojas and Memons, it is still a high number, signaling perhaps a forward movement toward community involvement in education. In higher education, there are 7 Muslim managed colleges in Maharashtra, besides an engineering college and a school of architecture.[114]

Very little is known as far as the Muslim percentage in the state employment at all three levels is concerned. For instance in 1958, a *Civil List* reports only 69 Muslims as gazetted officers in a total of several thousand.[115] The only reliable figures known today are those in the police department of Maharashtra. It is represented by 17,775 SCs, 11,006 STs, but only 5,950 Muslims; while the rest, presumably upper caste Hindus, Christians, and Parsis number 98,283 according to an official source.[116] In an attempt to address this imbalance, the Maharashtra State Minorities Commission has sponsored coaching classes to enable minority candidates to successfully compete and qualify for police posts.[117] In Mumbai itself, there evidently are only 653 Muslims out of a total police force of 30, 600 according to a news report.[118] In the state judicial service, the Muslim percentage in 1981 was reported to be a mere 3.09 percent.[119] In a study of Vidarbha Muslim youth, Jyoti Punwani found them too backward to be able to "stand a chance of competing with the OBC Hindus for state aid," thus meriting a separate quota for reservations in education and employment.[120] Barring a handful of communities, Muslims as such do not qualify for reservation, and their situation does not find a voice in the political system given the insignificant cabinet portfolios held by Muslims.[121] Most Muslims have of course not been touched by the new affluence that characterizes the middle class in Maharashtra towns such as Aurangabad.[122] Unlike the stereotypical image of Muslim women, a study in Aurangabad found that Muslim women are not averse to earning their own living, if conditions are proper.[123] A complete picture of Muslims in employment or out of it can emerge only if the state is willing to disclose the information it gathers. In early 1990s, for example, the state government provided statistics about the registration and placement of minority candidates for jobs, indicating that it is possible to find such statistics despite frequent denials that religion-wise statistics are not kept.[124] The State Minorities Commission established in April 1992 should undertake a thorough study of the socio-economic condition in the entire state on the model of those done in Andhra Pradesh and Karnataka.[125] For instance, the Commission has rightly pointed that while *Kathiks*, the Hindu butchers have been declared as a backward community entitling them to educational and employment benefits, such has not been the case with Muslim butchers known as *Qasais*.[126] Evidently there are more than 19 Muslim groups waiting for affirmative action by the state, since their Hindu counterparts have already been availing benefits offered by reservation.

Muslim Waqf Board

Like other states, the Waqf properties in the state are numerous, most numerous in Marathwada,[127] a legacy of the Nizam's rule, but many are in the illegal occupation, among others of the government, exemplified by the case of Ismail Yusuf College land in Mumbai.[128]Only a small number of properties have been released from illegal hands, such as the Masjid-i Kharbuza in Aurangabad.[129] When and if the *waqf* lands and properties are inventoried, returned to rightful owners and developed, there could be a major boost to welfare for Muslims.

Notes

1 "The Konkani Muslims: An Introduction," *Islamic Culture* 74, no. 1 (January 2000): 127-53.

2 N.A.G. Khan, *A Socio-Economic Survey of Muslims of Poona*, unpublished PhD dissertation, University of Poona, 1952, is probably the only one available and that too for just one town, and is now dated.

3 *Gazetteer of Aurangabad District*, 1884, cited in Masood Ali Khan, "Intergenerational Mobility Among Muslims in Aurangabad: A South Indian City," *Journal Institute of Muslim Minority Affairs* 8, 1 (January 1987): 88-108, citation on p. 91.

4 A.K. Vakil and K.P. Dhongde, "Economic Status of Muslims and Their Political Awareness," *Muslim India* (September 1991), p. 424.

5 Omar Khalidi, Konkani Muslims, pp. 140-141.

6 Omar Khalidi, "African Diaspora in India, op.cit.

7 Omar Khalidi, Konkani Muslims, p. 145.

8 Constituent Assembly of India, *Legislative Debates*, November-December 1949 (New Delhi: Manager of Publications, 1947-49), p. 16.

9 "Text of Memorandum to the Prime Minister on Inequity in the Application of Land Ceiling Laws in Maharashtra," *Muslim India* (June 1983), p. 281.

10 David W. Attwood, *Raising Cane* (Boulder, CO: Westview Press, 1992).

11 Dionne Bunsha, "The Hutatma Model," *Frontline* 20 (2003) Internet edition; a press report "Farmer Commits Suicide in Maharashtra," *NDTV* (22 June 2005), Internet edition, identifies the farmer as Yusuf Tandel in Pimpalwadi village of Junnar district.

12 Interview with Nasim Siddiqi, Mumbai 02 January 2005.

13 Moin Shakir and U.B. Bhoite, "Maharashtrians," pp. 467-469, in *Muslim Peoples: A World Ethnographic Survey*, edited by Richard V. Weekes (Westport, CT: Greenwood Press, 1984).

14 Telis are large enough to form an organization, Muslim Teli Samaj, which met in Pune in 2004.

15 Asiya Siddiqi, "Ayesha's World: A Butcher Family in Nineteenth Century Bombay," *Comparative Studies in Society and History* 43, 1 (January 2001): 101-129, is a rare glimpse into the subaltern Muslim life.

[16] Once ubiquitous in colonial Bombay, the Pathans, employed mainly as security have nearly disappeared in contemporary Mumbai. The Pathans' deployment by oil mill-owners to break a labor strike in December 1928 gave the dispute a communal color, see, K.B. Krishna, *The Problem of Minorities or Communal Representation in India* (London: George Allen & Unwin, 1939), Chapter 3, The Bombay Riots, pp. 268-69.

[17] S.P. Punelekar, "Family, Community and Social Terrain: Gleanings from the Autobiography of a Muslim Activist," *Economic and Political Weekly* (14 March 1998): 607-614.

[18] Taya Zinkin, *Challenges in India* (New York: Walker, 1966), pp. 160-161.

[19] Ibid,p . 161.

[20] Ibid, p. 161.

[21] Mumin Muhiuddin, *Mumin Ansari Biradari ki Tahzibi Tarikh* (Bombay, 1994).

[22] Douglas E. Haynes and Tirthankar Roy, "Conceiving Mobility: Weavers Migration in Pre-Colonial and Colonial India," *The Indian Economic and Social History Review* 36, 1 (January-March 1999): 35-67, reference to p. 62.

[23] Douglas E. Haynes and Tirthankar Roy, "Conceiving Mobility: Weavers Migration in Pre-Colonial and Colonial India," *The Indian Economic and Social History Review* 36, 1 (January-March 1999): 35-67, for an excellent map showing the route of migration.

[24] Peter Harnetty, "Deindustrialization Revisited: The Handloom Weavers of the Central Provinces of India, c. 1800-1947," *Modern Asian Studies* 25, 3 (1991): 455-510.

[25] S.J. Andrews, *A Study of the Socio-Economic Conditions of Momin Koshtis in Mominpura, Nagpur,* MA dissertation, Department of Sociology, University of Nagpur, 1964.

[26] "Declaration of Ansaris of Maharashtra as an OBC," *Muslim India* (November 1992), p. 522, the article was initially published in *The Times of India,* though reproduced without date attribution .

[27] "Four More Castes in OBC List," *Deccan Chronicle* (22 October 1999), Internet edition.

[28] Yogesh Pawar, "Malegaon Riots Hit Power Loom Workers Most," *India Abroad* (09 November 2001), p. 15.

[29] M.H. Lakdawala, "Bhiwandi in the Grip of Reverse Migration," *The Milli Gazette* (16-31 May 2003), p. 6.

[30] *Tenth Annual Report of the Minorities Commission for the Period from 1-4-1987 to 31-3-1988* (New Delhi: Controller of Publications, 1990), p. 36.

[31] Moin Qazi, "Himroo's Struggle for Survival," *The Times of India* (11 December 1986),p . 17. Many Himroo workshops are owned by Bohras with Muslims as workers.

32 Interview with Ijaz Ahmad Qureshi, Jaafar Gate, Mondha Road, Aurangabad, 11 January 2000.

33 Kalpana Sharma, *Rediscovering Dharavi: Stories from Asia's Largest Slum* (New York: Penguin, 2000).

34 Zubair Ahmad, "Bombay's Billion Dollar Slum," *BBC News* 03 March 2004, Internet edition

35 Farah Baria, "Dharavi: From Dust to Dreams," *India Today* (15 July 1996), p. 87.

36 M. Rahman, "Dharavi: Poor and Polarized," *India Today* (15 March 1993), p. 49.

37 Ibid.

38 Milnid Palnitkar, "Garments and Jewelry Worst Hit," *India Abroad* (29 January 1993), p 20.

39 M.H. Lakdawala, "Ten Thousand Tales of Lost Childhood," *Radiance* (8-14 August 2004), pp. 18-17.

40 M.H. Lakdawala, "Hawking as a Way of Life," *The Milli Gazette* (16-31 May 2004), p. 8.

41 M.H. Lakdawala, "Facing Chinese Onslaught: Muslim, Jain, Sikh Businessmen Bear the Brunt," *The Milli Gazette* (16-31 July 2003), p.3.

42 Badruddin Tyabji, *Memoirs of an Egoist* (New Delhi: Roli, 1988), p.147-148, Khatau chided Tyabji for his "communal proposal"!

43 Asghar Ali Engineer and Sunil Dighe, "A Survey Report on Employment Pattern of Muslims in Bombay," *Muslim India* (June 1987), pp. 273-274.

44 Shama Futehally, *Reaching Bombay Central* (New Delhi: Viking, 2002), Anu Kuma, "In Memoriam: Shama Futehally", *Economic and Political Weekly* (18 December 2004), pp. 5371-5372.

45 "V.H. Dalmiya's Letter to Hindu Industrialists", *Surya India* (July 1984), as reproduced in *Muslim India* (October 1984), p. 484.

46 Shamim Ahmed Shamim, "Haji Mastan Tells His Story," *The Illustrated Weekly of India* (06 October 1974): 18-19; and the obituary by Milind Palnitkar, "Haji Mastan, Ex-Underworld Boss," *India Abroad* (01 July 1994), p.12.

47 Theodore P. Wright, Jr., "Muslim Mobility in India Through Peripheral Occupations: Sports, Music, Cinema and Smuggling," *Asie du Sud,* edited by Marc Gaborieu and Alice Thorner (Paris: Editions du CNRS, 1979), pp. 271-278.

48 P.G. Jogdand, "Reservation in Private Sector: Legislation in Maharashtra," *Economic and Political Weekly* (24 July 2004): 3344-3346.

[49] Omar Khalidi, "Indian Muslim Society and Economy," *Oriente Moderno* 84, 1 (2004): 177-202.

[50] Jonah Blank, *Mullas on the Mainframe* (Chicago: University of Chicago Press, 2001); Hanna Papanek, "Pakistan's Big Businessmen: Separatism, Entrepreneurship, and Partial Mobilization," *Economic Development and Social Change* 21, 1 (1972): 1-33; Sergey Levin, "The Upper Bourgeoisie from the Muslims Commercial Community of Memons in Pakistan," *Asian Survey* 14 (1974): 231-243.

[51] Christine Dobbin, *Urban Leadership in Western India: Politics and Communities in Bombay City, 1840-1885* (Oxford: Oxford University Press, 1972), p. 15; the China trade was routed via Calcutta, where Roghay built the famous Nakhuda Mosque.

[52] Amalendu Guha, "More About the Parsi Shetias," p. 123, in *Business Communities of India: A Historical Perspective,* edited by Dwijendra Tripathi (New Delhi: Manohar, 1984).

[53] *The Muslim Yearbook of India and Pakistan and Who's Who,* compiled by S.M. Jamil (Bombay, 1949), lists hundreds of Muslim business houses in Bombay around 1947-49.

[54] Claude Markovits, "Businessmen and the Partition of India," pp. 236-258, in *Inventing Boundaries: Gender, Politics and the Partition of India, edited by* Mushirul Hasan (New Delhi: Oxford University Press, 2000), reference on p. 253.

[55] K.A. Hamied, *An Autobiography: A Life to Remember, 1898-1972,* (Bombay: Lalvani, 1972).

[56] Theodore P. Wright, Jr. "Muslim Self-Reliance in India: The Model of the Business Communities," Indian Journal of Politics 31, nos. 3-4 (1997): 49-55; idem, "The Indian State and its Muslim Minority: From Dependency to Self-Reliance, pp. 313-339, in *India: Fifty Years of Democracy and Development,* edited by Yoigendra K. Malik and Ashok Kapur (New Delhi: APH Publishing Corp., 1998).

[57] See its website for most recent profile http://www.biopharmalink.com/companies/5443.htm

[58] Michael Spector, "Annals of Medicine: India's Plague," *The New Yorker* (17 December 2001), p. 85; and www.businessweek.com/magazine/content/01_27/b3739090.htm

[59] http://www.rizvi.com/rizvi/rizvibuilders/; Munawwar Ali Khan Lodhi, "Development of Muslim Industrial Entrepreneurship in India, 1947-1981," *Journal Institute of Muslim Minority Affairs* 6, 1 (January 1985): 71-87.

[60] "Square Deal," *Business India* (19 January-01 February 2004),p . 141.

[61] K.S. Ramkumar, "Indian Firm Seeks Engineering Goods Market," *Arab News* (Jeddah, 22 July 1992), p.2.

[62] Sekhar Seshan, "Tracking Trucking," *Business India* (25 November-08 December 2002), p. 125.

[63] www.middaymultimedia.com/; Jawid Jamaluddin, *Abulhamid Ansari: Inqilabi Sahafi* (Mumbai: Inqilab, 2003).

[64] Safi Abdurrahim, "Al-Kabeer: A Giant Name in Meat Industry," *Arab News* (Jeddah) (6 February 1996), p. 6. Al-Kabeer is run in partnership with S.C.Subberwal, a Hindu. In 1981 out of 4, 3 directors were Hindus, see "Controversial Abattoir Near Bhiwandi," *Muslim India* (February 1984), p. 89.

[65] Ivan Fera, "The Sorrow of Bhiwandi," *The Illustrated Weekly of India* (3 June 1984), p. 23.

[66] Merle Almeida and Austin Lobo, "Costing the Carnage," *Business India* (1 February-14 February 1993), pp. 65-67.

[67] Anthony Spaeth, "India's Strife Slows Foreign Investment," *The Christian Science Monitor* (14 April 1993), p. 9.

[68] Syed Firdaus Ashraf, "Muslim Hoteliers Pick on Coke, Pepsi to Break US Backbone," *India Abroad* (9 November 2001), p. 15.

[69] "Sholapur Burns," *Radiance* (27 October-2 November 2002), p. 10.

[70] S.G. Bhanushali, *Entrepreneurship Development* (Bombay: Himalaya Publishing House, 1979), p. 227.

[71] Pierre Lachaier, "Artisans et petit entrepreneurs musulmanes en zone urbaine," *Lettre d'information,* Programme de recehereches interdisciplinaire sur le monde musulmanes peripherique, no. 14 (June 1994), pp. 59-68.

[72] Sadiq Dalvi's interview with S.E.A. Hashimi, Managing Director of MAAAVM, Mumbai 25 October 2004 on the present writer's behalf.

[73] Vidya Pitre, "Urban Cooperative Banks: Issues and Prospects," *Economic and Political Weekly* (12 April 2003): 1505-1513.

[74] M.A. Hamid, "Banking and Insurance," *The Muslim Yearbook of India and Pakistan and Who's Who*, compiled by S.M. Jamil (Bombay, 1949),pp. 483-496.

[75] Rahmatullah, "Islamic Banks in India," *Journal Institute of Muslim Minority Affairs* 13, 2 (July 1992): 317-324.M.G.I. Bagsiraj, *Islamic Financial Institutions of India: Progress, Problems and Prospects* (Jeddah: Scientific Publishing Center, King Abdulaziz University, 2003), outpaces are research published so far on this topic and Mumbai has the largest number of such institutions.

[76] Ausaf Ahmad, "Comments on Islamic Banks in India," *Journal Institute of Muslim Minority Affairs* 14, 1 & 2 (January-July 1994), p. 256.

77 Shariq Nasir, "Muslim Para Bank Crucified by the Media," *The Milli Gazette* (1-15 September 2003), p. 8.

78 Christine Dobbin, *Urban Leadership in Western India: Politics and Communities in Bombay City, 1840-1885* (Oxford: Oxford University Press, 1972), p. 229.

79 Ibid. p. 16, 31, 44,48, 112, 164, .231.

80 Ibid., p. 164.

81 *The Anjuman-i Islam: Memorandum and Articles of Association* (Bombay: The Anjuman, 1986); S.S. Desnavi, *Synopsis History of Anjuman-i Islam* (Bombay: The Anjuman, n.d.).

82 Husain B. Tyabji, *Badruddin Tyabji: A Biography* (Bombay: Thacker, 1952), p. 69. There are at least five sects of the Bohras: Alawi, Daudi, Mahdi Bagh Wala, Sulaymani, and Sunni.

83 Christine Dobbin, op. cit. 241.

84 Ibid.. p. 241.

85 Ibid., p. 242.

86 Ibid., p. 243.

87 Charles E. Buckland, *Dictionary of Indian Biography* (London: Sonnenschein, 1906), p. 384.

88 Ibid., p. 242.

89 Muniruddin Chughtai, "Post-1857 Economic and Administrative Policies of the British in India and the Muslims," *Pakistan Economic and Social Review* (Autumn 1974), p. 245, *India Army and Civil List*, 1872.

90 *Selections from the Records of the Government of India* (Home Department) No. CCV (Calcutta, 1886), p. 242 as cited in Muniruddin Chughtai, "Post-1857 Economic and Administrative Policies of the British in India and the Muslims," *Pakistan Economic and Social Review* (Autumn 1974), p. 247.

91 Ibid.,p. 243.

92 Government of India, Home Department, Proceedings, Education, 1871, p. 478, as cited in Hafeez Malik, *Sir Sayyid Ahmad Khan and Muslim Modernization in India and Pakistan* (New York: Columbia University Press, 1980), p. 147.

93 S. Shabbir, "Educational Development of Muslims in Vidarbha from 1882 to 1923," pp. 494-513, in *Pura-Prakasa: Dr Z.A. Desai Commemoration Volume*, I, edited by A.K. Sharma et al (Delhi: Bharatiya Kala Prakashan, 2003), citation on p. 495.

94 Joachim Oesterheld, "Muslims and Primary Education in the Central Provinces and Berar (1920-1947)," *Oriente Moderno* 84, 1 (2004): 245-262.

95 *Progress of Education in India*, 1927-32, II (Delhi: Manager of Publications, 1932), Table 99, as cited in Aparna Basu, "Growth of Muslim Education and Muslim Separatism, 1919-1939, pp. 223-243, in *Essays in Modern Indian History*, edited by B.R. Nanda (Delhi: Oxford University Press, 1980), citation on p.226.

96 Kanchanmoy Mojumdar, "Majority-Minority Syndrome in Regional Politics: The Central Provinces and Berar, 1919-1047," p. 449, in *Pura-Prakasa: Dr Z.A. Desai Commemoration Volume*, I, edited by A.K. Sharma et al (Delhi: Bharatiya Kala Prakashan, 2003).

97 For the Berar and Central Provinces refugees of 1947-48 in Hyderabad, see *Suqut-i Hyderabad*, edited by Omar Khalidi and Muinuddin Aqil (Hyderabad: Majlis-i Taamir-i Millat, 1998).

98 David E.U. Baker, "The Muslim Concern for Security: The Central Provinces and Berar, 1919-1947," pp. 221-47, in *Communal and Pan-Islamic Trends in Colonial India*, edited by Mushirul Hasan (New Delhi: Manohar, 1985); for a general statement, see Omar Khalidi, "From Torrent to Trickle: Indian Muslim Migration to Pakistan," *The Bulletin of the Henry Martyn Institute of Islamic Studies* 16, 1 & 2 (January-June 1997): 32-45.

99 A.R. Kamat, "Educational Progress in Rural Maharashtra," *Economic and Political Weekly* (05 October 1968): 1534-1536, citation on p. 1535.

100 Anita Dighe, "Deconstructing Literacy Primers," *Economic and Political Weekly* (1 July 1995): 1599-1561.

101 Joachim Oesterheld, "Muslims and Primary Education in the Central Provinces and Berar (1920-1947)," *Oriente Moderno* 84, 1 (2004): 245-262.

102 Sushila D'Cruz, "Textbook Muddle with an Absence of Malice," *The Illustrated Weekly of India* (30 January 1983), p. 35; Nirmala Chinu Panchal, " A Textbook Case," *India Today* (15 February 1983), pp. 137-138; Arvind Deshpande, "Reason, Emotion and History," *Communalism Combat* (March 1994), p. 5; "Muslim Students Forced to Sing Polytheistic Poems," *Radiance* (4-10 October 1998), p. 10.

103 "Bombay High Court Rules against Reservation for SC/St in Minority Institutions," *Muslim India* (June 1985), p. 273; "Muslim Institutions Denied Recognition," *Radiance* (26 December 1993-01 January 1004), p.1. M.H. Lakdawala, "Maharashtra Pressurizing Minority Institutions," *The Milli Gazette* 16-31 July 2002): 10.

104 Malika Mistry, "Muslim Students Top Exams in Maharashtra," *Radiance* (13-19 August 2000), pp. 13-14; M.H. Lakdawala, "Meriting Attention: Maharashtra's Muslim Schools are Claiming Top Scores in Public Exams," *Islamic Voice* (July 2000) Internet edition, idem "We Mean Business and We Expect the Best," *Islamic Voice* (August 2003) Internet edition; idem, "Go to Pakistan Taunt Led to Quality School," *The Milli Gazette* (1-15

June 2003), p. 7. Mushtaq Madni, "Pune's Azam Campus: A Beehive of Education," *The Milli Gazette* (1-15 February 2004), p. 32; "Education New Muslim Buzzward," *The Times of India* (25 October 2004) Internet edition; Parbhani ke Muslim College se 64 Doctors, 50 Engineers," *Rahbar-i Sanat wa Tijarat* (February 1998), pp. 69-70; Sweta Ramanujan, "Beyond the Veil: Things are Changing, We are Coming Forward," *Express India* (24 June 2004) Internet edition.

105 Omar Khalidi, " Politics of Official Language Status for Urdu in India," *Journal of South Asian and Middle Eastern Studies* 27, 3 (Spring 2004): 53-77.

106 Denzil Saldanha, "Literacy Campaigns in Maharashtra and Goa: Issues, Trends and Directions," *Economic and Political Weekly* (20 May 1995), p. 1188.

107 M.H. Lakdawala, "Urdu Medium Schools Luring New Converts," *Radiance* (4-10 April 2004), pp. 18-19.

108 Personal interview with Ishaq Jamkhanawala, 02 January 2005 in Mumbai. For a flattering account of the Anjuman's President see, Adam Shaikh, *Portrait of a Pragmatist: Life & Contributions of Dr. Ishaq Jamkhanawala* (Mumbai:Nensey Publishing House, 2001).

109 K.M. Aarif, personal interview, Mumbai 12 December 2004, during which he gave me several handouts elaborating on his allegations.

110 Personal interview with Ishaq Jamkhanawala, 02 January 2005 in Mumbai.

111 Jyoti Punwani, "The Changing Face of Pune Schools," *The Hindu* August 22, 2003, internet edition; and M.H. Lakdawala, "Grooming for Excellence," *Islamic Voice* (July 2001), Internet edition; Mushtaque Madni, *P.A. Inamdar: A Living Legend* (Pune: Usool Publications, 2005); idem, "Munawar Peerbhoy," *The Milli Gazette* (1-15 October),p. 18.

112 Mohammed Qamar Ishaq, *Directory of Muslim Educational, Religious and Welfare Organizations in India* (New Delhi: Institute of Objective Studies, 1995), pp. 77-85; updated by Rahat Abrar and Mohammad Qamar Ishaque, *Directory of Muslim Educational Institutions in India* (New Delhi: Institute of Objective Studies, 2002), pp. 223-265.

113 *Directory of Social Service Organizations of Muslims in Maharashtra* (Mumbai: All India Council of Muslim Economic Upliftment, 1998).

114 "Muslim Managed Degree Colleges," *Muslim India* (July 1996),p. 319.

115 *All India Civil List*, issued Half Yearly, corrected up to July 1st , 1958, pp. 209-220.

116 Omar Khalidi, *Khaki and the Ethnic Violence in India*, pp. 84-88, National Crime Records Bureau, *Crime in India* (New Delhi: Ministry of Home Affairs, 2000).

[117] *Maharashtra State Minorities Commission, Circular* no. MSMC/CC/2116/2004 dated 19 July 2004.

[118] Sweta Ramnujan, "No Shades in City's Khaki," *The Indian Express* (22 December 2004) Internet edition.

[119] "Representation of Muslims in Judicial Service in 1981," *Muslim India* (December 1983), p. 552. This includes M.C. Chagla, and M.N. Daud.

[120] "Jyoti Punwani's Plea for Reservation for Muslims as a Community," *The Midday* (03 May 1999, reprinted in *Muslim India* (August 1999),p. 364.

[121] Omar Khalidi, "Muslim" Ministers in the State Cabinets: The Case of Maharashtra," *Radiance* 15-21 September 2002: 10-11.

[122] James Traub, "Keeping up with the Sindhyes," *The New York Times Magazine* (15 April 2001), pp. 32-37.

[123] Masood Ali Khan, Social Change among Muslims of Aurangabad City," pp. 89-112, in *Problems of Muslim Women in India*, edited by Asghar Ali Engineer (New Delhi: Sangam Books, 1995).

[124] *National Commission for Minorities Second Annual Report (Financial Year 1994-95)* (New Delhi: Controller of Publications, 1997) pp. 112-114.

[125] According to Chairman Nasim Siddiqi, the Commission is interested in precisely such a project but unable to do so for lack of funds. Interview 02 January 2005, Mumbai.

[126] *Report of the Maharashtra State Minorities Commission* (Mumbai: The Commission,1994), p. 15. See also *First Report of the Maharashtra State Minorities Commission* (Mumbai: The Commission, 2002), the Commission was dissolved by the Shiva Sena government in 1995, and there was no Commission until it was reconstituted in April 2000.

[127] Hasanuddin Ahmad and Ahmedulla Khan, *Strategies to Develop Waqf Administration in India* (Jeddah: Islamic Research and Training Institute, Islamic Development Bank, Research Paper, 50, 1998) see "Marathwada Waqf Board," pp.16-147.

[128] "Government of Maharashtra Faces PIL for Misappropriating Wakf Property," *Radiance* (29 August-04 September 1999), pp. 10-11.

[129] "Masjid-I Kharbuza ki Arazi Musalmanon ko Wapis," *Munsif* (16 September 2004) Internet edition.

SUMMARY AND CONCLUSIONS

This study of Muslim community reveals patterns of the largest minority's share in the national economy of India. The study discovered that for the most part, the earliest Muslims were confined to the trade enclaves of the western coast and played a minor role in the economy of the region. The Muslims of various ethno-national groups arriving as conquerors from the twelfth century confined themselves merely to the opportunities in the military, bureaucracy and traditional education, leaving the rest to the upper caste Hindus. Even the tiny, traditional business communities among Muslims, the Bohras, Khojas, Labbes, and Memons belonged to the Hindu merchant communities before embracing Islam. Though several groups of artisans and peasants converted to Islam and improved their social standing at various points in time and in different regions, yet conversion did not necessarily improve their economic status. The pattern of economic stratification among Muslims — a community of a miniscule numbers in trade, slightly larger numbers in military and bureaucracy, larger numbers of artisans, and the largest number as landless peasants— continues into our own times.

Contrary to popular and journalistic perceptions, Muslims coming from the military, bureaucratic and learned backgrounds did take to modern education during the colonial era, except in Bengal, and some of the provinces constituting present-day Pakistan. In Bombay, Central Provinces, Hyderabad and Mysore states (contemporary Andhra Pradesh, Karnataka, and Maharashtra), Delhi, Bihar, and the United Provinces (present day U.P.), Muslims did well in modern education, sometimes even outpacing Hindus. Consequently, they were represented far in excess of their population percentages in government employment, particularly in the erstwhile Hyderabad State and U.P. In the Government of India services, they were adequately represented, especially since the reservation granted in 1925. The British Indian army had a percentage of Muslims to the tune of 30-36%, against the 23 percent Muslims in the national population in the 1941 census. The condition of Muslim artisans and peasants did not change any differently than of those belonging to other religious groups.

Since Independence

Independence and partition impacted various segments of Muslims differentially. Those most negatively affected in the immediate aftermath of 1947-48 were the propertied classes, who saw their immovable assets frozen by the dreaded Custodian of Evacuee Property, until 1956. Although, a clearly progressive and healthy measure, the land reforms in UP and old Hyderabad were not as effectively implemented as they were in Kashmir, Kerala and West Bengal. The land reforms in Hyderabad in 1949 and in Uttar Pradesh in 1950 rendered large number of absentee landlords among Muslims poor. The land reforms also negatively affected large numbers of hangers-on and the artisans dependent on the landlords' patronage. Significant number of educated Muslim families migrated to Pakistan, as did those already in the civil service and armed forces. Since the poorer Muslims were left behind in India, not many could compete for either the civil service or the armed forces' employment. The events of 1947-48 saw a vast reduction in the political voice of the Muslims. Abolition of the

Separate Electorates in 1949 and of reservation of jobs in the Government of India similarly affected the Muslims' presence in governance. Muslims' preponderance of civil service and army jobs in Hyderabad met a similar fate around the same time. Muslims, like other citizens of India, could not and have not been immune from the larger processes and trends in the country. For instance, the central and state governments in the country introduced reservations in education and employment for Scheduled Castes and Tribes, which does not include Muslims by law. In addition to reservation, the SCs and the STs are also eligible for job competition in the unreserved arena. The reservation system made competition that much more difficult for poor Muslims, whose educational condition has not been any better than those of the SCs and STs. Muslims' entry into civil and military service achieved through UPSC examinations is contingent upon educational attainment. For lower level jobs, political patronage is critical, which Muslims lack given that most Muslim ministers routinely do not get important cabinet portfolios of finance, revenue, home, education and the like. Finally, there is a perception of discrimination against Muslims, though not always easy to demonstrate.

Probably no country in the world can claim that the distributive benefits of its economic success and employment simply mirrors its societal diversity. It is perhaps not possible for each ethnic, religious segment of the society to be proportionally represented in each sector of the economy. Nonetheless, economic disparities when found along ethno-religious divide create a political problem. Thus the picture for Muslims in public employment is dismal. However, there are patches of bright spots here and there. Some Muslims prospered by making and marketing traditional crafts, and through small businesses and small- scale industries. New markets have been created or expanded the businesses in which either Muslims have specialized or which have been simply left to them by others. A substantial number of expatriate Muslims have become prosperous as a consequence of the "Arabian Interlude" by working in the rich states of the Persian Gulf and beyond. The "petro-remittances" financed real estate purchase, modern education, and sometimes profitable investments. On the other hand, the modest prosperity of some Muslims has ignited the Hindutvavadis, resulting in riots leading to destruction of property in a number of towns. The community's collective efforts have borne some fruit in education through the opening of a large number of technical and professional schools, though much remains to be done. On the political front, the example set by Andhra Pradesh, Karnataka and Kerala governments by giving reservation to Muslims as a whole have been welcomed in the community as a right step. There certainly is debate and plurality of opinion within and outside the Muslims community on the benefits and political costs of the reservations, but it must be remembered that a middle class was in fact created among the SCs and STs where none existed previously through the instrument of reservations. Thus the entry of some Muslims into entrepreneurship, hitherto confined to Bohras, Khojas, Labbes, and Memons, receipt of foreign remittances, opening of professional colleges, the introduction of reservations represents progress in the economic development of Muslims, however modest in scale. Barring a repetition of Mumbai and Gujarat pogroms of 1992-93 and 2002 respectively, one can safely predict further advances in these matters in the near future.

On the negative side, riots and pogroms have taken a huge toll on an already poor, impoverished community. The repeated failure of the state to predict, preempt, and once broken-out, to quell violence and protect life and property of all citizens represents a setback to minority interests, particularly because of the economic losses that it has entailed. The miniscule number of Muslims in the state employment in all these states is a direct consequence of poor education and training in technical and professional education. The bane of Muslims has been lack of progress in Science, Technology, Engineering, and Mathematics (STEM). Unless it improves, it would be futile to expect advances in the future. Given the repeated cycles of poverty and unemployment, the state needs to intervene on a scale larger than it has so far, particularly because sharp economic disparities between religious groups can accentuate differences with potential to accelerate violence. The state intervention requires either favorable political environment through national consensus or through pressure brought upon by legislators seeking justice for Muslims. For Hindu-Muslim relations to improve within India, relations between South Asia's twins—India and Pakistan have to improve. A resolution of Kashmir conflict—along with other India-Pakistan issues— is thus critical to a durable peace for minorities in both nations. Under conditions of peace and absence of threat to life and property, forces of progress in social and educational matters have the potential to grow within the Muslim community leading to the advancement of the entire community. Furthermore, whatever political measures the state needs to take at the central and state level for Muslims' improvement must not be at the expense of poor Indians of any religious affiliation. Muslims' economic interests are not in competition with or at the expense of poor classes of all Indians. The improvement of Muslims' economic condition can only be a part of the general program of poverty alleviation of all. Given the political price of poverty alleviation of Muslims, the state will need to formulate, present, and implement that program in a manner that will not be misconstrued as appeasement of minorities.

APPENDIX

CENTRAL GOVERNMENT SCHEMES AND COMMISSIONS FOR MINORITIES

The central government has notified five religious communities viz Muslims, Christians, Sikhs, Buddhists and Zoroastrians (Parsis) as minorities. These five communities constitute about 17% of the country's population. The educational and economic development of this section of the society and their mainstreaming is crucial for achieving the major national goals. It is deemed necessary to create conditions in which the minorities are assured that their constitutional and legal rights are safeguarded, and educationally and economically they are at par with the mainstream.

The schemes/organizations related with welfare of minorities are as follows:

Centrally Sponsored Scheme of Coaching and Allied Assistance for Weaker Sections Including Scheduled Castes, Other Backward Classes and Minorities

National Minorities Development and Finance Corporation

Fifteen Point Programme for the Welfare of Minorities

National Commission for Minorities;

National Commission for Religious & Linguistic Minorities

National Commission for Minority Educational Institutions

The Prime Minister's High Level Committee for...the Muslim Community of India

Maulana Azad Education Foundation

Special Officer for Linguistic Minorities

Development of Urban Waqf Properties

Area Intensive and Madrasas Modernization Programme

Area Intensive and Madrasas Modernization Program

In 1986, the then Ministry of Education issued a document entitled New Education Policy, which included proposals for government intervention in madrasa education through a Madrasa Modernization Program. The government's revised plan of action document in 1992 suggested introduction of subjects like mathematics, science, English and Hindi in the madrasas. The government offered to bear the cost of teaching the new subjects. The Ministry of Human Resource Development, which inherited the Ministry of Education, runs this program. In the Tenth Five Year Plan the government has allocated an amount of Rs. 160.00 crores, with an annual plan requirement of Rs. 31.50 crores for 2002/03. The implementation of this program has run into criticism both from some madrasas as well as some bigoted bureaucrats in the states of Bihar, Madhya Pradesh and Uttar Pradesh.[1]

Centrally Sponsored Scheme of Coaching and Allied Assistance for Weaker Sections Including Scheduled Castes, Other Backward Classes and Minorities

This scheme is run by the Ministry of Social Justice and Empowerment. The scheme aims at assisting students belonging to weaker section, SCs, OBCs and Minorities by way of special coaching for:

Admission to institutions imparting technical, vocational courses such as engineering, medicine, agriculture, management, information technology and service related courses, both in public and private sectors.

Recruitment to services under Groups 'A' and 'B' under the Central and State Governments, Public Sector Undertakings, Banks as well as in Private sector.

National Minorities Development and Finance Corporation (NMDFC)

On 15 August 1994, Prime Minister P.V. Narasmiha Rao announced the creation of NMFDC as his government's gesture toward the Muslim community, which was deeply hurt by his government's failure to prevent the demolition of Babri Masjid in Ayodhya on 6 December 1992.

NMDFC was set up by the Government of India to provide a "special focus to economic development of minorities." The people belonging to five communities i.e. Muslims, Christians, Sikhs, Buddhists & Parsis have been notified as minorities under the National Commission for Minorities Act, 1992. The prime mandate of NMDFC has been to provide concessional finance to the minorities living below double the poverty line for self-employment. NMDFC functions under the administrative control of the Ministry of Social Justice & Empowerment, Government of India.

The authorized share capital of NMDFC is Rs. 500 crores. The paid up share capital (till 31/03/2003) was Rs. 318.21 crores, of which Rs. 258.42 crores has been contributed by the Government of India and Rs. 59.79 crores by various State Governments as well as Union Territory Administrations. Evidently, both the Central Government and State governments have not given the amounts that were expected. No private individual or organization has come forward with any money up till 2005. In May 2005, a delegation of Andhra Pradesh Muslim leaders met Sonia Gandhi, leader of the Congress Parliamentary Party seeking her intervention to increase the share capital to 400 crores.[2]

NMDFC is a National level apex financing body. It has two channels to reach the ultimate beneficiaries - one through the State Channelising Agencies (SCAs) nominated by the State Governments and the other, through the Non Government Organizations (NGOs). Through the SCAs, individual beneficiaries are assisted under Term Loan and Educational Loan schemes, and through NGOs, Micro Credit is provided for the members of Self Help Groups (SHGs). Presently, NMDFC has 34 operational State Channelising Agencies in 25 States and two Union Territories, and a network of more than 100 NGOs across the country. Newly created states of Uttranchal, Jharkhand and Chhatisgarh have also become operational.

Over the years, the activities of NMDFC have progressively increased. It has been able to finance more than Rs. 556.17 crores for about 20, 6728 beneficiaries under the twin schemes of Term Loan and Micro-Financing.

Financial Assistance Schemes of NMDFC

Term Loan: This is the main activity of NMDFC, which is undertaken through the SCAs. Loans to individual beneficiaries are provided for projects with a maximum unit cost of Rs. 5.0 lakhs. The pattern of funding envisages 85% NMDFC share, and the SCA and beneficiary contribute the remaining 15% with minimum 5% share from the beneficiary. NMDFC provides loans to the SCAs at 3% rate of interest.

Micro Financing Scheme: NMDFC has taken the lead to start a parallel channel of micro financing. This initiative has been taken in order to reach the poorest among the target group, especially the minority women scattered in remote villages and urban slums who are not able to take advantage of the formal banking credit, or of the NMDFC program through its SCAs. Under this scheme small loans up to a maximum of Rs. 10,000 per beneficiary are provided through the network of NGOs and SHGs. Funds are given to the NGOs at an interest rate of 4%, who further lend to the beneficiaries directly or through the SHGs at an interest rate of 10%.

Educational Loan Scheme: NMDFC introduced its Educational Loan Scheme with the objective of facilitating job-oriented education among the weaker sections of minorities. The loan is available for professional and technical courses of short duration (up to a maximum of 2 years) having good employment potential.

Maximum loan of Rs. 75,000 is given to the eligible persons belonging to minorities. The loan is available at 3% interest and is repayable in a period of 5 years, to begin 6 months after completion of the course or getting employment, whichever is earlier. The scheme is implemented through the State Channelising Agencies of NMDFC

Capacity Building of Targeted Groups Vocational Training Scheme: The vocational training scheme aims at imparting skills in the targeted beneficiaries leading to self/wage employment. NMDFC provides 85% grants for conducting such vocational training programmes through the State Channelising Agencies.

Mahila Samridhi Yojana Scheme: A unique scheme linking Micro credit with training to the women members organised in SHGs in the trades such as tailoring, cutting and embroidery etc. has been launched by NMDFC. The scheme is being implemented through the State Channelising Agencies of NMDFC

Marketing Assistance Program: NMDFC provides marketing support to the artisans belonging to minorities for undertaking marketing of their products through participation in various National as well as State Level exhibitions.

Achievements of NMDFC have been as follows:

Table I

Term Loan (Year wise achievements) Up to March 31, 2004

Year	*Funds disbursed (Amount in Rs. Lakhs)*	*Beneficiaries covered*
1994-95	3003.9	9570
1995-96	649.13	4797
1996-97	4423.4	10749
1997-98	2341.3	4932
1998-99	5939	14333
1999-00	6077.9	22510
2000-01	7243.66	20274
2001-02	9206	21489
2002-03	7103.71	16348
2003-04	8224.47	18184
Total	54,212.47	143186

Table II
Term Loan (State Wise Achievements) Up to March 31, 2004

State/UT	*Beneficiaries*	*Amount disbursed*	*State*	*Beneficiaries*	*Amt. disb.*
Andhra	25671	2481	Manipur	2095	202
Assam	1700	389	M.P.	5144	1200
Bihar	9120	1757	Mizoram	9945	2790
Chandigarh	141	57	Nagaland	2695	1355
Chhatisgarh	36	15	Orissa	4447	745
Delhi	350	175	Pondicherry	98	50
Gujarat	14354	5501	Punjab	3665	1729
H.P.	707	277	Rajasthan	3246	355
Haryana	4002	1321	Tamil Nadu	9891	755
J & K	2220	1274	Tripura	383	166
Kerala	21078	7640	Uttar Pradesh	33193	11122
Karnataka	14301	3967	Uttranchal	1115	31
Maharashtra	6092	2059	West Bengal	31183	8206
Total	206872	55619			

Table III
Micro Financing (Year Wise Achievements) Up to March 31, 2004

Year	*Amount disbursed*	*Number of beneficiaries*
1998-99	43.08	3,281
1999-00	52.41	7,359
2000-01	100.15	11,418
2001-02	477.67	24,529
2002-03	290.44	7,540
2003-04	442.39	9415
Total	1406.14	63542

A government-appointed chairman heads the NMFDC. Qari Miyan Muhammad Mazhari, an obscure journalist has this position since 2000. According to Syed Shahabuddin, "compared to the [national] banking system, the NMFDC's credit outlay to the minorities is less than a peanut. The NMFDC in a nutshell, is an exercise in tokenism."[3] Instead, Shahabuddin has suggested "the government to establish a National Bank for Micro Financing modeled after the Bangladesh

Grameen Bank, which has placed on record its experience that small borrowers repay their loan on time, unlike the big borrowers who cheat the banks through collusion and legal skullduggery. Such a bank could also extend micro-credit to the NGOs and local institutions for vocational training and upgrading skills and facilitation of marketing by artisans."[4] The National Commission for Minorities in its Annual Report for 1997-98, noted having "received a large number of complaints regarding inaction, mismanagement, prejudices, bias, even corruption against the State Channelising Agencies of the NMDFC."[5]

15/20 Point Program for the Welfare of the Minorities

The 15-Point Program for Welfare of Minorities was launched in May 1983.The Program is in the nature of guidelines to the States/UTs and aims at giving a sense of security and for ensuring rapid socio-economic development of minority communities. The 15-Point Program is based on a 3-pronged approach, namely, (i) to tackle the situation arising out of communal riots, (ii) ensuring adequate representation of the minority communities in employment under the Central and State Governments as well as Public Sector Undertakings and (iii) other measures, such as ensuring flow of benefits to the minority communities under various development programmes, maintenance and development of religious places, Waqf properties and redressal of grievances of the minorities.

Upon his coming to power in June 1984, Rajiv Gandhi added five more points thus making it a 20 Point Program.[6]

The State Governments/UTs and the concerned Ministries/Departments of Government of India implement the program and send half-yearly reports to the Ministry of Social Justice & Empowerment, which monitors the implementation of the 15-Point Program at the national level. The Ministry obtains reports in respect of points 1 to 8 from the Ministry of Home Affairs. Half-yearly reports in respect of points 11 to 14 are obtained from the State Governments/Departments. The information received from concerned agencies is compiled, analyzed, reviewed, and the deficiencies noticed in the implementation of the program are brought to the notice of the authorities concerned for remedial action.

At the State level, the progress under the programme is monitored at the level of Chief Minister/Chief Secretary. In the districts the Deputy Commissioner/ District Magistrate monitors the program.

The implementation of the 15/20 Points Program has been far from satisfactory. The Implementation Report's published extracts point to the lukewarm reception of many state governments.[7] Despite the Program's commitment to increase minorities' recruitment in state employment, Minister for State for Welfare, Sumati Oraon, told Syed Shahabuddin that her "Government is not interested in monitoring representation in public employment."[8] On 10 July 1989, Minister for Welfare, Rajendra Kumari Bajpai, claimed "that the implementation of ...the 15 Point Program has helped to create a sense of reassurance among the minorities..."[9] Union Minister for Human Resource Development, Arjun Singh, wrote to Members of Parliament inviting suggestions for the 15 Point Program in July 1991 in an attempt to infuse new life into the programme.[10] But nothing seems to have come of it. Matters worsened when Bharatiya Janata Party came to power at the Center in 1999. The Government "has not even bothered to monitor the implementation of the much tom-tommed program," commented one newspaper.[11] A report prepared by the National Commission for Minorities for internal circulation found that "the 15 Point Program has failed to achieve the desired results. The lack of interest on the part of States and Union Territories is so much that they do not even bother to send any feedback to the Center as to what they are doing in this connection."[12]

National Commission for Minorities

The National Commission for Minorities (NCM) was established in January 1978, in the wake of the first non-Congress government, Janata Party's coming to power a year earlier. For nearly a decade and a half the Commission was without a statute. On popular demand from minorities and the democratic forces, the Government passed an Act in May 1992 in the Parliament making the National Commission for Minorities a statutory body. The Commission has been set up to perform a number of functions for the effective implementation of safeguards provided under the Constitution for protection of the interests of minorities and to make recommendations in this regard to the Central Government or State Government, as the case may be.

The Commission receives approximately 3000 complaints/ representations in a year. The complaints received in the Commission are broadly related to atrocities by the police, service matters, disputes relating to religious places and complaints relating to Minority Educational Institutions. After taking cognizance of the complaints, reports are called for from the concerned authorities. On receipt of the reports, the Commission makes appropriate recommendations to the concerned authorities. The Chairman, Vice Chairman and Members of the Commission undertake visits to States/UTs during the period to review problems relating to Minorities.

The Commission has also constituted a Minority Education Cell to exclusively look after the problems being faced by minority educational institutions in regard to recognition, affiliation, grants-in-aid, etc. The annual reports of the Commission often contain useful data not available anywhere else. Thus it performs a useful function.

However, the Commission's effectivity is limited as it lacks authority. It does not have powers to adjudicate in disputes between religious groups in India. Its work is merely advisory. Many state governments have not formed Minorities Commissions at their level. The recommendations of the Minorities Commission are not binding on governments. In the words of lawyer and journalist A.G. Noorani, "The Congress' manifesto had promised to endow the Minorities Commission with the necessary powers to carry out its duties effectively. Instead, its functions and duties have been curtailed; its powers restricted, and its members deprived of any security of tenure. It was a half-hearted, insincere implementation of a solemn promise."[13] The Commission is also handicapped by the small amount of money it has at its disposal to carry out its functions.[14] The National Minorities Commission has "failed because it attempted too much and too little; too much because its jurisdiction exceeded its powers, and too little because its procedure of acting upon grievances narrowed its attention to symptoms rather than underlying causes of minority problems."[15] The Commission's failures are frankly evident in a former chairman's book titled "*Minorities Commission: Minor Role in Major Affairs*."[16]

National Commission for Religious & Linguistic Minorities (NCRLM); National Commission for Minority Educational Institutions (NCMEI); The Prime Minister's High Level Committee for...the Muslim Community of India (PMHCMCI)

By October 2005, there were as many as five commissions, committees appointed by the Government of India, including the long-established (1957) Commissioner for Linguistic Minorities, National Commission for Minorities (1978). The newer ones are: NCRML headed by Justice Ranganathan Mishra; NCMEI headed by Justice M.S.A. Siddiqui, and PMHMCI established in May 2005 and chaired by Justice Rajindar Sachar. Why are there so many commissions? Is there coordination among them? Are their reports ever made public? The ones printed by the NCM are not tabled before the Lok Sabha as it involves an Action Taken Report. In the meanwhile, rodents have been eating up the printed reports, some not available even in the NCM's own Library as the present writer discovered in December 2004! In the end, nothing happens, as has been the fate of Gopal Singh Panel, and they remain largely exercises in public relations. For a departure from past practice, these commissions must be made effective.

Commissioner for Linguistic Minorities

The Office of the Special Officer for Linguistic Minorities (commonly known as the Commissioner for Linguistic Minorities) was created in July 1957, in pursuance of the provision of Article 350-B of the Constitution.

The Commissioner for Linguistic Minorities in India has his Headquarters at Allahabad with three Regional Offices at Kolkata, Belgaum and Chennai. The

CLM takes up all matters pertaining to grievances arising out of non-implementation of the Constitutional and Nationally Agreed Scheme of Safeguards provided to linguistic minorities that come to its notice or are brought to its knowledge by the linguistic minority individuals, groups, association or organizations at the highest political and administrative levels of the State Governments and UT Administrations, and recommends remedial actions to be taken.

The Commissioner for Linguistic Minorities in India submits Annual Reports, which are sent to the concerned Ministries/Departments of the Central Government and the Governments of various States/UTs for follow up action after placing them in Parliament. The CLM has submitted 38 Annual Reports, so far. As far as the question of Urdu is concerned, the CLM has not been able to do anything, not even prevent the state-sponsored closure of Urdu classes all over Uttar Pradesh where the largest number of Urdu-speakers is located.[17]

Maulana Azad Education Foundation

Maulana Azad Education Foundation (MAEF) is a voluntary, non-political, non-profit organization established for promotion of education amongst the educationally backward minorities. The Maulana Azad Education Foundation was established in July 1989 as a Society under the Societies Registration Act. It is fully funded by the Ministry of Social Justice & Empowerment, Government of India. Presently the Foundation has a Corpus Fund of Rs.70.01 crore. The Minister for Social Justice & Empowerment is ex-officio President of the Foundation. In July 1997 the Union Government sanctioned Rs. 100 crores as the corpus to the MAEF, with a promise that each additional year another 100 crore rupees would be added. Evidently this has not happened in the budget presented in March 2005, according to a press report.[18]

The aim of the Foundation is to formulate and implement educational schemes and plans for the benefit of the educationally backward minorities in particular and weaker sections in general. The Foundation provides financial assistance to NGOs for various educational activities.

Main schemes:

At present, the MAEF provides grant-in-aid to NGOs under following Schemes:

Financial assistance for establishment/expansion of schools/residential schools/colleges

Financial assistance for purchase of lab equipments and furniture etc.

Financial assistance for setting-up/ strengthening of Vocational/Technical Training Centers/Institutes
Financial assistance for construction of hostel buildings
Financial assistance for Remedial Coaching.

Achievements:
Up to 31st March 2003, the Foundation had assisted 474 NGOs with a grant of Rs.64.68 crore, since inception. Apart from this, the Foundation arranges training programme for teachers of the institutions assisted by the Foundation. The Foundation has provided free training to more than 3000 girls at the Vocational Training Centers run by the Foundation in collaboration with South Delhi Polytechnic at Ajmeri Gate, Delhi in the following trades:

Cutting & Tailoring, Textile Designing, Beauty Culture, Arts & Crafts & Computers.

The following new schemes have been launched in the current financial year:

Maulana Azad National Scholarship for meritorious students belonging to minorities
Maulana Abul Kalam Azad Literacy Awards
Establishment of Maulana Azad Sadbhavna Kendras=Maulana Azad Centres.

According to National Commission for Minorities, there "has been a simmering discontent with its functioning…the demand that the Foundation should pay greater attention to the (officially declared) educationally backward minorities than the educationally advanced minorities was met with stiff resistance by the then Welfare Minister."[19]

Development of Urban Waqf Property
Objective:
To improve the financial position of Waqfs and Waqf Boards, to save the properties from likely encroachment and enlarge the area of their welfare activities, the Central Waqf Council assists the Waqf Institutions and Waqf Boards in developing their urban Waqf properties.

How the Scheme Works:
The projects approved under the scheme involve construction or reconstruction of commercially viable buildings on Waqf lands like residential flats, commercial complexes, marriage halls etc.

Eligibility:
Only the Waqf institutions and Waqf Boards having urban Waqf land free from all encumbrances and having potential for development, could apply for assistance.

Funding Pattern:
The scheme is funded by the Central Government by giving an annual grant-in-aid to the Central Waqf Council, a statutory body established by the Government of India under the Waqf Act, 1995. The Central Government has (up to 31-3-2004) released a sum of Rs. 2540.11 lakh as grant-in-aid to the Central Waqf Council, which includes Rs. 150 lakh for the financial year 2003-2004. The budget provision for the current financial year 2004-05 is Rs. 1.70 crore.[20]

Nature of Assistance:
The Council gives loans up to 75% of the estimated cost of the project, which is released in installments. There is no upper limit for the cost of the project.

Notes

1 Irshadul Haq, "Bureaucrats Foil Madrasah Education Modernization Program," *The Milli Gazette* (1-15 October 2002), p. 23; Yoginder Sikand, "Madrasa Reform and the Indian State," *Economic and Political Weekly* (25 October 2003), pp. 4503-4506; "Modernization of Madrasas in U.P." *The Milli Gazette* (1-15 April 2005), p. 19.

2 Email from Asaduddin Owaisi, MP, 22 May 2005.

3 Syed Shahabuddin, "NMFDC's Poor Impact...Flow of Bank Credit to the Minorities," *The Milli Gazette* (16-31 May 2003), p. 12.

4 Ibid.

5 *National Commission for Minorities Annual Report, 1997-98* (New Delhi: NCM, 1999), pp. 21-22.

6 "New Light on 20-Point Program," *Radiance* (12-18 June 1994), p. 2.

7 "PM's 15 Pont Directive on Minorities' Welfare: Implementation Report by Ministry of Welfare," *Muslim India* (January 1987), pp. 6-7.

8 Government not Interested in Monitoring Representation in Public Employment." *Muslim India* (July 1988), p. 195.

9 "Statement of the Conference of State Ministers on 15-Point Program..." *Muslim India* (January 1990), p. 7.

[10] "PM's Program for Welfare of Minorities," *Muslim India* (December 199), p. 190.

[11] "Minority Schemes in Peril," *Deccan Chronicle* (December 9, 2000), Internet edition.

[12] Ibid.

[13] A.G. Noorani, "Minorities Act: Congress (I) Pledge not Fulfilled," *Radiance* (2-8 August 1992), p. 8.

[14] M.A. Siraj, "Shortage of Funds, Personnel Cripple Minorities Commission," *Saudi Gazette* (12 March 1992), p. 8.

[15] Theodore P. Wright, Jr., "The Failure of the Minorities Commission of India, 1977-81," *Indian Journal of Politics* 20, 1 & 2 (January-June 1986): 1-8.

[16] Tahir Mahmood, *Minorities Commission: Minor Role in Major Affairs* (New Delhi: Pharos Media, 2000).; idem *Amid Gods and Lords: My Life with Votaries of Religion and Law* (New Delhi:Amity Press, 2005)

[17] Conversation with R.K. Syed, IAS, Commissioner of the Linguistic Minorities in 1992, in Minneapolis, Minnesota, in August 22, 2004; "Fate of One Report and Two Institutions," *Muslim India* (October 1987), p. 439.

[18] "Interests of Muslims Ignored in the Budget," *The Milli Gazette* (16-31 March 2005), p. 13'"Step-Motherly Treatment to Maulan Azad Education Foundation," *The Milli Gazette* (1-16 June 2005), p. 9.

[19] *National Commission for Minorities Annual Report, 1997-98* (New Delhi: NCM, 1999), p.33. The Minister in question was Balwant Singh Ramoowalia, a Sikh.

[20] There is apparently large-scale misuse of the funds, according to Lok Sabha member Hannan Molla, "Reconstitute Central Waqf Council," *The Milli Gazette* (16-30 September 2005), p. 3.